Received Via Ma

In Their Own Words:

THE DEMOCRATIC PARTY'S PUSH TOWARDS A COMMUNIST AMERICA

By
Terry D. Turchie and Donagh Bracken

HISTORY PUBLISHING COMPANY LLC
Palisades, New York 10964

This publication is designed to provide authoritative and accurate information in regard to the subject matter covered. It is sold with the understanding that the publisher is not engaged in rendering legal, accounting, or other professional services. If legal advice or other expert assistance is required, the services of a competent professional person should be sought.

Ordering Information:
Quantity sales. Special discounts are available on quantity purchases by corporations, associations, and others. For details, contact the publisher at the address above.

Orders by U.S. trade bookstores and wholesalers. Please contact Big Distribution: Tel: (845) 359-1765; or visit historypublish@aol.com.

SAN: 850-5942
Research contributions by Donald Joseph Bracken
Market contributions by Kevin Turchie

This text is printed on acid-free paper by
History Publishing Company LLC
Palisades, New York 10964
First Edition

Printed in the United States of America

ABOUT THE AUTHORS

Terry Turchie spent thirty years in the FBI- as a clerical support employee from 1972-1976, and as an FBI agent from 1976 until his retirement in May 2001, as the Deputy Assistant Director of the FBI's Counterterrorism Division. He received many promotions, Letters of Commendation, and Incentive Awards during his career, including the FBI Director's Award for Management and Attorney General's Award for Distinguished Service. In 1986, he and his partners arrested Gennady Zacharov, a Soviet KGB officer in New York City, for espionage. The Assistant Director of the FBI, New York called him, "a key figure in the Soviet Division and our effort to neutralize Soviet intelligence services." He led the UNABOM investigation from 1994 to 1998, drafting the search warrant for the cabin of Theodore Kaczynski. The FBI Director appointed him as the Inspector in Charge of the fugitive hunt for Eric Robert Rudolph, who detonated a bomb at the 1996 Summer Olympics in Atlanta and murdered a police officer in Birmingham, Alabama, in January 1998. In March 2000, he traveled overseas with former FBI Director Louis Freeh to facilitate joint investigations of international terrorism and al-Qaeda in the Far East. Upon his retirement from the FBI in 2001, he went to work at the Lawrence Livermore National Laboratory, as the head of the counterintelligence program.

Donagh Bracken, a native New Yorker born in Manhattan, raised in the Bronx and educated in Riverdale, went to Manhattan Prep (Manhattan College High School), then walked across campus and attended Manhattan College and earned a B.B.A. After graduation, he entered the United States Army and was assigned to the Tenth Infantry at the Combat Development Experimentation Center (CDEC)and worked on the development of nuclear warfare tactics. Following his military experience and inspired by John F. Kennedy, he entered the Democratic

Party in suburban New York. He coordinated campaigns for candidates on the local and congressional level, including the successful 28th CD re-election of Congressman John Dow, who opposed the Gulf of Tonkin Resolution. He achieved success as an entrepreneurial businessman until retirement in 2000. He came out of retirement in 2008 and founded The History Publishing Company with two imprints. One featured an analysis of the American Civil War through computer technology utilizing the data compiled by the National Park Service. The other imprint, books about the FBI and the military. Today, a broader spectrum of interest is contained in seven imprints. He is also the author of *The Words of War*, an analysis of the contrasting newspaper reportage of *The New York Times* and *The Charleston Mercury*.

FOREWORD

The Democratic Party of Franklin Roosevelt, Harry Truman and John F. Kennedy no longer exists. This fact is well documented *In Their Own Words, the Democratic Party's Push Towards a Communist America*, by two distinguished authors who write from personal knowledge and experience, backed up by superb research.

Terry Turchie, a native of California, had a stellar career with the FBI. In his thirty years with the Bureau, he made significant contributions to the safety and security of our great nation.

Donagh Bracken is a native New Yorker, with vast affiliations with the Democratic Party before its push toward a Communist America.

The Democratic Party reacted to the election of President Donald Trump in 2016 with resistance, accusations, investigations and impeachment. To the millions of voters who cast their ballots for President Trump, the Democratic Party sent a clear message-those voters were deplorable, racist, and part of an America that was plagued by systemic and institutional racism.

When the Democratic Party took back control of the House in 2018, instead of working to create a vibrant economy, creating jobs for all Americans, and protecting the rule of law, the Party's leading Presidential candidates have called for a restructuring of American society, bigger government, and socialism. They have resurrected the battle cries of radical revolutionaries of the 1960's and 1970's who sought to topple the United States Government and replace it with communism.

To all Americans who believe in our system of government and support capitalism, In Their Own Words will be exceedingly informative and will cause you great concern for the way a once great political party has been taken over by avowed Socialists and Communists. Their words and actions reveal their true intentions.

To the Millenniums who are caught up in the Socialist Movement, be aware of who you are listening to and following. This book is a must read for you. It should be no surprise that the Communist Party of the United States of America (CPUSA) totally supports Bernie Sanders for President. If you didn't know that already, this book will remind you that the CPUSA believes that "defeating Trump and the right in 2020 means moving the electorate to the left". The CPUSA also believes that the most effective force to defeat the President is the campaign of Bernie Sanders. The CPUSA believes America needs a revolutionary transformation to socialism and then communism-and views the Democratic Party as the best path to get there.

This book adds a clear lens from which to view what is, and has been, happening in America-and the Democratic vision for America's future - a vision of communist utopia and international solidarity through the destruction of our constitutional Republic. It is a must read for every American who believes in freedom of choice and the right to "life, liberty and the pursuit of happiness."

Cecil E. Moses
Retired Member of The FBI's Senior Executive Service.

TABLE OF CONTENTS:

PART ONE

Introduction

Vermont Senator Bernie Sanders and newly elected Representative Alexandria Ocasio-Cortez, a thirty year -old former bartender from New York's 14th Congressional District, believe that the United States needs socialism. Both are willing to destroy America's constitutional Republic to get what they want. Congresswoman Ocasio-Cortez has said that "capitalism is irredeemable," and that "this is about a movement that has been decades in the making."

In Their Own Words explains the movement that Ocasio-Cortez stands for and how it has infected today's Democratic Party. She is correct. It has been decades in the making. It is the Democratic Party's push towards a communist America, under the cloak of "democratic socialism." And it comes straight from the pages of the strategy of the revolutionary Weather Underground and the violent Black Panther Party of the 1960's and 1970's.

In 2008, *Homeland Insecurity, How Washington Politicians Have Made America Less Safe (HI)*, argued that the primary motivation of politicians in Washington, D.C. was power. Working counterintelligence, counterterrorism and criminal investigations in the FBI for a combined 60 years, the co-authors of *HI* watched elected officials from both parties attempt to compromise, gain favor with, or get in the way of an FBI investigation, if it interfered with their quest for power.[1]

---

[1]   *Homeland Insecurity, How Washington Politicians Have Made America*

HI described in detail how only seven years after the surprise attack on American soil by Islamic terrorists, many influential Democrats and Republicans, tried to use the 9/11 hearings to blame the FBI for failing to prevent one of the most horrific events in the history of our nation.

The reality is that the seeds of 9/11 were planted decades earlier when a brazen burglary of the Democratic Headquarters at the Watergate Hotel brought down an American President. Then, it turned on the counterintelligence activities of the FBI. It was the pursuit of political power that put an end to legitimate FBI domestic intelligence gathering inside the United States. The absence of an effective domestic intelligence capability to protect America contributed to the 9/11 surprise terrorist attacks on the United States. It was the U.S. Congress that eliminated the FBI's domestic intelligence capability.

The Republican Party was torn apart by Watergate, even as most Republican politicians joined with their Democratic colleagues to roundly condemn the abuse of power by President Richard Nixon and his staff. The Republican Party learned from what happened. The Democratic Party did not.

- Over the decades that followed the Watergate burglary and coverup, Democratic Party politicians pushed programs that led to more government interference in people's lives, motivated by their desire to install "socialist democracy" in the United States.

- Democratic Party loyalists and an FBI investigation characterized by poor judgment and criminality, have created the appearance that U.S. intelligence agencies mounted an operation designed to remove President Donald Trump from the White House after his successful election in 2016.

- The Democratic Party has been completely hijacked by those espousing the ideology of communism as advocated by the

Less Safe, by Terry D. Turchie and Kathleen L. Puckett, History Publishing Company, Palisades, New York, 2008

1970's revolutionaries.

Known as the Weather Underground, this group of domestic terrorists described itself as "communist minded men and women." Forming a loose alliance with the Black Panther Party of Self-Defense, both organizations recognized they would need to install a temporary socialist government structure inside the United States before they could transform America into a full-blown communist utopia.[2]

In 2008, *HI* named names. *HI* identified politicians who constantly placed their pursuit of power before the interests of the American public. Their quest for power placed them on a confrontation course with the FBI. It was inevitable that a Democratic Party on a path to install a democratic socialist government in America would eventually collide with the FBI's national security responsibilities. The 2008 election of President Barack Obama would be the intersection of such a collision-but the stage was set decades earlier.

COINTELPRO and the Foreign Intelligence Surveillance Act (FISA)

Most Americans have no idea that President Richard Nixon wanted to remove the legal restraints governing intelligence community activities directed against left wing groups in the late 1960's and early 1970's.

FBI Director J. Edgar Hoover objected that the risk of such a plan was greater than the potential benefit. When Hoover died on May 2, 1972, President Nixon named Department of Justice Assistant Attorney General L. Patrick Gray as the Acting FBI Director. Gray was quickly co-opted by White House Counsel John Dean into a relationship with the White House. It would eventually result in Gray's decision to destroy documents given to him by Dean that implicated the White House staff in a coverup of the Watergate burglary.

---

[2]   *The Politics of Revolutionary Anti-Imperialism, Political Statement of the Weather Underground,* Bernardine Dohrn, Billy Ayers, Jeff Jones, Celia Sojourn, Communications Company, San Francisco, CA., 94110

Following President Nixon's resignation, Congressional hearings focused on the FBI's role in domestic intelligence. As a result, the American public came to know of an FBI counterintelligence program code-named COINTELPRO. It was highly controversial. Supporters credited the program with crippling the violent revolutionary communist movement of the 1970's that sought to overthrow the U.S. government.

U.S. Senator Frank Church from Idaho viewed the FBI as trampling on the civil rights and freedom of speech of Americans. The *Church Committee*, Democrats, Republicans in Congress, as well as the news media, universally condemned the FBI's COINTELPRO. Congress passed legislation leading to reform in the intelligence community called the Foreign Intelligence Surveillance Act (FISA).

The FISA legislation established an artificial barrier between FBI agents conducting criminal investigations and those who were engaged in long-running national security investigations of individuals and groups who supported the overthrow of the United States Government. FISA created the FISA Court system to see and hear requests for investigative techniques like wiretaps and various search warrants, separate from the criminal courts. FBI agents working national security investigations using the FBI's chain of command for counterintelligence cases were not allowed to share information they gained with colleagues working criminal investigations. Inside the FBI and Department of Justice (DOJ), this became known as the FISA wall or *The Wall.*

Senator Church was made aware that his hearings risked the exposure of extremely sensitive FBI sources and could have vast repercussions on America's national security. This didn't stop him and many other politicians from using the information at their disposal to tarnish the Bureau in the eyes of the American public. The Department of Justice had long been well aware of COINTELPRO and why it was developed.[3]

---

[3] *Homeland Insecurity: How Washington Politicians Have Made America Less Safe,* by Terry D. Turchie and Kathleen L. Puckett, History Publishing

The FBI closed down its Domestic Intelligence Section. It stopped most of its national security collection programs. During 1987-1988, the FBI closed its long-running investigation of the Communist Party of the United States (CPUSA).

The FBI's shift- away from active domestic intelligence collection, removed its agents from street contact with police departments across the country. This deprived law enforcement of everyday sharing and information exchanges, helpful in the identification and prevention of crime trends and national security problems.

When Islamic terrorists attacked America, the 9/11 Commission held extensive bipartisan hearings, just like Watergate. They wrote a report, just like Watergate. They made recommendations on how to prevent terrorists from striking the country again. In the course of the hearings. Jamie Gorelick, Deputy Attorney General for Bill Clinton, argued that the FISA wall didn't really exist. There was never any rule to prevent FBI agents from sharing FISA gained intelligence with each other and /or the CIA. Jamie Gorelick was wrong. Every FBI agent and every Department of Justice employee familiar with national security work

---

Company, Palisades, New York, 2008, page 34. Jack and Morris Childs were the FBI's counterintelligence assets in the most important espionage operation the United States ever conducted against the former Soviet Union. The FBI operation was codenamed *SOLO*. The FBI assets had access to the highest levels of the leadership of the Soviet Union. They provided the information that helped the FBI identify KGB funding of the Communist Party of the United States of America. Their reporting was the basis of the FBI investigation of Soviet agents in America, Stanley Levison and Jack O'Dell. Both Levison and O'Dell were associates of Dr. Martin Luther King. King's relationship with O'Dell and Levison, formed the predication for the Department of Justice authorization of the FBI's investigation of Dr. King himself. After Senator Church was briefed on this information, he said, "I am satisfied that there was every reason in the world for the FBI to be investigating King...I want none of this talked about...None of this is to leave this room."

knew the meaning of the wall and the consequences of violating it.[4]

The Insider Threat and Agents of Influence

When America's political parties shut down the FBI's domestic intelligence gathering, they made it all but impossible to prevent the hiring of individuals by U.S. Government agencies who believed in the subversive ideology of communism. The gates were unlocked. The external threat became an *insider threat.* Many who worked to destroy our government institutions in the 1970's rushed through the unlocked gates. Today, they've taken up residence inside the Democratic Party.[5]

The intelligence services of enemies of the United States (Russia, China, Cuba, Iran, Islamic jihadists) focus on the recruitment of *agents of influence* inside America's political parties. These agents of influence can pass legislation or use their positions to promote public policies that are hostile to America's interests. Through their covert operations, they can easily compromise or otherwise undermine trust in U.S. Government agencies and our institutions dedicated to the rule of law.

In addition to fully recruited *agents of influence,* elected officials sympathetic to the causes of hostile countries can subvert our political system, while fulfilling the goals of worldwide communism. America is the only nation since the end of World War II to consistently fight the spread of the ideology of communism. America's constitutional Repub-

---

[4]   *Homeland Insecurity: How Washington Politicians Have Made America Less Safe,* by Terry D. Turchie and Kathleen L. Puckett, History Publishing Company, Palisades, New York, 2008, page 49-50.

[5]   U.S. Government counterintelligence agencies have always been concerned with the "insider threat." The intelligence services of America's enemies work hard to penetrate the FBI, CIA, branches of Congress, the U.S. military, critical industries and technology firms through the recruitment of trusted employees or *"insiders."* With their knowledge of other employees, security systems in place to protect people and classified or sensitive information, extensive damage can be done when these employees turn into traitors.

lic, built on the back of the rule of law, is the reason. Intentional efforts to undermine the rule of law is a primary objective of the ideology of communism.

Sanctuary Cities

Look no further than sanctuary cities. There are 564 cities, counties and states across America that have declared themselves sanctuaries. Their defining characteristic is the prohibition of funds to aid enforcement of Federal immigration laws. They interfere with the communication among law enforcement officers at the local, state and Federal level. They hamper terrorism investigations. They get police officers and citizens alike seriously injured or killed. Incrementally, they will destroy the rule of law.[6]

If Americans are to make rational choices concerning the direction of the nation, it is imperative they re-learn the dangers of modern-day communism.

In Their Own Words identifies the individuals undermining the way we live as Americans. Our freedom is at stake. There should be little doubt that passionate and incremental actions are under way inside our government to deprive Americans of life, liberty and the pursuit of happiness. The FBI has been rendered inoperable to effectively expose and stop it.

Through deceit, subversion, fraud and force, the Democratic Party is purging free expression inside the United States. They are pursuing international solidarity at the expense of long dependable allies. Through the pursuit of policies and initiatives such as sanctuary cities, they are destroying the fabric of the rule of law that binds fifty states, thousands of cities, and hundreds of thousands of law enforcement officers into an effective force of crime prevention and protection of the civil liberties of all Americans.

---

[6] *"FAIR Report: Sanctuary Jurisdictions Have Nearly Doubled Since Trump Took Office," Federation for American Immigration Reform, 2019*

The Importance of International Solidarity to the Socialist Movement

The alliance involving Russia, China, Cuba and Iran is responsible for the resurrection of the ideology of communism across the globe. Under the guise of democratic socialism, an aggressive campaign is underway inside the United States, to incrementally move America in the same direction. The passionate advocates of democratic socialism include some of the key leaders of the Democratic Party.

The underlayment of the ideology of communism is international solidarity. America is not immune from its reach. Democratic leaders view the Resistance movement of the 1970's as one of America's revolutions. They view the Resistance movement of today as its political equivalent. The Weather Underground and Black Panther Party recognized that the overthrow of America's Constitutional Republic would result in a temporary period of socialism-followed by communism.

Communism went dormant after the collapse of the former Soviet Union. But years of rule by Vladimir Putin and his worldwide mischief making, have brought it back to life.

Venezuela's rule by so-called socialist Hugo Chavez was bolstered by international solidarity with sympathetic Americans and elected officials who viewed him as another in a long line of benevolent revolutionaries, in the image of Fidel Castro of Cuba. The Venezuelan experiment in democratic socialism was the talk of the liberal elite in America-until it wasn't.

The consolidation of power by China's Xi Jinping, China's positions on Taiwan, its aggressive stance on continued economic freedom in Hong Kong and a resurgence of China's relationship with Cuba and South America are intended to further its global ambitions.

The development of relationships with the ayatollahs who rule Iran proves the importance of international solidarity in furthering the ideology of communism. Russia, China, Cuba and Iran are the modern version of President Ronald Reagan's "axis of evil," from the 1980's. They are looking to establish a home base inside the United States.

Communism, Marxism, globalism, have resurrected and reinvented themselves in the pursuit of absolute power. Just like the 1980's, America is the primary target.

The spreading of the deceptive message of democratic socialism to a generation that never faced communism and doesn't understand its insidious nature goes unabated.

This book connects the past to the present. It offers a plan to protect America's future. The information in it is from real people who stood on the front lines of the Cold War. They were real actors in the 1980's "decade of the spy," and understand the inner workings of Russian, Chinese, Cuban and Iranian espionage in America.[7]

This book presents the evidence showing the penetration of the Democratic Party by political revolutionaries promoting democratic socialism, as a cover for the ideology of communism. The proof lies in their own words.

---

[7]   *"1985, The Year of the Spy," Wikipedia*

CHAPTER ONE

"Revolution is a fight by the people for power…" Weather Underground

---

Appointed by Attorney General Harlan Fiske Stone, J. Edgar Hoover became the Director of the Bureau of Investigation in 1924. Hoover assumed command of an agency that had close to 650 employees, 441 of them Special Agents. Taking on complaints of corruption within the Agency he led, Hoover tightened requirements for his agents, established tough rules for new hires, and began the process of revolutionizing law enforcement with the addition of fingerprint and forensic laboratory services to the Bureau's operations. By 1935, the Bureau of Investigation had become the Federal Bureau of Investigation-the FBI.[8]

Years of hard work and adherence to integrity and the rule of law by thousands of men and women who entered its ranks, made the FBI the most legendary crime-fighting agency in the world. Director J. Edgar Hoover remained on the job for fifty years, turning a U.S. Government agency into a brand name. Adding national security, counterintelligence, espionage and sabotage to its list of responsibilities as America entered World War II, Director Hoover and the Bureau became synon-

---

[8] *"The FBI and the American Gangster, 1924-1938," FBI, A Brief History, fbi.gov*

ymous with truth, justice and the American way.

It didn't take long for Hollywood to adopt the FBI's relentless pursuit of spies, bad guys, crooks and cons to its movies and television shows. A legend was born. In 1972, the agency could do no wrong and continuously topped polls of American citizens as one of their most trusted institutions. The FBI's shootouts with violent mobsters, capture of Nazi saboteurs, and identification of Soviet "moles," living inside the United States under deep cover identities made Americans from all walks of life ages, feel safe and protected by the agency that never slept.

America was besieged by the ambush and murder of police officers and terrorist bombings in the 1970's, inspired by "communist-minded" Weather Underground revolutionaries and the Black Panther Party. Politicians turned to the FBI to stop the violence, identify those responsible, and bring them to justice.[9] The FBI responded. A domestic counterintelligence program, code-named COINTELPRO, was launched to stop the violent attacks on America's institutions.[10]

The Weather Underground and Black Panther Party described themselves as Marxist/Communist. Their goal was toppling the U.S. government. The Weather Underground was involved in attacks on police stations, U.S. government installations, and targeted bombings. The Black Panther Party and Black Liberation Army were responsible for upwards of 70 attacks on police officers between 1970 and 1976, resulting in 15 police officers murdered.[11]

The FISA Wall and 9/11

American political leaders in both parties were aware that the FBI had taken aggressive steps to stop the violence tied to these organiza-

---

[9]   Ibid. *Prairie Fire,* page 5.

[10]   *"FBI Records: The Vault-COINTELPRO," vault. fbi.gov*

[11]   *"Police History: The Black Panthers and the rise of anti-cop violence," Police One, Tactical Analysis with* Mike Wood

tions. But when COINTELPRO came to light following Watergate, Democrats and Republicans alike condemned the FBI's spying on American citizens.[12]

The consequences were immediate and sweeping. The FBI closed its Domestic Intelligence Section and ended all of its domestic intelligence gathering activities. Many of its routine contacts and information sharing with local law enforcement ended as well.[13]

New guidelines were established and implemented by Attorney General Robert Levi for the conduct of foreign counterintelligence investigations. Congress passed legislation in the form of the Foreign Intelligence Surveillance Act (FISA), which created a separate FISA Court to consider requests for national security related wiretaps and searches.[14]

FBI agents working counterintelligence investigations were not permitted to share what they had gained with fellow agents conducting criminal investigations. This prohibition became known as *the Wall*. It was common knowledge inside the Department of Justice and the FBI. Everyone knew that violating the rules of *the Wall* could potentially cost an agent his or her job, if reported to the Intelligence Oversight Board.[15]

The Wall was in place when terrorists slammed airplanes into the Twin Towers of the World Trade Center, crashed another into the Pentagon, and a third into a field outside Washington, D.C. on September 11, 2001. When this act of war was committed against the United States, FBI agents in the New York City Office were in hot pursuit of Khalid-al-Mihdhar, for his role in the bombing of the U.S.S. Cole in Yemen in October 2000.

---

[12]   Ibid. *"FBI Records: The Vault"*

[13]   Ibid. *"FBI Records: The Vault"*

[14]   Ibid. *Homeland Insecurity,* pages 43-44.

[15]   Ibid. *Homeland Insecurity*, pages 49-50.

FBI Headquarters didn't share counterintelligence information with New York criminal agents because of *the Wall.* The FISA legislation passed by Congressional politicians with great fanfare in the 1970's to curb potential FBI abuse, resulted in the end of liberty for over 3000 people murdered in the simultaneous terrorist attacks on American targets. Had FBI agents assigned to criminal investigations been able to use the information collected from counterintelligence investigations of al-Mihdhar, perhaps the outcome on 9/11 would have been different.[16]

Appointment of FBI Director Robert Mueller and Politics in the FBI

President George W. Bush appointed Robert Mueller to become Director of the FBI during the summer of 2001. Mueller took office just a week before the 9/11 terror attacks. A former United States Marine, war hero, career prosecutor and Deputy Attorney General, Mueller's appointment was hailed by both political parties. During his confirmation process, which was ongoing in the weeks leading to 9/11, Mueller appeared at hearings held by Democratic Senator Patrick Leahy and Republican Senator Charles Grassley.

The political environment of the day was captured in this summary *from Homeland Insecurity, How Washington Politicians Have Made America Less Safe.*

"On August 2, 2001, 39 days prior to the 9/11 terrorist attacks on the United States, Democratic Senator Patrick Leahy delivered thirteen pages of remarks urging his colleagues to vote for former Assistant Attorney General Robert Mueller III to replace former FBI Director Louis Freeh.Seventy-four times during his remarks, Leahy, in his oversight role on the FBI as chairman of the Senate Committee on the Judiciary, focused on threats he said the Bureau posed to civil liberties in the United States. He characterized the power of the FBI as 'extraordinary,' and deplored the problematic nature of the 'FBI culture...'

---

[16] Ibid. *Homeland Insecurity,* pages 45-46.

"Appearing to speak more in sorrow than in anger, Senator Leahy said that since the role played by the FBI in combating sophisticated cases of terrorism and espionage was so critical to the nation, Congress needed to 'forge a constructive partnership with the Bureau's next director to get the FBI back on track.'"[17]

Senator Charles Grassley echoed Leahy's feelings, "I think there's a management culture that's at fault. I call it a cowboy culture…It's the kind of culture that puts image, public relations and headlines ahead of the fundamentals of the FBI."[18]

During his first ten years as FBI Director, Mueller complied as Senators Leahy and Grassley worked to exert political pressures on the FBI to have a greater say in how the Bureau was managed. Again, from Homeland Insecurity, published in 2008:

"In February 2002, Grassley joined with Senator Leahy in the hands-on approach Leahy had mentioned at Director Mueller's confirmation hearings the previous year and co-sponsored the FBI Reform Act…

"The FBI Reform Act of 2002 gives Congress the hands-on approach it has long desired in managing the FBI. Although he acknowledged that increased funding for FBI counterterrorism operations was an immediate necessity, Leahy made it clear that more money for the FBI meant more congressional involvement in management decisions…

"'…this bulking up of the FBI must be accompanied by increased congressional oversight. The hands-off approach to the FBI that Congress has taken in the past is no longer an option…'"[19]

Caving to the political pressures of the day, Director Mueller spent his first ten years on the job changing the FBI culture, just as Leahy and Grassley demanded. Bringing Maureen Baginski to the Bureau from

---

[17]   Ibid. *Homeland Insecurity*, page 76.

[18]   Ibid. *Homeland Insecurity, page 81.*

[19]   Ibid. *Homeland Insecurity, pages 82-83.*

the National Security Agency and Philip Mudd from the CIA, Mueller placed intelligence collection on an equal footing with the FBI's criminal investigations. He created Field Intelligence Groups, called FIGs in FBI field offices, and instructed them to answer to FBI Headquarters.

Investigations, the FBI's "bread and butter" began to take a backseat to analysis inside the FBI, resulting in a thirty per cent reduction in criminal investigations during Mueller's first few years on the job. When Mueller decreed that experienced field supervisors would be brought to FBI Headquarters whether they liked it or not, the FBI Agents Association painted the bleak picture to come:

"The FBI Agents Association, which represents about 80% of the Bureau's 12,000 agents conducted a survey of nearly 1,000 supervisors assigned at 56 field offices affected by the order and found that more than 50 percent of them intended to leave management or retire as a result of the order."[20]

The Agents Association worry became reality as Director Mueller approached the end of his ten -year term limit as head of the FBI. By this time, FBI agents promoted from the field to FBI Headquarters often had three or fewer years of experience as street agents prior to their transfers. Their lack of investigative experience was second only to their lack of knowledge of the FBI's culture. Their inability to hold their ground with senior officials when there were disagreements marked a major reversal in the FBI's longstanding independence from the Department of Justice. As Mueller's time at the FBI was coming to an end, the Bureau he led was becoming compromised by politics.

Against this backdrop, President Barack Obama asked Mueller to extend his stay as Director in 2011. By the time Mueller left the FBI in 2013, replaced by his protégé James Comey, many of the Bureau's employees, both agents and support, were deeply concerned about its future and the influence of politics on its independence. Not since J. Edgar Hoover had been appointed Director of the FBI in 1924, had its employees become so concerned about political corruption in its ranks.

---

[20]   *"5 Years Up Costs FBI Top Managers," Washington Times,* May 23, 2008.

FBI Employees' Letter to FBI Director James Comey

When James Comey entered office, he was presented with a five-page letter signed by "hundreds" of FBI employees representing a broad cross section of the FBI rank and file, identifying major issues within the FBI. The letter asked Comey to reset the FBI's course, and the employees pledged their loyalty on such an historic journey. Comey never acknowledged or further commented on the letter he was presented. Here is the final paragraph of the letter, which is included in the Appendix of this book.

"... Fidelity, Bravery and Integrity. It is the motto of the FBI and something that should be at the very core of the Bureau's Mission, always and everywhere. The Bureau is still an amazing law enforcement and national security agency, full of dedicated employees who march valiantly to protect the citizens of this beloved Nation. We know that our work is ultimately good vs. evil and that anything that takes us away from this Mission is a diversion, a calculated distraction that makes us less than we ought to be. **We pray that you recognize the dangerous territory into which the FBI has been purposefully led**. It can only be corrected with Godly wisdom, strength and fortitude; and you have our prayers and our support as you embark on this historic journey.

"The FBI once enjoyed the reputation as the finest law enforcement agency, serving the citizens of the greatest nation on earth. We believe that place of honor is still within our reach."[21]

Several years after James Comey replaced Robert Mueller as FBI Director, America plunged into the depths of darkness as an FBI intelligence operation spiraled out of control. The explosive debris of political interference in the Bureau's operations lay tangled in the wreckage of a political coup against a duly elected President. Americans still don't know the truth about what happened-and likely still is happening.

---

[21] From 5 Page Letter Given to FBI Director James Comey.

Some FBI employees saw the coming storm winds during President Obama's watch:

- Robert Mueller sold out the Bureau for power in 2001. Following his first major hearing with Leahy and Grassley, they both pressed him to change the "Bureau culture." After President Obama extended him for two more years as FBI Director, Mueller accelerated the pace of change in the FBI.

- Mueller brought in Maurine Baginsky and Philip Mudd from the NSA and CIA respectively, using them to place intelligence collection on an equal footing with criminal investigations inside the FBI.

- Mueller brought a few non-agents into the FBI to take over some of the Assistant Director positions, replacing FBI agents. These outsiders had Mueller's ear.

- Mueller left a morning meeting one day, glanced at the head of the Career Board and said, "this is not the way I want my Executive Staff to look." The Career Board got the message. Almost overnight, diversity seemed to become more important than competency and experience as a qualification for promotion and entry into the FBI.

- Andrew McCabe had three years of experience as an FBI agent in Chicago when he was first promoted to FBI headquarters. He had entered the FBI around 1998. By the time McCabe was appointed FBI Deputy Director, he had limited experience working cases on the street.

- By the time Barack Obama entered the White House, Mueller made clear to his Executive Staff that they better not embarrass him when representing the FBI in front of the President. If they did, they knew it could harm their chance for future promotions.

- Mueller invited executives from the Council on American Islamic Relations (CAIR) into the FBI to act as advisers on training FBI agents working terrorism investigations. When he was told that this was not a good idea and that CAIR would be listed as an unindicted co-conspirator in an upcoming terrorist financing trial on the Holy Land Foundation, he left his policy unchanged. It was not until an FBI agent testified in the Holy Land trial regarding CAIR, that Mueller ended the FBI's relationship with them. The Holy Land Foundation was convicted. An Appellate Court Judge ruled that there was "ample evidence," to include CAIR as an unindicted co-conspirator in the criminal case.

- While the FBI was being advised by CAIR, references to jihad, Islam, etc., were removed from FBI training manuals and exercises. An FBI Assistant Director supervised the effort. As a consequence, agents undergoing terrorism training received "politically correct" training, which had the potential to impact the judgements they might make in assessing investigations.

- When Army Major Nidal Hasan was involved in the Fort Hood massacre in November 2009, FBI agents attended a meeting at the Department of Justice, requesting subpoenas to obtain bank records in the case. The agents were told by Department of Justice (DOJ) officials that the case was not a terror case-it was a case of workplace violence and the DOJ would be handling it. The agents were told by the Department of Justice not to bring the matter up again.

- Mueller began placing Department of Justice (DOJ) attorneys into FBI field office Principal Legal Advisor (PLA) positions. The PLA plays a critical role in an FBI field office. It allows the Special Agent in Charge to discuss the legal aspects of investigative strategies. Replacing the PLA position with a DOJ attorney has the potential to directly interfere with the independence of an FBI investigation.

- As the Deputy Assistant Director of the Washington Metropolitan Field Office, Andrew McCabe was confronted by field agents at an All Agent Conference about his wife's acceptance of money from Terry McAuliffe and the Democratic National Committee, as she ran for political office in Virginia. The agents in Washington Field were concerned at the ethical issues involved and the perception of impropriety. McCabe did not address their concerns.

- When James Comey replaced Robert Mueller as FBI Director, morale was so low, and worry so high, that Mueller had completely decimated the FBI, a number of people signed the letter and presented it to the new Director to advise him of their concerns and suggestions on how to reverse course. Comey never mentioned, nor referred to the letter after he received it.

Was the FBI compromised during the latter years of the Obama Administration?

If so, did the compromise involve the Democratic Party, Democratic National Committee, and Terry McAuliffe?

Was the compromise part of a larger political intelligence operation to ease the way for the Democratic Party to implement their agenda for democratic socialism in America?

And did it eventually extend to efforts to undermine an American presidential election in 2016 by the intelligence community at large?

The answers lie in the changing culture at the FBI during the sixteen years it was led by Robert Mueller and James Comey. The answers lie in understanding the mission and the role of the FBI in American society.

The Weather Underground (WU), Black Panther Party (BPP), and Revolution

As any street agent working counterintelligence in New York City, Washington, D.C. and San Francisco learned, one of the objectives of the FBI's counterintelligence efforts was to identify and sort out known and suspected KGB and GRU intelligence officers from Soviet nationals who were in the country to perform legitimate diplomatic missions.

They did the job by evaluating what these people were saying to friends, colleagues and acquaintances. They assessed their contacts inside the United States. They analyzed their activities. They monitored their travel and financials. They compared them to the normal for intelligence officers who had been coming to the United States for decades.

It's reasonable to apply this assessment model to the Democratic Party and its political leaders and use the words from their 2016 party platform to understand where the progressives intend to take America. It's no coincidence that the party's strategy, and many of its words, themes, and objectives come directly from the pages of the Black Panther Party *Ten Point Program* and the Weather Underground's *Prairie Fire.*

Proclaiming themselves a "guerrilla organization," the Weather Underground made it clear, 'we are communist women and men, underground in the United States for more than four years.' We are deeply affected by the historic events of our time in the struggle against US imperialism." [22]

Weather Underground (WU), Coalition of the Masses, and the Democratic Party 2016 Platform

The Weather Underground strategy to topple the U.S. Government as the Vietnam War raged on, was to organize the "masses" to mount widespread demonstrations that would stop government in its tracks,

---

[22]   Ibid. *Prairie Fire*, page 10.

wreak havoc on cities and states, and stress police and fire services to the breaking point. The resulting instability in America would help the Weather Underground begin their transformation of our society. In *Prairie Fire*, the Weather Underground explained why revolution was necessary:

"Revolution is a fight by the people for power. It is a changing of power in which existing social and economic relations are turned upside down. It is a fight for who run things, in particular, for control by the people of what we communists call the means of production-the means by which people eat, work, protect themselves from the cold and the rain, get around, raise children and build..."[23]

In passage after passage in their *Prairie Fire* Manifesto, the Weather Underground identified the people whom they would target to build the mass resistance to launch the revolution:

"PRAIRIE FIRE is written to all... who are engaged in armed struggle against the enemy. It is written to prisoners, women's groups, collectives, study groups, workers' organizing committees, communes, GI organizers, consciousness-raising groups, veterans, community groups and revolutionaries of all kinds..."

"...the Black, Puerto Rican, Chicano, and Indian people... women...the Native American movement..."

"...the left must make clear at every point its unswerving and militant support for the liberation of Black, Puerto Rican, Chicano, Native American and all Third World peoples..."

"The Black Nation...Native Americans...the Chicano Struggle... Women...the Women's Movement...Revolutionary Women...Youth... Youth Culture...the Revolutionary Youth Movement...women against sexism..."[24]

As learned in the FBI years ago, while conducting an intensive decades long investigation of the Communist Party of the United States, identifying the "masses;" organizing and equipping them with all the

---

[23] Ibid. *Prairie Fire,* page 12.

[24] Ibid. *Prairie Fire*, page 5.

appropriate signs, slogans and symbols; and then launching mass demonstrations in a pre-selected American city was part of their strategy for successful revolution in America.

The Weather Underground understood the importance of the masses when they wrote *Prairie Fire's* political strategy.

"…We need a revolutionary communist party in order to lead the struggle, give coherence and direction to the fight, seize power and build the new society. Getting from here to there is a process of coming together in a disciplined way around ideology and strategy, developing an analysis of our real conditions, mobilizing a base among the US people, building principled relationships to Third World struggle, and accumulating practice in struggle against US imperialism."[25]

It's no surprise that the following categories of people identified in the 2016 Democratic Party platform, who are the focus of the party's efforts, look a lot like the same categories of people the Weather Underground identified decades ago:

"…African American, Latino, Asian American and Pacific Islander (AAPI), and American Indian teenagers and youth with disabilities…"

"…African Americans… Latino Americans…American Indians and certain Asian American subgroups…"

"…African Americans and Latinos, Native Americans and Alaska Natives, students with disabilities, and youth who identify as LGBT…"

"…Women…Women of Color…Women and Girls… Lesbian, Gay, Bisexual, and Transgender People…Young People…Religious Minorities…Refugees…"[26]

---

[25]   Ibid. *Prairie Fire*, page 4.

[26]   The 2016 Democratic Platform

Weather Underground (WU), Racism and the Democratic Party 2016 Platform

To keep the masses sufficiently motivated to sustain the *"resistance,"* the Weather Underground effectively stoked the flames of racism. They knew that the racism cry was inherently divisive and allowed for the creation of an enemy class (white people), against whom they could direct the anger of the masses. Connecting racism to the fairness of the criminal justice fueled the fire even more, directly challenging the notion that "all men are created equal," and that justice is blind.

The effect of this is to remove the rule of law as the foundation of the American Republic. Allowing a subversive organization like the Black Panther Party to demand that an entire race of people live by different rules because they are black "…we believe that all Black people should be released from the many jails and prisons because they have not received a fair and impartial trial," would effectively end the rule of law that has built America. It's the same rule of law that has acted as a restraint on government authority.[27]

Throughout the *Prairie Fire* document, the Weather Underground found many ways to label America and large categories of its population "racist."

"The Black movement was pushed forward into a revolutionary movement for political power, open rebellion and confrontation with the racism of white people and the racism of institutions…"

"The creation of an anti-racist white movement is the necessary foundation for the functional unity of Third World and white enemies of the empire. Anti-racist organizing and action can create this unity."

"Racism as a prime social and cultural dividing line was born in North America, out of slavery—it was born out of greed for profit, perpetrated by deception and a monopoly of firearms, not of biological superiority real or imagined…"

---

[27]   *Marxist History: USA: Black Panther Party, The Ten-Point Program, 10/15/66.*

"The US invented a new kind of racism and a more horrible form of slavery. It has been building on this ever since; and exporting its variety of racism to the rest of the world..."

"Racism is not only directed at Black people -it is also aimed at controlling whites to keep Black people in slavery, and the rulers firmly in command..."

"Racism is imperialism's most deadly weapon for brainwashing, controlling and mobilizing the LIS population in support of wars of conquest...They also draw on xenophobia and national chauvinism."

"Racism is the chief justification for US expansion and colonial ventures. The imperial army has been rallied with vile epithets since "the only good Indian is a dead Indian" and led into conquest by men like Teddy Roosevelt..."[28]

The Democratic Party platform of 2016 stressed "Ending Systemic Racism" and "Closing the Racial Wealth Gap." The platform sounds just like the Weather Underground's Prairie Fire Manifesto, the Black Panther Party Ten Point Plan, and the Marxist/Leninist ideology of communism.

"...Democrats will fight to end institutional and systemic racism in our society. We will challenge and dismantle the structures that define lasting racial, economic, political, and social inequity..."

"...our nation's long struggle with race is far from over...race still plays a significant role in determining who gets ahead in America and who gets left behind. We must face that reality and we must fix it."

"...Democrats support removing the Confederate battle flag from public properties, recognizing that it is a symbol of our nation's racist past that has no place in our present or our future. We will push for a societal transformation to make it clear that black lives matter and that there is no place for racism in our country."

"...Democrats will always fight to end discrimination on the basis of race, ethnicity, national origin, language, religion, gender, age, sexual orientation, gender identity, or disability."

---

[28]   Ibid. *Prairie Fire*, page 24, under caption "Racism."

"We have been inspired by the movements for criminal justice that directly address the discriminatory treatment of African Americans, Latinos, Asian Americans and Pacific Islanders, and American Indians to rebuild trust in the criminal justice system."

"Low income communities and communities of color are disproportionately home to environmental justice "hot spots," impacts of climate change will also... affect low-income and minority communities, tribal nations, and Alaska Native villages—all of which suffer the worst losses during extreme weather and have the fewest resources to prepare.... this is environmental racism."[29]

Weather Underground (WU), White Supremacy and Democratic Party 2016 Platform

If America is characterized by systemic racism and racist institutions, then there must be a social force that built and continues to foster racism in the United States. The revolutionary Weather Underground, the Black Panther Party and today's Democratic Party agree that there is such a force. That force is white supremacy, white nationalism, or white privilege. If white supremacy exists, it legitimizes the argument that America is an inherently racist society. Racism and white supremacy drive the divisive politics of the Democratic Party and have become institutionalized throughout their political agenda.

This is the formula the Weather Underground created to topple the American Government in the 1970's. It is the same formula the Democratic Party is using today on their march to a communist America.

The Weather Underground communist manifesto, *Prairie Fire,* explains how racism, white supremacy and white nationalism are connected and interrelated:

"...racism is not only directed at Black people-it is also aimed at controlling whites to keep Black people in slavery, and the rulers firmly in command. The institutionalizing of white supremacy created a struc-

---

29   The 2016 Democratic Party Platform.

ture to divide the white worker and small farmer from the Black slave. Coupled with the economic bribe of white privilege, it is the cornerstone of US history, the rock upon which capitalism and imperialism have been erected.[30]

The Black Panther Party for Self-Defense, in their Ten Point Program, reached the same conclusion, applying it to multiple issues impacting black communities:

"…we believe that if the White American businessmen will not give full employment, then the means of production should be taken from the businessmen…we believe that if the White Landlords will not give decent housing to our Black community, then the housing and the land should be made into cooperatives…Black people, are being victimized by the White racist government of America. We will protect ourselves from the force and violence of the racist police and the racist military, by whatever means necessary…"[31]

The Democratic Party platform of 2016 has adopted the language and issues the self-described "communist men and women" preached fifty years ago:

"It is unacceptable that the median wealth for African Americans and Latino Americans is roughly one- tenth that of white Americans…"

"We condemn Donald Trump's demonization of prisoners of war, women, Muslims, Mexicans, and people with disabilities; his playing coy with white supremacists…"

"Women of color who are disproportionately impacted by discriminatory pay practices…"

"We will also expand programs to prevent displacement of existing residents, especially in communities of color…"

"We will nurture the next generation of scientists, engineers, and entrepreneurs, especially women and people of color…"

"The racial wealth and income gaps are the result of policies that

---

[30]   Ibid. *Prairie Fire,*

[31]   *Marxist History: USA: Black Panther Party, The Ten-Point Program, 10/15/66.*

discriminate against people of color…"

"We recognize our current marijuana laws have had an unacceptable disparate impact in terms of arrest rates for African Americans that far outstrip arrest rates for whites.[32]

WU, Black Panther Party, Wealth Disparity, Capitalism and the Democratic Party 2016 Platform

The Democratic Party platform of 2016 is highly critical of today's "extreme levels of income and wealth inequality." They wrote the platform after eight years of a Democrat in the White House and wanting to elect yet another Democrat as President who advocated continuing on the same economic path. [33]

The U.S. economy has been far stronger since President Barack Obama left the White House and the nation's economic course was changed, following President Trump's election. More jobs have been added than in decades, the country's economic growth has set records, and the unemployment rate for all, including minorities, has fallen dramatically.

But that doesn't matter to the Democratic Party because the march to communism mandates the continued attack on capitalism in America.

"…we need an economy that prioritizes long-term investment over short-term profit-seeking, rewards the common interest over self-interest…we believe that today's extreme level of income and wealth inequality—where the majority of the economic gains go to the top one percent and the richest 20 people in our country own more wealth than the bottom 150 million—makes our… politics poisonous…ordinary Americans work longer hours for lower wages, while most new income and wealth goes to the top one percent…at a time of massive income

---

[32] The 2016 Democratic Platform

[33] Ibid.

and wealth inequality, we believe the wealthiest Americans and largest corporations must pay their fair share of taxes…we will ensure those at the top contribute to our country's future by establishing a multimillionaire surtax to ensure millionaires and billionaires pay their fair share… "[34]

The Black Panther Party demanded all of these same results in more generalized terms. "…we want full housing for our people…We Want Land, Bread, Housing, Education, Clothing, Justice and Peace."[35]

The Black Panther Party gave a warning as to what would happen if their demands weren't met:

"…When, in the course of human events, it becomes necessary for one people to dissolve the political bands which have connected them with another, and to assume, among the powers of the earth, the separate and equal station to which the laws of nature and nature's God entitle them, a decent respect of the opinions of mankind requires that they should declare the causes which impel them to the separation."[36]

The 2016 Democratic Party platform called for unity but outlined policies and ideas that build and spread division, anger and conflict. The Black Panther Party presented their list of wants, but then bluntly stated if their wants were not addressed, they would move for "separation."

This passage, from the Weather Underground's *Prairie Fire,* explains why their revolutionary movement was comparable to the Black Panther Party vision then, and fits within the Democratic Party ideology today, fifty years after *Prairie Fire* was written:

"The spirit of resistance inside the US was rekindled by Black people. The power and strategy of the civil rights movement, SNCC, Malcolm X, and the Black Panther Party affected all other rebellion.

---

[34] Ibid.

[35] *Marxist History: USA: Black Panther Party, The Ten-Point Program, 10/15/66.*

[36] *Marxist History: USA: Black Panther Party, The Ten-Point Program, 10/15/66*

They created a form of struggle "called 'direct action'; awoke a common identity, history and dignity for Black people as a colonized and oppressed people within the US; drew out and revealed the enemy through a series of just and undeniable demands such as the vote, equal education, the right to self-defense, and an end to Jim Crow. The police, the troops, the sheriffs, the mass arrests and assassinations were the official response. The Black movement was pushed forward into a revolutionary movement for political power, open rebellion and confrontation with the racism of white people and the racism of institutions…"[37]

The Democratic Party is fueling the division in America today, just as the Weather Underground promoted in its communist manifesto, *Prairie Fire*.

The Democratic Party 2016 platform aggressively advocates for division between black and white Americans. It creates other categories of minorities to further that division- Latinos, Native Americans, undocumented immigrants. It calls for broad based U.S. Government policies which would further institutionalize racial divide and create more racial conflict in America.

The only agency that had the capability and power to evaluate why the Democratic Party would use division to accomplish its political agenda was the FBI. The only agency trusted enough by the public to neutralize a uniquely American coup involving a major American political party was the FBI. Was the FBI compromised internally beyond its ability to handle the job? If it was, did it become wittingly, or unwittingly, a part of the vision for successful revolution in America outlined by the Weather Underground's- *"communist- minded men and women."*

---

[37]   Ibid. *Prairie Fire,*

CHAPTER TWO

"Don't tell me words don't matter..."
Barack Obama

Senator Barack Obama hadn't even won the Presidential election of 2008 when he exhorted cheering crowds that, "we are five days away from fundamentally transforming the United States of America." While fighting Hillary Clinton for the Democratic Party nomination, he defended the rousing speeches he gave that brought people to their feet. "Don't tell me words don't matter," he engaged with Clinton, when she accused him of being all talk and no experience during one of their debates. Of course, Obama was right. Words do matter. [38]

Barack Obama's "Fundamental" and Huey Newton's "Total" Transformation of America

What did the newly elected president mean when he described the changes his Presidency would bring to America? What would the im-

---

[38] "In Context" What Obama Said About Fundamentally Transforming the Nation," by Tim Ryan, February 6, 2014, *Politifact.* "An Obama Refrain Bears Echoes of a Governor's Speeches," by Jeff Zeleny, February 18, 2008, *The New York Times.*

pact of those changes be on America's future? Change. Progressive. Transformation. Imported directly from the 1960's and designed to topple the U.S. government during the days of the Vietnam War, these were the words of the radical and violent communist movement inside America then.

These same words are shaping the democratic socialist movement inside the Democratic Party now. President Obama's administration co-opted the words of the violent "communist-minded men and women" of the Weather Underground terrorist organization and the Black Panther Party for Self-Defense to announce his fundamental transformation of America. Today, his Democratic Party has adopted their strategy to implement that transformation. [39]

The Democratic Party is moving forward with these same words and strategies at a feverish pace. This is the "fundamental transforming of America" that Obama spoke of and it is in high gear as the 2020 presidential election approaches.

President Obama's expressed intention to fundamentally transform America sounded a lot like the words of Huey Newton, who, along with Bobby Seale, founded the Black Panther Party in Oakland, California in the mid-1960's. Huey Newton gave a speech at Boston College in 1970, telling his sympathetic audience America was a country of racists and fascists, responsible for fascism, aggression, brutality and murder. His solution, "in order to change it, there must be a total transformation...The Black Panther Party is a Marxist-Leninist Party..."[40]

Invoking the memory and philosophies of both Karl Marx and Vladimir Lenin, Newton told his audience that "society goes from a slave class to a feudalistic class structure to a capitalistic class structure to a socialistic class structure to communism. Or in other words from socialist state to capitalist state to non-state communism...in order for a revolution to occur in the United States you would have to have a redis-

---

[39]   Ibid. *Prairie Fire.*

[40]   "Huey Newton Introduces Revolutionary Intercommunalism, Boston College, November 18, 1970, *libcom.org.*

tribution of wealth...on an inter-communal level."[41]

Almost 20 years after Newton gave the speech at Boston College, he was asked during an interview if he saw the Black Panthers as a local organization or a revolutionary organization. He explained that the Black Panthers thought if they could chase the "oppressive army of police" out of Oakland, they would gain national attention. The attention would lead to an alliance with the international communist movement, worker's movement, and international proletariat.[42]

As a result, the Black Panther Party would become more connected to the Cuban revolution. Newton viewed the black community as nothing more than a pawn to be used in creating and intensifying race as an issue that would lead to conflict and transformation.

"... I think I had read a book called the...Imperial, Materialism and Empirical Criticism...by I.V. Lenin... there were many contradictory social forces and if you knew what to increase or decrease at a particular time that you could cause the transformation...so we were trying to increase the conflict that was already happening and that was between the White racism...the police forces in the...various communities in the Black communities in the country...We felt that we would take the conflict to so high a level that some change had to come."[43]

When Obama first used the words describing his intentions as to "fundamentally transforming," America, there were people across the country who became immediately concerned. They understood the significance of his choice of words. And they realized that words do matter.

"We Americans generally don't do fundamental transformation. We make changes, yes, small and large, but who among us—other than

---

[41] Ibid. libcom.org.

[42] "Eyes on the Prize II Interviews, Interview with Huey P. Newton," by Louis Massiah, May 23, 1989, *Washington University Digital Gateway Texts*.

[43] Ibid. *Washington University Digital Gateway Texts*.

the most radical revolutionaries—actually want to fundamentally transform the nation?...Ask professors who teach history or political ideologies (as I have for two decades) and we will tell you that totalitarianism is the ideology that fundamentally transforms. Indeed, the textbook definition of totalitarianism...is to seek to fundamentally transform—specifically, to fundamentally transform human nature via some form of political-ideological-cultural upheaval..."[44]

Barack Obama Reintroduces Police Racism to America

An incident seven months after Obama's inauguration would establish the tone of his entire presidency. Americans didn't realize it then, but Obama's reaction to a routine police incident in Massachusetts formally reintroduced revolution and "police racism" to America, as the President embarked upon his fundamental transformation of the country.

Following a neighbor's report of a possible residential break-in, Cambridge, Massachusetts, police Sergeant (Sgt.) James Crowley went to the home of Harvard professor, Henry Louis Gates. Finding an individual inside, Crowley asked that he identify himself. The individual, who would later be identified as Gates, said, "No, I will not."[45]

Another officer who had arrived on the scene, wrote in a police report, "the gentleman was shouting out to the Sgt. that the Sgt. was racist and yelled 'this is what happens to black men in America.'"[46]

Professor Gates refused to calm down, continued yelling at the

---

[44] "How Obama Made Good on His Promise to Fundamentally Transform USA," by Dr. Paul Kengor, January 16, 2017, *CNS News.*

[45] "2 Cambridge Worlds Collide in Unlikely Meeting," by Don Van Natta, Jr. and Abby Goodnough, July 26, 2009, *The New York Times.*

[46] "Cambridge Mayor: Gate's Arrest Shouldn't Have Happened," July 24, 2009, *CNN.*

officer, was arrested and taken to the Cambridge Police Department. When Sergeant Crowley refused to apologize for his handling of Gates, the mayor of Cambridge, Denise Simmons, apologized to the professor during a phone call. Simmons told CNN's American Morning, "this can't happen again in Cambridge."[47]

Before having all the facts, President Obama went public with his opinion:

"But I think it's fair to say, No. 1, any of us would be pretty angry; No. 2, that the Cambridge police acted stupidly in arresting somebody when there was already proof that they were in their own home; and, No. 3 ... that there's a long history in this country of African-Americans and Latinos being stopped by law enforcement disproportionately." The incident, Obama said, shows "how race remains a factor in this society."[48]

After a week of taking criticism for his comments, President Obama called Sgt. Crowley, but stopped short of apologizing to him. "The fact that this has become such a big issue I think is indicative of the fact that... race is still a troubling aspect of our society. Whether I were black or white, I think that me commenting on this and hopefully contributing to constructive, as opposed to negative, understandings about the issue is part of my portfolio."[49]

Throughout his next seven years in the White House, President Obama used tragedies on America's streets to unfairly tag the police with the racist label. Resurrecting the racial divide in America was President Obama's portfolio. And he used his own Department of Justice, led by his "wingman," Attorney General Eric Holder to fan the flames of that racial divide. Consider these examples:

---

[47]   Ibid. *CNN.*

[48]   Ibid. *CNN.*

[49]   "Statement by the President," July 24, 2009, Office of the Press Secretary, The White House.

George Zimmerman and Trayvon Martin

In October 2012, two Florida residents, George Zimmerman and African- American Trayvon Martin, age 17, got involved in an altercation late at night in the gated community where they lived. Zimmerman shot Martin, who died of his wounds.

President Obama reacted to photos of a much younger Trayvon Martin, saying, "you know. If I had a son he'd look like Trayvon." He added, "when I think about this boy, I think about my own kids...I think every parent in America should understand why it is imperative that we investigate every aspect of this."[50]

Zimmerman called the shooting self-defense. When all the facts were in, a local jury agreed. He was acquitted of murder and manslaughter at his trial. An FBI civil rights investigation of the circumstances of the shooting took three years. When finally completed, it exonerated Zimmerman of committing a hate crime.

Michael Brown

During August 2014, African- American Michael Brown, age 18, of Ferguson, Missouri was stopped on a neighborhood street by Officer Darren Wilson. Brown had been reported as a suspect in the robbery of a convenience store. Brown weighed close to 300 pounds and stood 6 feet 4 inches tall. When Brown didn't cooperate with Officer Wilson, there was a struggle. Wilson shot and killed him. A witness claimed that Brown stood with his hands up in the air surrendering, and Officer Wilson shot him anyway. Peaceful and non- peaceful protests broke out around the country with the cry, "Hands Up, Don't Shoot."[51]

---

[50] "Obama on Trayvon Martin: 'If I Had a Son, He'd Look Like Trayvon,' by Krissah Thompson and Scott Wilson, March 23, 2012," *Washington Post.*

[51] "'Hands Up, Don't Shoot,' Ranked One of Biggest 'Pinochios' of 2015, by Nick Gass, 12/14/2015," *Politico.*

When all the investigations were completed, the local police and District Attorney found that Officer Wilson acted in self-defense. An FBI civil rights inquiry determined the same. The witness who said he saw Brown with his hands up had been lying. Nonetheless, Officer Wilson was forced to leave the department and his hometown.

Attorney General Eric Holder launched a separate Department of Justice inquiry that he controlled, directed at the Ferguson Police Department itself. Holder's inquiry concluded there was a systemic pattern of unlawful conduct. Following the release of the report, President Obama told the country the white police force was "systematically biased," and placed minorities into an "oppressive and abusive situation."[52]

Freddie Gray

Police in Baltimore were very familiar with Freddie Gray as they engaged in a foot pursuit of him on an April evening in 2015. When Gray was finally captured and placed in a police van for allegedly possessing a switchblade knife (illegal under Baltimore law), he suffered a spinal cord injury on the way to jail. He died several days later.

Rioting broke out in Baltimore for a number of days, as the police tried to control the crowd, while pelted with rocks and bottles. Looters ransacked businesses and set buildings on fire at the height of the violence. But the police were ordered from the highest levels of city government to stand down and not react.

Marilyn Mosby, Baltimore's City Attorney took to the microphones as the city was being attacked. She announced in a fiery and impassioned voice to the crowd, "I heard your call for 'No justice, no peace.' Your peace is sincerely needed as I work to deliver justice on

---

[52]　"Remarks at a Town Hall Meeting and a Question-and-Answer Session at Benedict College in Columbia, South Carolina," March 6, 2015, *Administration of Barack Obama, 2015.*

behalf of this young man. ... Our time is now!"[53]

Within two weeks of Freddie Gray's death, Mosby filed murder and manslaughter charges against six Baltimore police officers. Her conduct led famed Harvard Attorney Alan Dershowitz to say, "these... officers may have made a mistake, but they are not guilty of criminal conduct...she's a part of a larger problem...Black Lives Matter is endangering the fairness of our legal system. Because they're rooting for outcomes based on race. Started a long time ago. Started with the O.J. Simpson case."[54]

After a mistrial was declared in one of the officer's trial and three officers were found not guilty, the trial judge dropped all of the charges against the remaining officers. The Federal government also declined to file any civil rights related charges. Five of the officers caught up in Mosby's prosecution recently secured a victory in Federal Court, with a judge ruling they can proceed with the Discovery process in a malicious prosecution case against Mosby.

Prior to the officers being charged, President Obama told the country, "this has been going on for a long time. This isn't new and we shouldn't pretend that it's new."[55]

Alton Sterling

In early July 2016, *The Washington Post* was one of many media outlets rushing to judgment with dramatic headlines following the shooting of Alton Sterling by police in Baton Rouge, Louisiana. Declaring that Sterling's death appeared to be legal and preventable, the paper

---

[53]   "Read the Transcript of Marilyn J. Mosby's Statement on Freddie Gray," May 1, 2015, Time Magazine.

[54]   Alan Dershowitz, "Black Lives Matter is Endangering the Fairness of Our Legal System," by Ian Schwartz, May 25, 2016, *Real Clear Politics*.

[55]   Baltimore Sun, April 28, 2015.

went on to post videos of a police search of Sterling, accompanied by the statements of a witness that Sterling was complying with the requests of the officers when he was shot.

An opinion piece in *The New York Times* was even more severe. It asserted that black lives matter until they don't. It added Sterling's name to the list of black citizens who have fallen as victims of police brutality because they are black. The writer portrayed Sterling as "selling CDs in front of a convenience store," as if the police are a menace to anyone standing on a random street corner.[56]

Police had responded to a complaint call involving Sterling. When he didn't comply with their instructions during the stop, a struggle ensured. The police officers believed Sterling was reaching for a weapon. He was shot. Two previous attempts to subdue him by use of a taser were ineffective. As it later turned out, Sterling was in possession of a .38 caliber revolver. The Department of Justice (DOJ) launched a Civil Rights investigation. It took a year to complete, concluding in 2017. There was not enough evidence to support any charges.

As part of the extensive investigation, FBI agents and Department of Justice attorneys interviewed dozens of witnesses. They reviewed video from a variety of sources, assessed crime scene forensics, and interviewed the two officers involved in the shooting. They also reviewed the video with two independent use- of- force experts. Those experts concluded that "the officer's actions were reasonable under the circumstances and thus met constitutional standards."[57]

President Obama released a statement telling Americans that there was a significant disparity in the numbers of police actions taken against blacks and other minorities. "And when incidents like this occur, there's a big chunk of our fellow citizenry that feels as if because of the color of their skin, they are not being treated the same. And that hurts. And

---

[56] "Alton Sterling and When Black Lives Stop Mattering," by Roxane Gay, July 6, 2016, *The New York Times.*

[57] "Federal Officials Close Investigation into Death of Alton Sterling," Department of Justice, Office of Public Affairs, May 3, 2017.

that should trouble all of us."[58]

Philandro Castile

On July 6, 2016, Minneapolis police officer Jeronimo Yanez shot and killed Philandro Castille during a car stop. Castille told the officer he had a weapon. He began reaching for something, as the officer yelled for him to stop. When he didn't follow the officer's instructions, he was shot. Castille's girlfriend said he was reaching for his identification. The stop and the conversation between the officer and Castille, was captured on the police dash-cam. Yanez was charged with three felonies, including manslaughter.

President Obama, who was traveling in Europe, issued a statement on the shooting within 24 hours, "..Americans, should be troubled by these shootings, because these are not isolated incidents." "They're symptomatic of a broader set of racial disparities that exist in our criminal justice system."[59]

Yanez was acquitted of all the charges a year later by a trial court jury.

The Ambush and Murder of Dallas Texas Police Officers

When lone sniper, Micah Johnson, killed five law enforcement officers and wounded seven others in a shooting spree in Dallas, Texas several days after the shooting of Alton Sterling, it was because he "wanted to kill white people, especially white officers."[60]

---

[58] "Statement by the President, The White House," Office of the Press Secretary, July 7, 2016.

[59] "Statement by the President, The White House," Office of the Press Secretary, July 7, 2016.

[60] "Police in Dallas: 'He Wanted to Kill White People, Especial-

Johnson had served in the U.S. Army and been deployed to Afghanistan. But investigators found his social media pages laced with indications he'd adopted the ideology of the Black Panthers, Black Lives Matter and the Black Power movement. Johnson chose a peaceful march where people were using the streets of Dallas to protest Alton Sterling's death. As the shots rang out, America's so-called brutal and over-militarized police, rushed to the sounds of the guns, risking their lives to protect those protesting against them.

At a memorial service for the slain Dallas officers, President Obama addressed each of them by name and had nice things to say about their sacrifice and the necessity of preserving the rule of law in America.

Then he said, "... when African Americans from all walks of life, from different communities across the country, voice a growing despair over what they perceive to be unequal treatment; when study after study shows that whites and people of color experience the criminal justice system differently, so that if you're black you're more likely to be pulled over or searched or arrested, more likely to get longer sentences, more likely to get the death penalty for the same crime...it hurts."[61]

The Ambush and Murder of Police Officers in Baton Rouge

Less than two weeks after the attack on police in Dallas, three law enforcement officers were ambushed and murdered in Baton Rouge by Gavin Eugene Long, clad in black, wearing a mask and carrying a rifle near a shopping complex. Long fired 43 rounds in 14 minutes, before he

---

ly White Officers,'" by Matt Zapotosky, Adam Goldman, and Scott Higham July 8, 2016, *Washington Post.*

[61] "Remarks by the President at Memorial Service for Fallen Dallas Police Officers," The White House, Office of the Press Secretary, July 12, 2016.

was killed by police. In a suicide note found at his residence, Long, who was honorably discharged after serving five years in the U.S. Marines, said he wanted good and bad cops killed, because even the good ones were part of a criminal justice system that committed crimes against his "people."

Racism-the Common Underlayment for Marxist Style Transformations

President Obama's comments on every case mentioned above disregarded the fact patterns. His judgments on each one was never supported by Federal civil rights investigations or jury decisions. But Obama's own words may have been a factor in the attacks on police in Dallas and New Orleans. Did the president use the tragic incidents in America's streets to promote his true "fundamental transformation?"

Here is how one author discussed the importance of transformation in the conflict between capitalism and communism.

"Marx stated that "between capitalist and communist society lies the period of the revolutionary transformation of the one to the other...

"Marx failed to provide a specific name to this period of fundamental change, but his intellectual successor, Vladimir Ulyanov, did. Ulyanov — better known as "Lenin" — named this transitional period "socialist...

"Since capitalist oppression is based upon the private ownership of the means of production, the only way to "cure" oppression is to eliminate private property... When the socialist goal of abolishing private property is accomplished, the theory goes, oppression will no longer exist, and society will evolve to the classless, utopian "synthesis" of capitalism and socialism — the communist mode of production...

"In his book, Dialectical and Historical Materialism, Stalin officially adopted Marxist theories as the official "world outlook" of the Soviet Union. While the Soviet Union may have fallen, the Left's belief in Marxist theory of societal evolution — and socialism — continues. Therefore, when leftists praise socialism and call for "change" or "progress," Americans must ask: "Change to what?" and "Progress towards what?" The answer to both questions is communism."[62]

The Weather Underground, Black Panther Party and President Obama's Fundamental Transformation

The blueprint for President Obama's fundamental transformation comes directly from the pages of the Black Panther Party *Ten Point Program* and the Weather Underground *Prairie Fire*, communist manifesto. The current Democratic Party agenda is an extension of Obama's fundamental transformation and built on the back of the same words, plans and strategies that characterized the subversive efforts to topple the American government during the 1970's.

The Black Panther Party's *Ten Point Program* encompassed the following demands. Their purpose was the mobilization of the oppressed "masses," of Black Americans in preparation for a socialist America, based on the Marxist-Leninist model:

- "We Want Freedom. We Want Power to Determine the Destiny of our Black Community. We believe that Black people will not be free until we are able to determine our destiny.

- "We believe that the federal government is responsible and obligated to give every man employment or a guaranteed income. We believe that if the White American businessmen will not give full employment, then the means of production should be taken from the businessmen and placed in the community so that the people of the community can organize and employ all of its people and give a high standard of living...

- "We believe that this racist government has robbed us, and now

---

[62] "Socialism and Marx's Theory of Societal Evolution," by Jayme Sellards, March 27, 2019, *American Thinker.*

we are demanding the overdue debt of forty acres and two mules. Forty acres and two mules were promised 100 years ago as restitution for slave labor and mass murder of Black people...

- "We believe that if the white landlords will not give decent housing to our black community, then the housing and the land should be made into cooperatives so that our community, with government aid, can build and make decent housing for its people...

- "We want education for our people that exposes the true nature of this decadent American society. We want education that teaches us our true history and our role in the present-day society...

- "We Want All Black Men to Be Exempt from Military Service. We believe that Black people should not be forced to fight in the military service to defend a racist government that does not protect us. We will not fight and kill other people of color in the world who, like Black people, are being victimized by the White racist government of America. We will protect ourselves from the force and violence of the racist police and the racist military, by whatever means necessary.

- "We believe we can end police brutality in our Black community by organizing Black self-defense groups that are dedicated to defending our Black community from racist police oppression and brutality...

- "We believe that all Black people should be released from the many jails and prisons because they have not received a fair and impartial trial...

- "We want all Black people when brought to trial to be tried in court by a jury of their peer group or people from their Black communities...

- "Prudence... will dictate that governments long established should not be changed for light and transient causes...But, when a long train of abuses and usurpations, pursuing invariably the same object, evinces a design to reduce them under absolute despotism, it is their right, it is their duty, to throw off such government, and to provide new guards for their future security."[63]

The Weather Underground's (WU) *Prairie Fire* manifesto called for organizing the masses and building a base of solidarity with the hungry, angry, poor and working people of America. They were Black, Puerto Rican, Chicano, Native American and Third World. The WU viewed these categories of people as undeveloped revolutionaries to be organized and directed at white supremacy, imperialism, corporations, sexism and racism. Their goal was the toppling of the American Republic, "the empire" from the inside.

- "Throughout its history, the rulers of the U.S. have maintained their power by creating privileged sectors among the people and letting us fight over the privileges... their main weapon is white supremacy...

- "Our job is to tap the discontent seething in many sectors of the population, to find allies everywhere people are hungry or angry, to mobilize poor and working people against imperialism...

- "The corporate myth of limitless consumption is based on control of Third World resources. The ruling class depends upon petrochemical products, high horsepower and excessively heavy cars, plastics and synthetics and nitrogen fertilizers. The failure to develop good sources of energy (such as fusion or

---

[63] "The Ten Point Program," by Huey P. Newton and Bobby Seale, October 15, 1966, *Marxist History Archive.*

solar energy) is not based on priorities for a better life, but on profit…

- "There are two currents of thought and activity that conspire to hold back the power of the movement. They are American exceptionalism and reformism…They are both racist in effect…

- "The lack of a national organization, embracing and based in popular movements, unified around anti-imperialism is a most severe weakness. People need organization. Organization unites, gives direction and breadth to particular political work. The lack of organization affects all other problems…

- "Sexism. The full participation and leadership of women is necessary for successful and healthy revolution…The development of the independent women's movement as well as active struggle against the institutions and ideas of sexism are the basis for ensuring that the revolution genuinely empowers women…

- "Racism. The left must make clear at every point its unswerving and militant support for the liberation of Black, Puerto Rican, Chicano, Native American and all Third World peoples. It must refuse to compromise this active support for short-term "gains," or to win the approval of whites we are trying to organize at the workshop, in the schools or the communities.

- "This is true for the whole movement and for every individual in the movement. The creation of an anti-racist white movement is the necessary foundation for the functional unity of Third World and white enemies of the empire. Anti-racist organizing and action can create this unity. Where this kind of work has begun, it should be broadened and extended…"

- "Opposition to racism. The spirit of resistance inside the US was rekindled by Black people…the Black movement was pushed forward into a revolutionary movement for political power, open rebellion and confrontation with the racism of white people and the racism of institutions...

- "It is the responsibility of mass leaders and organizations to encourage and support revolutionary armed struggle, in open as well as quiet ways...There are many faces to militant resistance and fighting, a continuum between guerrilla and mass work. An examination of recent history points to acts of resistance . . . draft card burnings, sabotage in the military, on the job, in government, and attacks on the police; mass demonstrations . . . Marches on the Pentagon, Stop the Draft Week, African Liberation Day rallies. International Women's Day marches, Chicano Moratorium marches; demands for control and power through seizures of institutions...

- "The, true history of the Americas begins with the original peoples of the hemisphere...Columbus noted his first day on American soil that 'the people are ingenious and would make good servants'...Historically, the cultural and social justification of slavery had been religious...

- "Racism as a prime social and cultural dividing line was born in North America, out of slavery—it was born out of greed for profit, perpetrated by deception and a monopoly of firearms... The notion that slavery is somehow based upon racial and cultural inferiority of African and other Third World peoples has been deeply embedded into every US institution as the chief means of brainwashing and using the white population...

- "The institutionalizing of white supremacy created a structure to divide the white worker and small farmer from the Black slave..."

- "Imperialism—which everything points to as being the last

stage of capitalism—was a historical necessity, a consequence of the development of the productive forces and of the transformation of the methods of production in the general contour of humanity as a whole in movement. A necessity, just as the national liberation of the peoples, the destruction of capitalism, and the arrival of socialism are at present...

- "We have an urgent responsibility to destroy the empire from within in order to help free the world and ourselves from its grasp...Our final goal is the destruction of imperialism, the seizure of power, and the creation of socialism.

- "Our strategy for this stage of the struggle is to organize the oppressed people of the imperial nation itself to join with the colonies in the attack on imperialism. This process of attacking and weakening imperialism involves the defeat of all kinds of national chauvinism and arrogance; this is a precondition to our fight for socialism."[64]

Barack Obama Adopts the Racism Strategy of Weather Underground Terrorists and Black Panther Party

After decades of relative calm, the election of Barack Obama returned America to an era of words, symbols and slogans to fan the flames of a new generation of revolutionaries-however, this time the propaganda and misinformation comes from inside the U.S. government.

Racism as an issue is alive and well again in America-not because Americans refused to confront their racial past, but because the Democratic Party, with President Obama's election, has painted the police and America's institutions with the sweeping stroke of racism to build

---

[64] Ibid. Weather Underground, *Prairie Fire.*

the foundation for their fundamental transformation of American society. It would be built on the strategy prescribed decades earlier by "communist minded men and women."

Writing in the *New York Post*, John R. Lott, Jr. said, "Inflammatory, false claims about police racism not only endanger the lives of police officers, they can also lead to higher crime rates—especially in heavily black areas. If Obama really cares about poor blacks, he should be more careful getting his facts right."[65]

Eldridge Cleaver, Bobby Hutton and Black Panther Party Ambush the Oakland Police

Getting the facts straight, as Mr. Lott said, is vital. However, in dealing with the ideology of communism and the "communist minded men and women" who preach it, intentionally spreading false facts is a part of the gospel. Take the example of young Black Panther Party (BPP) member Bobby Hutton, Eldridge Cleaver, the party's information minister, and an "ambush" in Oakland, California on April 6, 1968.

"The first recruit to sign up for the BPP was 15 year -old Bobby Hutton, who met Newton and Seale at an anti-poverty program in downtown Oakland. He was so young, the story goes, that Newton and Seale had to get his mother's permission for him to join. Hutton became the Party's national treasurer and a close running buddy of Newton, Seale and eventually Cleaver. In April 1968, Bobby Hutton became a symbol of the police brutality against black Americans...

"On 6th April 1968 eight BPP members, including Hutton, Eldridge Cleaver and David Hilliard, were traveling in two cars when they were ambushed by the Oakland police. Cleaver and Hutton ran for cover and found themselves in a basement surrounded by police. The building was fired upon for over an hour. When a tear-gas canister was thrown into the basement the two men decided to surrender...

---

[65] "Obama's False Racism Claims Are Putting Cops' Loives in Danger," by John R. Lott, Jr. July 8, 2016, *New York Post*.

"Cleaver was wounded in the leg and so Hutton said he would go first. When he left the building with his hands in the air, he was shot twelve times by the police and was killed instantly. "

"Oakland police, responding to the initial gunfire, engaged with BPP members for over 90 minutes, eventually arresting at least eight of them, including Cleaver. News reports flashed throughout the country that the BPP had been ambushed by the police and that "Little" Bobby Hutton was murdered...

"America's big city streets were already uneasy, just days following the assassination of Dr. Martin Luther King in Memphis, Tennessee. Tension was high. The criminal justice system clamped down on publicity and none of the police officers involved in the shooting were able to talk about what had happened from their perspective. For over twelve years the only version of events carved into America's history had been carefully choreographed by Eldridge Cleaver, the BPP and their defense attorneys..."[66]

The only thing better than having a live martyr like Huey Newton to attract recruits to the BPP, was having "Little" Bobby Hutton, "murdered" by the Oakland police. Eldridge Cleaver and his wife, Kathleen, fled the country before Cleaver could be tried for his role in the shooting. They lived in Cuba and Algeria before finally returning to the United States in 1980. By then, Cleaver had become a born-again Christian, turned his back on the communist revolution, and wanted to resolve the charges against him.

During a 1980 interview with a reporter, Cleaver was asked directly if he had arranged for the Black Panthers to ambush the police, contrary to the version of events that had been held up as truth for so many years.

"'Did you ambush the police back in 1968?' the reporter asked him." "'I wasn't charged with ambushing the police,' he answered evenly.

---

[66] By John Simkin, September 1997, updated August 2014, *Spartacus-Educational*.

"'I'm not asking about the charges. Did you deliberately ambush the cops?'"

"'...I don't want to be misunderstood,' he began in the slow, deliberate drawl that can be so irritating when he uses it to evade a direct question. 'I am no longer in favor of going after the police with gun"... With that context clear" he paused until I looked up from my notepad and met his eyes-'yes.'"[67]

For the first time, Oakland Police Officer Nolan Darnell was able to tell journalist Kate Coleman his recollections of April 6, 1968:

"Me and my partner were on routine patrol... Suddenly, without warning or any provocation, the bullets were coming at us from every angle... He (Darnell's partner) was hit like nine or ten times. I thought he was dead. Immediate panic set in. As I got out of the car to get a better aim, I got hit."[68]

Jensen was wounded thirteen times. Darnell was shot in the shoulder. Over 50 bullets and bullet fragments were later discovered in their patrol car. Huey Newton had lied about his responsibility for the death of Oakland Police Officer John Frey. Eldridge Cleaver lied about his responsibility for the ambush of the Oakland police. They saw themselves as the vanguard of a communist revolution in America. The police provided a perfect symbolic target for the imagery they needed to assemble recruits.

Without portraying the police as the enemy, the BPP lacked victimhood. As Newton so carefully explained at Boston College, the BPP had to use the issue of black racism and paint the police as the oppressors, to create the conflict necessary to bring about the transformation of America.

---

[67] "Souled Out, Eldridge Cleaver Admits He Ambushed Those Cops," *New West Magazine*, by Kate Coleman, May 12, 1980.).

[68] Ibid. "Souled Out..." *New West Magazine*. May 12, 1980.

Using Racism, President Obama Ignites the Occupy Movement, Black Lives Matter

Obama skillfully used the policing incident in Connecticut involving Professor Henry Lewis Gates to lecture America that, "there is a long history in this country of African Americans and Latinos being stopped by police disproportionately... It's a sign of how race remains a factor in this society.""[69]

During President Obama's time in office, the country watched the creation and growth of *Occupy Wall Street* and *Black Lives Matter*, with the latter engaging in highly flammable rhetoric, resurrecting the image of the first iteration of the Black Panther Party in Oakland, California.

Here's a CBS version of at least one incident involving *Black Lives Matter* in Minnesota in 2015, "protesters in a Black Lives Matter march held outside the Minnesota State Fair over the weekend were captured on video yelling 'pigs in a blanket, fry'em like bacon,' a statement that some law enforcement members viewed as targeting police officers..."[70]

President Obama Pursues International Solidarity as a Message to the Socialist Movement

President Barack Obama's fundamental transformation of America began early in his Presidency when he traveled to other countries of the world, issuing various statements of apology for America. For example, before the Turkish Parliament, Obama had this to say, "The United States is still working through some of our own darker periods in our history...Our country still struggles with the legacies of slavery

---

[69] "Obama Criticizes Arrest of Harvard Professor," by Helene Cooper, July 22, 2009, *The New York Times*.

[70] "'Pigs in a Blanket' Chant at Minnesota State Fair Riles Police," *CBS News*, August 31, 2015.

and segregation, the past treatment of Native Americans...''[71]

President Obama's fundamental transformation didn't stop with resurrecting the revolutionary messages of international solidarity and division inside the United States. His policies abroad were even more potentially devastating than his apologies for America. For example, the Obama Administration threw its support behind the Muslim Brotherhood in Egypt, although the Brotherhood was one of Iran's closest allies in spreading Islamic jihad.

An adviser to Iran's Supreme Leader, Ayatollah Khamenei said, "the Brotherhood is closest to Tehran among all Islamic groups." Even when the Egyptian people revolted against the Muslim Brotherhood's Mohammed Morsi in a successful coup attempt, Obama's Secretary of State Hillary Clinton demanded Morsi's release from jail.[72]

The Obama Administration learned very little from the example involving the Muslim Brotherhood. By 2016, Obama's State Department gave $350,000 to an Israeli organization, One Voice. One Voice had one focus during the Israeli elections- to oust Israeli Prime Minister Benjamin Netanyahu."[73]

The same State Department observed from afar as Libya collapsed; the transnational terrorist organization, ISIS, grew throughout the Middle East, attacking Christians and Muslims alike; Syria used chemical weapons against its own citizens, ignoring Obama's red line; China busied itself expanding its military and building islands in the strategically important South China Sea; and revolutionary movements spurred by China, Cuba and Russia, resumed in South America.

---

[71] "Obama's Top Ten Apologies (So Far)," by Mark Tapscott, *Washington Examiner,* June 4, 2009.

[72] "Why Did the Obama Administration Support Morsi's Muslim Brotherhood," by Irina Tsukerman, July 28, 2018, *The Jerusalem Post.*

[73] "NGO Connected to Obama's 2008 Campaign Used US Tax Dollars Trying to Oust Netanyahu," by Jennifer Rubin, July 12, 2016, *Washington Post.*

President Obama's Misuse of U.S. Government Agencies in Furtherance of the Transformation

The Tea Party and Domestic Dissent

President Obama's Internal Revenue Service spent several years harassing the Tea Party and affiliated organizations, which had been instrumental in handing the Republicans a majority in both houses of Congress during the 2012 elections. By 2017, after countless lawsuits and the discovery process, "in a legal settlement that still awaits a federal judge's approval, the IRS 'expresses its sincere apology' for mistreating a conservative organization called Linchpins of Liberty—along with 40 other conservative groups—in their applications for tax-exempt status."[74]

The Misuse and Abuse of America's Intelligence Agencies

Of course, whether the issues were domestic or international, they involved national security policy. Obama's key national security advisers included Ben Rhodes, John Brennan and Susan Rice. All three proved themselves to be serial liars.

As a Senate Intelligence Committee investigated the use of torture by the CIA in the Middle East, CIA officers covertly penetrated the network computers used by the Senate investigators. Senator Dianne Feinstein's comments weren't pleasant after she found out about the CIA's activities.

"I have grave concerns that the CIA's search may well have violat-

---

[74] "IRS Apologizes for Aggressive Scrutiny of Conservative Groups," by Peter Overby, *NPR*, October 27, 2017.

ed the separation of powers principles embodied in the United States Constitution... have asked for an apology and a recognition that this CIA search of computers used by its oversight committee was inappropriate. I have received neither."[75]

President Obama's CIA Director Brennan was furious that his agency would be so accused.

"Nothing could be further from the truth...We wouldn't do that. That's just beyond the scope of reason in terms of what we'd do."[76]

Months later, a CIA investigation found that CIA officers had engaged in the use of torture-and had indeed penetrated the computer network of the Senate Intelligence Committee, as it was preparing its own report on the Agency's interrogation tactics.

Nothing happened to John Brennan or his officers as a result of the torture and the lies. In fact, Brennan's stature grew with President Obama throughout the president's second term in office. So did the lying.[77]

To be fair, former CIA Director John Brennan wasn't always a liar. When he sat down to take a polygraph test to get into the CIA, he decided to come clean about how he had voted in the 1980 presidential election. His choice-Gus Hall, the Chairman of the Communist Party of the United States. The admission didn't stop him from employment or promotion within the CIA. It didn't stop him from becoming President Obama's major intelligence asset. And it didn't stop Brennan from offering an even more aggressive explanation of his decades old vote in 2016.

"I said I was neither Democratic or Republican, but it was my way,

---

[75] "Feinstein Drops CIA Bombshell," by Jeremy Herb, Alexander Bolton and Ramsey Cox, 3/11/2014, *The Hill*.

[76] "A Brief History of the CIA's Unpunished Spying on the Senate," Conor Friedersdorf, 12/23/2104, *The Atlantic*.

[77] "*A Brief History of the CIA's Unpunished Spying on the Senate*," by Conor Friedersdorf, *The Atlantic*, 12/23/2014).

as I was going to college, of signaling my unhappiness with the system, and the need for change. I said I'm not a member of the Communist Party, so the polygrapher looked at me and said, 'OK,' and when I was finished with the polygraph and I left and said, 'Well, I'm screwed'[78]

Talking to the Congressional Black Caucus at a conference on diversity in the intelligence community, Brennan said:

"'We've all had indiscretions in our past... I would not be up here if that was disqualifying... [79]

"So if back in 1980, John Brennan was allowed to say, 'I voted for the Communist Party with Gus Hall' ... and still got through, rest assured that your rights and your expressions and your freedom of speech as Americans is something that's not going to be disqualifying of you as you pursue a career in government.[80]

It's reassuring that President Obama's national security advisers, responsible for the safety and security of 320 million Americans, view freedom of speech as a means to harbor those who advocate the overthrow of our constitutional Republic.

Brennan was a good liar, but in the Obama Administration, he just barely made the varsity lying team. Susan Rice, President Obama's United Nations Ambassador wins the go-to prize when the Obama players needed a really good lie. After four Americans, including the U.S. Ambassador to Libya, were killed in a large-scale terror attack mounted against the American diplomatic compound in Benghazi on 9/8/2010, Rice told the America public:

"Based on the best information we have to date, what our assessment is as of the present is in fact what began spontaneously in Benghazi as a reaction to what had transpired some hours earlier in Cairo

---

[78] "CIA Director Reveals He Was Once a Communist Sympathizer" by Eric Levitz, 9/22/2016, *New York Magazine.*

[79] "Polygraph Panic: CIA Director Fretted His Vote for Communist," by Tal Kopan, September 15, 2016, *CNN.*

[80] Ibid. *CNN.*

where, of course, as you know, there was a violent protest outside of our embassy-- --sparked by this hateful video. But soon after that spontaneous protest began outside of our consulate in Benghazi, we believe that it looks like extremist elements, individuals, joined in that--in that effort with heavy weapons of the sort that are, unfortunately, readily now available in Libya post-revolution. And that it spun from there into something much, much more violent."[81]

As Rice pedaled the story, others in the administration fell into line with her rhetoric. Secretary of State Hillary Clinton echoed the video defense of the tragedy in Benghazi. Documentary evidence showed that President Obama's National Security adviser Ben Rhodes provided Rice her talking points. Rice dramatically pedaled the Rhodes' script into a lying act deserving of a Hollywood Oscar.

In a release of documents pursuant to a lawsuit brought by *Judicial Watch*, it was revealed that Rhodes had prepped Rice to appear on television news Sunday talk shows several days following the Benghazi attacks. Her task- to stress the terror attacks were spontaneous and based on a video when the administration knew the attacks were pre-planned all along and the video had nothing to do with them.

One of the State Department documents released to *Judicial Watch* was sent to Susan Rice. It highlighted the following passage, which the Obama Administration planned to use in defending its story that the attacks were a result of the video.

"This story is absolutely wrong. We are not aware of any actionable intelligence indicating that an attack on the U.S. Mission in Benghazi was planned or imminent. We also see indications that this action was related to the video that has sparked protests in other countries."[82]

This talking point was a lie. The entire Obama national security team was in on it. Protecting President Obama from the fallout in a

---

[81]   "Flashback: What Susan Rice Said About Benghazi," 11/16/2012, *Wall Street Journal*

[82]   Forty-one Documents Released by the Department of State to Kate Bailey, Judicial Watch, enclosed in letter dated /17/2014.

political election season was the priority. Telling the truth about Benghazi was not. Hillary Clinton told Congress as much, in a stinging insult to the families of those who died there- "what difference does it make?" the words she uttered, while under oath, to a congressional committee.

Rice didn't suffer from her unwavering loyalty to the president. When Ben Rhodes left his position, Susan Rice became President Obama's National Security adviser and stayed in the position until he left office.

John Brennan, Susan Rice, Ben Rhodes, Hillary Clinton. All of their names continue to surface as America tries to determine what truly happened in the Clinton email investigation, the Donald Trump Russian investigation, and the unmasking of intelligence information during the waning days of the Obama years.

President Obama and Bill Ayers, Weather Underground Terrorist and Mentor to the President

The "transparency" of the Obama Administration, highly touted by Attorney General Eric Holder and an adoring mainstream media, was simply an illusion in a two-term magic show. Perhaps the most stirring act in Obama's magical eight years in the White House was concealing any hint of a connection between he and former Weather Underground leader Bill Ayers.

To this day, Americans still do not know the specifics of Obama's relationship with Ayers, driven by his goal of overthrowing the U.S. Government in a revolutionary and bloody uprising. Obama's handlers have proven themselves to be the masters of lies designed to conceal Obama from the scrutiny he has always deserved, but never received. Is it a coincidence that today's Democratic Party speaks with the same words and strategies of the resistance that come directly from the pages of the Weather Underground's *Prairie Fire?* Was Barack Obama's fundamental transformation merely a return to the revolution of the 1970's?

The following summary appears to be as balanced as anything the authors have read or found, about the relationship between Obama and

Ayers.

"Bill Ayers was born into and raised on the wealthy side of Chicago. His father Thomas was the CEO and president of Chicago's electric utility company, Commonwealth Edison. He was also a close friend of Richard Daley, mayor of Chicago between 1989 and 2011. Bill Ayers attended a public and a prep school in Chicago before going to the University of Michigan. After becoming involved in various protests and demonstrations, he joined the Students for a Democratic Society...

"Bernardine Dohrn graduated from University of Chicago Law School, becoming an organizer for the National Lawyers Guild. She joined the SDS, breaking from them in 1969, along with Mark Rudd, who headed the SDS at Columbia. Both believed SDS had become too passive and had decided the only way to achieve their goals was violent revolution. Dohrn described herself as a revolutionary communist. Ayers' objective was the fight against American imperialism, using the Vietnam War as a means to build a revolutionary youth group...

"But attacking police and smashing windows was not enough to satisfy Ayers' appetite for destruction. Two months later he and several other Weathermen leaders set up an explosives' factory in a house in New York's Greenwich Village. They intended to make bombs to blow up Fort Dix, in New Jersey, and police headquarters in New York and Detroit...

"But one of the bombs accidently exploded, leveling the town house and killing three people. According to the Washington Post, the Weathermen claimed responsibility for 25 bombings, including the Pentagon in 1972 and the State Department in 1975. The 1976 FBI report detailed at least 30 bombings and attempted bombings by the Weathermen between October 1969 and September 1975...

"Ayers has always claimed that his bombings were designed to damage property. In fact, they killed at least seven people, three of whom were police officers. The worst, and perhaps most notorious, was the 1981 robbery of a Brinks armored truck in Nanuet, New York, in which two police officers and a Brinks guard were killed. Ayers was not directly involved, although Kathy Boudin and David Gilbert, two of his close Weatherman comrades, were...

"One former member of the Weathermen, Larry Grathwohl, became an FBI informant and later testified to the Senate Judiciary Committee that he had been in meetings with Ayers where it was made clear that Ayers wanted people killed or injured by his bombs. Grathwohl said that when "Billy Ayers gave me instructions on where and when to place explosives, I warned him that people would be killed. 'In a revolution,' Ayers replied, 'some people have to die... '"In February 1970, the Weathermen placed a bomb on a window ledge at a San Francisco police station; it killed one officer and injured eight others. According to Grathwohl's Senate Judiciary Committee testimony, Ayers told him that Bernardine Dohrn had planned, developed, and carried out the San Francisco bombing...

"Dohrn and 27 other Weathermen members traveled to Yugoslavia and Hungary in 1968 to meet with representatives of the Viet Cong and to discuss how further student unrest in the U.S. might assist the North Vietnamese and Viet Cong. She also maintained close relationships with members of the Cuban UN mission in New York. She made several trips to Cuba, where, according to the FBI reports, she met with Cuban and Vietnamese intelligence officers to plan strategies to frustrate American efforts in Vietnam. According to an FBI agent who followed her activities, in the late 1960s Dohrn lived in the San Francisco home of a Chinese Communist agent...

"Ayers, for his part, must have been in higher demand at home, and we know only of several trips to Canada. But not to go fishing- in one meeting with representatives of the North Vietnamese government in Toronto, Ayers was presented with a ring made from the metal of an American airplane shot down over North Vietnam. Later, he said he was so moved by the gesture that he "left the room to cry. I realized... America was evil...and that I was...living inside the belly of the beast...

"Both Dohrn and Ayers joined a number of boards and became active in all the usual liberal causes. They were welcomed by Chicago's liberal establishment, and in 1997, Mayor Richard M. Daley made Ayers "Chicago's Citizen of the Year." Dohrn had worked as a clerk at law firm Sidley and Austin in New York. Michele Obama had worked for the firm in Chicago...

"Re Obama connection- "Certainly they knew each other in the early 1990s, if not before, in Chicago when Obama was a community organizer and Ayers was working on juvenile justice and education reform. In 1993, Ayers worked closely with ACORN on school reform while Obama was ACORN's lawyer. They served on two foundation boards together in the mid-1990s. In 1995 Ayers and Dohrn hosted the famous party at their house for Obama when he announced his candidacy for the Illinois state senate..."

"...1998 interview with Connie Chung on ABC News, Dohrn said, "We'd do it again. I wish that we had done more. I wish we had been more militant." Ayers famously said almost the same thing in a New York Times interview published on September 11, 2001."[83]

The National Lawyers' Guild- "The U.S. Will Require a Vast Restructuring of Our Entire Society"

The National Lawyers' Guild, Bernardine Dohrn's former employer, is described on its webpage as:

"The National Lawyers Guild (NLG) was founded in 1937 as an association of progressive lawyers and jurists who believed that they had a major role to play in the reconstruction of legal values to emphasize human rights over property rights...

"Guild members defended FBI-targeted members of the Black Panther Party, the American Indian Movement, and the Puerto Rican independence movement and helped expose illegal FBI and CIA surveillance, infiltration, and disruption tactics that the U.S. Senate Church Commission detailed in the 1975-76 COINTELPRO hearings and that led to enactment of the Freedom of Information Act and other specific

---

[83]   "They're All in this Together," by Alfred S Regnery, 9/2/2011, *American Spectator.*

limitations on federal investigative power...

"During the McCarthy era, Guild members represented the Hollywood Ten, the Rosenbergs, and thousands of victims of anticommunist hysteria. Unlike all other national civil liberties groups and bar associations, the Guild refused to require "loyalty oaths" of its members; it was unjustly labeled "subversive" by the United States Justice Department, which later admitted the charges were baseless, after ten years of federal litigation. This period in the Guild's history made the defense of democratic rights and the dangers of political profiling more than theoretical questions for Guild members and provided valuable experience in defending First Amendment freedoms that informs the work of the organization today...

"The NLG supported self-determination for Palestine, opposed apartheid in South Africa at a time when the U.S. Government still labeled Nelson Mandela a "terrorist," and began the ongoing fight against the blockade of Cuba. During this period, members founded other important civil rights and human rights institutions, such as the Center Constitutional Rights, the National Conference of Black Lawyers, the Meiklejohn Civil Liberties Institute in Berkeley, San Francisco's New College School of Law and the Peoples Law School in Los Angeles. In the 1980s, the Guild pioneered the "necessity defense," supported the antinuclear movement, and began challenging the use of nuclear weapons under international law...

"In 1989, the Guild prevailed in a lawsuit against the FBI for illegal political surveillance of legal activist organizations, including the Guild. The suit, which had been filed in 1977, revealed the extent to which the government had been spying on the NLG. Since 1941, the FBI used over 1,000 informants to report on NLG activities and disrupt Guild meetings and conferences....

"In the 1990s, Guild members mobilized opposition to the Gulf War, defended the rights of Haitian refugees escaping from a U.S.-sponsored dictatorship, opposed the U.S. embargo of Cuba, and began to define a new civil rights agenda that includes the right to employment, education, housing, and health care...

"At the dawn of the 21st century, the globalization of information and economic activity is a fact of life, but so is the globalization of extremes in wealth and poverty. The U.S. population faces trends that will require a vast restructuring of our entire society if we are to avoid the social chaos that is already overtaking life in our major cities, or the militarized imposition of social peace that we see in other unstable societies and that is embodied in post-9/11 laws and policies. Guild members have long recognized that neither democracy nor social justice is possible, internationally or domestically, in the face of vast disparities in individual and social wealth. In short, the organization has always seen questions of economic and social class as inextricably intertwined with most domestic and international justice issues."[84]

Obama- "be Practical" and Just Choose What Works Between Capitalism and Socialism

When he left office, President Obama was riding atop the same apology horse that carried him through eight years as President. He and Eric Holder continue to talk about the amazing transparency and scandal free years of the Obama Presidency. Yes, those are lies as well. But there is a special truth that accompanies and rewards "communist minded men and women" and those who preach the ideology of communism. Lying is totally justified and permissible for the common good. CNN isn't going to question the lying Left.

Here is the message that President Obama gave to a group of students during a visit to Argentina as his days in the White House came to an end:

"So often in the past there has been a division between left and right, between capitalists and communists or socialists, and especially in the Americas, that's been a big debate...Oh, you know, you're a capitalist Yankee dog, and oh, you know, you're some crazy communist

---

[84] "History...Today and Tomorrow," Website, *National Lawyers' Guild*

that's going to take away everybody's property...

"Those are interesting intellectual arguments, but I think for your generation, you should be practical and just choose from what works. You don't have to worry about whether it really fits into socialist theory or capitalist theory. You should just decide what works..."[85]

Obama ended his administration as he started it, appealing to international solidarity. Urging everyone who would listen, that it wasn't necessary to decide between capitalists and communists or socialists-that people "should just decide what works," was Obama's outgoing message to the world.

In Obama's mind, the millions of people killed across the world as academic elitists and communist tyrants worked to establish socialist, and then communist utopias, at the expense of individual freedom and failed social engineering, was merely an "intellectual argument."

President Obama freely criticized police tactics and methods during the eight years he was in office. He took every opportunity he could to connect incidents and violence on the streets to a key phrase of the 1960's communist revolutionaries- systemic police racism. President Obama used his Department of Justice to hold open the door as purveyors of the ideology of communism worked to steal the Democratic Party's soul.

By the time Obama left office, his Department of Justice was enforcing consent decrees directed at fourteen of the nation's police departments, all in the spirit of Obama's legacy to reform America's police and rid them of "implicit bias"-bias they didn't even realize they possessed, since it was buried so deeply in their subconsciousness.[86]

To those supportive of communist ideology, reforming the police

---

[85]   "Obama: Forget the Difference Between Capitalism and Communism, 'Just Decide What Works,' by Tim Hains, March 25, 2016, *Real Clear Politics*.

[86]   "Sessions Wants a Review of Consent Decrees, Which Have Been Used for Decades to Force Reforms," by Mark Berman, April 4, 2017, *Washington Post*.

and making them the enemy in the eyes of the public, is the first step towards controlling the police. A federal government controlling the longstanding tradition of local policing in America, is a giant step towards communist style totalitarianism. Once the U.S. Government controls the police and treats their "implicit bias," controlling citizens of our country will not be far behind.

CHAPTER THREE

"Time for a Third Revolution...we had one in
1776...we had one in the 50's and 60's-"
Eric Holder

Eric Holder was President Obama's first Attorney General. He served for six years, until replaced by Loretta Lynch in April 2015. Holder made clear how he felt about racism in America- including inside the nation's police departments. Less than a month after President Obama's inauguration, Holder wrote a letter to the men and women of the Department of Justice, in commemoration of Dr. Martin Luther King Day.

"... the need to confront our racial past, and our racial present, and to understand the history of African people in this country, endures...." "...One cannot truly understand America without understanding the historical experience of black people in this nation." "...Simply put, to get to the heart of this country one must examine its racial soul." "...In things racial we have always been and continue to be, in too many ways, essentially a nation of cowards." "...this nation has still not come to grips with its racial past nor has it been willing to contemplate, in a truly meaningful way, the diverse future it is fated to have.

"...I fear however, that we are taking steps that, rather than advancing us as a Nation, are actually dividing us even further." "...there will be no majority race in America in about fifty years- the coming diversity that could be such a powerful, positive force will, instead, become a reason for stagnation and polarization." "…It is also clear that if we are to better understand one another, the study of black history is essential, because the history of black America and the history of this nation, are inextricably tied to each other." "…Black history is given a separate, and clearly not equal, treatment by our society in general and by our educational institutions in particular." "…But an unstudied, not discussed and ultimately misunderstood diversity can become a divisive force."[87]

The speech became one of the most powerful and controversial, during Holder's tenure as Attorney General. He called America a "nation of cowards," when it came to things "racial." Holder warned America that in a few decades there would be no majority race in the United States. If we lacked the courage to examine our "racial soul" and understand the linkage between the history of Black America and America itself, our fate would become one of division, stagnation and polarization.

America had just elected its first Black president. But in Eric Holder's mind, America hadn't done enough. America was racist. Its past was racist. Its institutions were racist. It hadn't "come to grips with its racial past." If there was any doubt as to how the Obama Administration was going to view race relations, Holder gave the country an early look at what to expect.

Holder eventually put his thinking and words about racism into context. He gave an interview to Michele Norris, of the Race Card Project. When the topic turned to the concept of revolutions, Holder responded:

"Time for a Third Revolution…we had one in 1776…we had one in the 50's and 60's…fifty years from that last revolution it may be time for us to take stock of where we are as a nation and rededicate ourselves to the principles of Dr. King and come up with answers for our time…

---

[87] "Attorney General Eric Holder at the Department of Justice African American History Month Program," 2/18/2009, *Office of Public Affairs.*

this is a revolutionary country…George Washington was revolution-ary…Benjamin Franklin was a revolutionary…they saw inequality, they saw unjust system and they resorted to revolution…"[88]

The interview with Norris is Eric Holder's signed statement that he is well aware of the intent and goals of the violent revolutionaries of the 1960's. President Obama's first attorney general concluded that present day America could use a third revolution.

The Weather Underground's Strategy for Waging Revolutionary War in America- *Prairie Fire*

In *Prairie Fire,* the Weather Underground (WU) announced its in-tent to forge an alliance with the Black Liberation movement to "wage war" to overthrow the U.S. government.[89]

Implementing the WU plan required direct attacks on the thin blue line-America's policing, "to retaliate for the most savage criminal at-tacks against Black and Third World people, especially by the police apparatus."[90] The Weather Underground claimed responsibility for tar-geted bombings of police stations across the country, including:

"Haymarket police statue, Chicago, October 1969 and October 1970; Chicago police cars, following the murder of Fred Hampton and Mark Clark, December 1969; New York City Police Headquarters, June 1970; Marin County Courthouse, following the murder of Jonathan Jackson, William Christmas and James McClain, August 1970; Long Island City Courthouse, in Queens, in solidarity with prison revolts tak-ing place in New York City, October 1970; Department of Corrections in San Francisco and Office of California Prisons in Sacramento, for the

---

[88]   "Modern day civil rights challenges," Michele Norris Interview of Attor-ney General Eric Holder, January 18, 2016, *Race Card Project.*

[89]   *Prairie Fire: The Politics of Revolutionary Anti-Imperialism, The Politi-cal Statement of the Weather Underground.*

[90]   Ibid. Prairie Fire.

murder of George Jackson in San Quentin, August 1971; Department of Corrections in Albany, N.Y., for the murder and assault against the prisoners of Attica, September 1971; 103rd Precinct of the New York City police, for the murder of 10-year-old Clifford Clover, May 1973."[91]

The Black Panther Party (BPP); Black Liberation Army (BLA); Weather Underground (WU); Students for a Democratic Society (SDS); Socialist Worker's Party (SWP); Communist Party of the United States (CPUSA) and other anti-war and revolutionary groups that wanted to overthrow the U.S. Government, turned out thousands of people to engage in mass demonstrations. University and college campuses became the scene of riots and violence in the streets. Institutions of higher learning- such as Columbia University, University of California at Berkeley, Pennsylvania State (Penn State), and others, exploded with anger and rage.

Holder himself was part of a sit-in at a Columbia University residence hall Reserve Officers' Training Corps (ROTC) lounge in 1970.[92]

Americans weren't clinging to a racial past they couldn't let go of when they voted for Barack Obama as President. Eric Holder and President Obama returned America to the crime scene of revolutionary violence committed decades earlier, under the guise of racial injustice. Why-so they could resurrect a racial divide in the United States as part of President Obama's fundamental transformation of America.

Holder's philosophy was converted into action early in the Obama administration. He decided that the Department of Justice would drop charges against members of the New Black Panther Party for voter intimidation. Prompted by an incident during the 2008 elections, "in which Black Panthers in intimidating outfits and wielding a club stood outside a polling place in Philadelphia.," Holder closed the investigation upon assuming office. When questioned before Congress about his

---

[91] Ibid. *Prairie Fire.*

[92] "Attorney General Eric Holder Speaks at the Columbia University School of Law Commencement," 5/14/2010, *Office of Public Affairs*, The United States Department of Justice.

decision, Attorney General Eric Holder launched a scolding lecture.[93]

"When you compare what people endured in the South in the 60's to try to get the right to vote for African Americans, and to compare what people were subjected to there to what happened in Philadelphia—which was inappropriate, certainly that... to describe it in those terms I think does a great disservice to people who put their lives on the line, who risked all, for my people...To compare that kind of courage, that kind of action, and to say that the Black Panther incident wrong thought it might be somehow is greater in magnitude or is of greater concern to us, historically, I think just flies in the face of history and the facts."[94]

Attorney General Holder relied on his version of past American history to justify intimidation of voters at polling locations. Holder's recall of the history of the Black Panther Party was incomplete.

The Weather Underground and Black Panther Party Unite to Overthrow the U.S. Government

The Black Panther Party and Weather Underground formed an alliance to topple the American government during the 1970's. Violence and division based on racial conflict was their strategy. President Obama and Eric Holder, the President's self-described "wingman," used the White House and Department of Justice to reintroduce racial conflict to the American public-from the inside.[95]

A rewrite of American history is underway to cast the Black Panther Party as a group of caring individuals who gave warm lunches to black school children in Oakland, California in the late 1960's and early 70's. Law enforcement officers on the ground have dramatically dif-

---

[93] "Eric Holder: Black Panther Case Focus Demeans 'My People,'" by Josh Gerstein, 3/1/2011, *Politico*.

[94] Ibid. *Politico*, 3/1/2011.

[95] "I'm Still the President's Wingman," by Josh Gerstein, 4/4/2013, *Politico*.

ferent memories. The FBI predicated a major investigation of some members of the Panthers and the Party itself, because of its involvement in killing police officers across the country.

Contrary to the image of Black Panther Party members acting as community organizers to feed the young and hungry, the FBI characterized the BPP as:

"...a black extremist organization founded in Oakland, California in 1966. It advocated the use of violence and guerrilla tactics to overthrow the U.S. government. In 1969, the FBI's Charlotte Field Office opened an investigative file on the BPP to track its militant activities, income, and expenses."[96]

Huey Newton was found guilty of manslaughter in the shooting death of Oakland police officer John Frey on October 28, 1967. In 1971 a California Appellate Court reversed Newton's conviction, citing prejudicial error. Newton had claimed he was lying unconscious in the street when Officer Frey was shot and killed. Eyewitness testimony to the shooting contradicted Newton's story. Newton later bragged that he was the person who shot Officer Frey in the back. Officer Frey was left to die in the early morning hours on the pavement of an Oakland street.

Newton's continuing journey as an activist and leader of the Black Panthers took him to China, where he was hailed as a hero. He traveled to Fidel Castro's Cuba, where he was welcomed with open arms and granted sanctuary. Ultimately, he returned to the United States and a life in and out of crime.

Newton's statement that the Black Panther Party he co-founded was a Marxist/ Leninist movement is important for all America to understand. Using the term "total transformation" in his Boston College speech calling for a communist revolt inside America, Newton forewarned our country of subversive forces working to destroy our Republic. President Barack Obama's fundamental transformation of America is the political version of that revolution.

While Huey Newton and the Black Panthers were ambushing the

---

[96]   FBI Records: The Vault- Black Panther Party.

police and inciting revolution, the Weather Underground, a violent break-away from the Students for a Democratic Society, was attacking national guard armories, police stations, government installations and American corporations.

By May of 1974, the Weather Underground was ready to distribute their plan for "action and unity" to bring about a communist revolution inside the United States. Called *Prairie Fire,* and written by Bernardine Dohrn, Jeff Jones, Celia Sojourn, and "Billy Ayers," *Prairie Fire* was written to "communist-minded people, independent organizers and anti-imperialists," to mobilize a base of people who would become the nexus of a "revolutionary communist party" that would "seize power and build the new society."[97]

In *Prairie Fire*, the Weather Underground explained that the:

"...revolution is a fight by the people for power. It is a changing of power in which existing social and economic relations are turned upside down. It is a fight for who run things, in particular, for control by the people of what we communists call the means of production -the means by which people eat, work, protect themselves from the cold and the rain, get around, raise children and build."[98]

The leaders of the Weather Underground were astute and educated in the use of communist propaganda. They realized the importance of forming a cohesive bond involving activists within the black community, inside prisons, and with other Third World people, who believed that America was an imperialist and evil nation.

The Weather Underground made clear that its intention was to forge alliances with the perceived victims of America's so-called empire building. The Weather Underground's ultimate objective was to topple the empire from the inside and through force, "... we realized the power of armed self-defense, mass rebellion and revolutionary violence

---

[97]   *Prairie Fire: The Politics of Revolutionary Anti-Imperialism, The Political Statement of the Weather Underground.*

[98]   *Prairie Fire: The Politics of Revolutionary Anti-Imperialism, The Political Statement of the Weather Underground.*

in the Black movement."[99]

Like Huey Newton and the Black Panther Party, the Weather Underground viewed their quest for power in terms of transformation moments in American history. *Prairie Fire* is replete with the transformation philosophy integrated into a communist revolutionary strategy:

"Militant confrontation politics **transformed us…**we broke with a powerless past."

"Black Power had become the slogan for the Black liberation movement, and its political thrust **transformed the civil rights movement**."

"SDS was faced with several urgent necessities: to draw broader masses of people into the struggle, and also to organize our cadre and **transform ourselves** into a force which could eventually contend for power."[100]

The Weather Underground went to great length in *Prairie Fire* describing the America that would emerge in place of the imperialist government they planned to topple:

"…Our final goal is the destruction of imperialism, the seizure of power, and the creation of socialism…socialism is…the rejection of empire and white supremacy…socialism is the violent overthrow of the bourgeoisie, the establishment of the dictatorship of the proletariat, and the eradication of the social system based on profit…power will be in the hands of the people…society will have to be reorganized…there will be some rebuilding to do."[101]

---

[99]   Ibid. *Prairie Fire.*

[100]   Prairie Fire: The Politics of Revolutionary Anti-Imperialism, The Political Statement of the *Weather Underground.*

[101]   Ibid. *Prairie Fire.*

The Marxist Influence on the Weather Underground and Black Panther Party

As self-described Marxist/Leninist communists, Huey Newton, the Black Panther Party, and the leaders of the Weather Underground, found a common foundation based upon the teachings of Karl Marx. Some experts recognize Marx as the father of modern communism.

Born into a middle -class German family in 1818, Marx became a journalist and philosopher, adopting hard left radical friends and ideologies when he went away to the University of Berlin. Marx came to believe that communism was the future and that the hard left needed to force change upon citizens by exerting pressure from the government and society. After years of research, writing, and study, Marx and Friedrich Engels wrote the Communist Manifesto.

They laid out the basis for a classless society, which would come after the citizens of the world joined together in a class struggle to end capitalism and the capitalist mode of production. They would replace it with socialism-and then communism. Marx regarded the industrial working class in capitalism as the proletariat and the owners of the means of production as the bourgeoisie.

Marx viewed capitalism as a history of class struggle against the proletariat. Only through a revolution and rejection of capitalism would workers be able to move towards a classless society. To achieve the desired revolution, Marx envisioned the proletariat initially making a series of demands.

The demands included a progressive income tax, the end of private property ownership and child labor, free education, nationalized communication and transportation networks, a national bank and increase in government owned businesses. Marx believed that through the establishment of a wide variety of transparent and subversive groups in countries around the world, the democratic socialist movement would grow. Through international solidarity, the movement would expand its influence and become the foundation of an alliance that would replace capitalism with communism.

The principle factor in moving from capitalism to communism would be the seizure of the means of production by the proletariat. Marx saw this transformation as key to the classless society. Marx realized that the leap from capitalism to socialism might require revolutionary force. He didn't back away from the potential of a bloody battle to reach his goals. He also justified the instability and social upheaval that would accompany the transformation from capitalism to communism. In the end, communism-classless and Godless, would be worth the sacrifice. According to Marx, "my object in life is to dethrone God and destroy capitalism."[102]

Black Extremism, the Congressional Black Caucus, and A.G. Eric Holder

In an August 3, 2017 FBI report on Black Extremism, the Bureau identified individuals targeting police over perceptions of police brutality. The Congressional Black Caucus, referencing COINTELPRO of the 1960's, fired off a letter to current FBI Director Christopher Wray, criticizing the report saying it, "conflates black political activists with dangerous domestic terrorist organizations."[103]

The Congressional Black Caucus has long been penetrated by advocates of the ideology of communism from the 1960's that is on the rise again today as a result of President Obama's fundamental transformation. Eric Holder's declaration that America does not want to confront its racist past has bolstered their resolve.

The American police are the victims of systemic group and individual violence, not the perpetrators of it. Huey Newton and the Black Panther Party of the 1960's and 1970's wanted Americans to believe the

---

[102]   "Do Marxism and Communism Have Anything in Common?" by Bill Flax, *Forbes,* May 12, 2011.

[103]   "FBI's Black Identity Extremists Assessment Spurs Question from Lawmakers," by Max Kutner, 11/29/2017, *Newsweek.*

police were brutal and racist, just as Barack Obama and Eric Holder want a new generation of Americans to believe that now. Only by making the police the enemy and the criminal justice system the problem, can they form their army of recruits to carry forth their revolution.

The Weather Underground recognized the importance of collaborating with the Black Power movement, as a means to divide black and white citizens, and to leverage the effectiveness of the armed struggle already identifiable with the Black Panther Party for Self-Defense.

"The development of guerrilla organization and armed activity against the state is most advanced in the Black community, where the tradition and necessity for resistance is highest. The crises of the society provide the training grounds; for Third World people the conditions of prison, the army, the streets and most oppressive jobs produce warriors, political theorists, and active strategists."[104]

The Black Panther Party *Ten Point Program* addressed the conflict between policing, criminal justice and the black community in three of its ten demands-they wanted an end to "police brutality and the murder of black people;" all black men held in jails and prisons to be released; and all black people tried by a jury of their peers-in their minds, only all black juries.[105]

Barack Obama, A.G. Holder, Consent Decrees, and Democratic Party Control of America's Police

Years before the drafting of the 2016 Democratic Party presidential election platform, the Obama Administration was engaged in resurrecting America's black/white divide, while putting the police and criminal justice system in their gun sites.

President Obama took every opportunity to paint the police as trig-

---

[104]   Ibid. *Prairie Fire.*

[105]   "Black Panther Party Ten Point Program," by Huey Newton and Bobby Seale, *Marxist History Archive,* 10/15/1966.

ger happy, racist gun slingers marauding through America's streets. His attorney general used civil rights investigations, speeches and consent decrees to whip America's police departments into shape. Racism was used as the justification to destroy trust between the police and the communities they served.

As Holder announced he was leaving the Department of Justice, the Reverend Al Sharpton rushed to the nearest news camera to say, "there is no attorney general that has demonstrated a civil -rights record equal to Eric Holder."[106]

Maybe, but Holder was also the only attorney general ever to say, "I am the attorney general of the United States. But I am also a black man." Imagine former A.G. Janet Reno saying, "but I am also a woman," or Jeff Sessions proclaiming, "but I am a white southern gentleman." Better yet, try and imagine the Reverend Al Sharpton's reaction to such statements.[107]

From the standpoint of one progressive publication, "the country will still need a voice like Holder's in the coming years." Pointing to the police involved shootings that had occurred during Holder's five years as the attorney general, the same publication concluded that, "the Justice Department's role in policing the police is in its infancy."

Holder was hailed as an advocate of criminal justice reform, body cameras for police, community policing, and keeping police out of public schools where they are often called to deal with severe disciplinary issues involving students. The Democrats believe if there are no police in public schools there will be no school to prison pipeline.[108]

Progressives are proud of the essence of Holder's approach towards the police:

"In the past five years, the Department of Justice has exercised its

---

[106]   "Eric Holder's Historic and Little Noticed Civil Rights Legacy," by Nicole Flatow and Ian Millhiser, 9/25/2014, *Think Progress.*

[107]   Ibid. *Think Progress.*

[108]   Ibid. *Think Progress.*

power to conduct investigations into police departments 20 times. That's more than twice as many as were opened in the prior five years, according to the Justice Department. These investigations have ended with scathing findings of police brutality, abuse of the mentally ill, and excessive deadly force, and agreements known as consent decrees that bind cities to federal monitoring and other reforms."[109]

The following is another viewpoint of Holder's days on the job. When all the words and actions are evaluated, people can make their own decisions about Holder's role in President Barack Obama's fundamental transformation of America, based on the real measure of criminal justice-the evidence.

"The 1994 Violent Crime Control and Law Enforcement Act, authored by then Democratic Sen. Joseph Biden of Delaware, gave the Obama administration (under Attorneys General Eric Holder and Loretta Lynch) a club with which to 'police the police…'

"That club – in the form of 'consent decrees' – was wielded to intimidate state and local government law enforcement authorities to buckle under various charges of civil rights violations…

"A consent decree is an agreement or settlement that resolves a dispute between two parties without admission of guilt (in a criminal case) or liability (in a civil case)

"Through court-ordered consent decrees, the Obama administration Justice Department (DOJ) has forced dozens of state and local law enforcement officials to plead guilty rather than fight a Justice Department investigation and civil or criminal complaint as well as accept to run their departments under direction of a court-ordered federal monitor…

"In effect, the Obama administration found a way to nationalize any state or local law enforcement department or agency that insisted on strict enforcement of immigration laws, or exerted diligence in policing crime-ridden minority inner cities to protect law-abiding citizens against the ravages of criminal, drug-dealing gangs…

---

[109]   Ibid. *Think Progress.*

"This 'federalization by consent decree' of state and local law enforcement reached its peak under the direction of Thomas E. Perez, chairman of the Democratic National Committee and a self-professed La Raza 'open borders radical.' Perez also served as Assistant Attorney General for the Department of Justice Civil Rights Division from 2009-2013.

"The radical hard-left of Bill Ayers and Saul Alinsky view police in the United States not as a dedicated force for good- willing to risk their lives daily to preserve law and order in communities across the United States, but as an 'occupying force' employed by capitalistic white elites hired to attack immigrants and suppress minorities, and apply enforce social control by the discriminatory exercise of deadly force and the power to arrest and imprison..."[110]

The words of the 2016 Democratic party platform conform to the demands of the Black Panther Party and the political statement of the Weather Underground. They lay out a methodical plan for the takeover and control of local and state police departments by progressive politicians. Nothing should be more frightening to the average citizen than any plan which asserts U.S. Government control of independent law enforcement in America.

"...We will work with police chiefs to invest in training for officers on issues such as de-escalation and the creation of national guidelines for the appropriate use of force. We will encourage better police-community relations, require the use of body cameras, and stop the use of weapons of war that have no place in our communities. We will end racial profiling that targets individuals solely on the basis of race, religion, ethnicity, or national origin, which is un-American and counterproductive. We should report national data on policing strategies and provide greater transparency and accountability. We will require the Department of Justice to investigate all questionable or suspicious po-

---

[110]   "How the Obama Justice Department Used Consent Decrees as a Club to Nationalize Law Enforcement," by Jerome R. Corsi, Ph.D. 4/11/2017, *Law Enforcement Charitable Foundation Incorporated.*

lice-involved shootings, and we will support states and localities who help make those investigations and prosecutions more transparent, including through reforming the grand jury process. We will assist states in providing a system of public defense that is adequately resourced and which meets American Bar Association standards. And we will reform the civil asset forfeiture system to protect people and remove perverse incentives for law enforcement to 'police for a profit.

"Instead of investing in more jails and incarceration, we need to invest more in jobs and education, and end the school-to-prison pipeline. We will remove barriers to help formerly incarcerated individuals successfully re-enter society by 'banning the box,' expanding reentry programs, and restoring voting rights. We think the next President should take executive action to ban the box for federal employers, and contractors, so applicants have an opportunity to demonstrate their qualifications before being asked about their criminal records..."[111]

The clear intent of the Democratic Party, as it relates to police operations inside the United States, is to dictate to local police departments the politically correct way to police their individual communities. The platform subverts long-standing court decisions that have recognized the importance of street smarts and police instinct when police officers routinely make decisions to detain citizens or to conduct a "stop and frisk."

The progressive ideology reflected in the platform would place police officers in dangerous situations, where any delay in making a decision could cost them their own life or that of an innocent citizen.

The police should not be taking orders from politicians in Washington, D.C. about the split-second judgments they often make on dangerous streets. Especially from people whose agendas are completely disconnected from effective law enforcement and favor political correctness over the rule of law. Democratic Party elitists are already teaching the rest of us how to use the right words when attacking America's police.

---

[111]   Our Platform, the 2016 Democratic Party Platform."

Caren Z. Turner, a Democratic partisan and former Commissioner of the Port Authority of New York and New Jersey, showed up at the scene of a traffic stop made by Tenafly New Jersey police officers. Turner's daughter was a passenger in the car stopped by police. When Turner demanded the police tell her what was going on, the officers declined and told her the driver was an adult and she could ask him what had occurred.

Turner launched into a blistering rant at the officers, mindless of the dangers posed to everyone by oncoming high-speed traffic, even after one of the officers suggested they all move to a safer position. In just a few short minutes, Turner had dropped the names of high- profile politicians (Turner had worked for Hillary Clinton), referenced her three homes, the prestigious schools attended by her kids, and the fact that the officers couldn't string together a single sentence.

The entire stop was caught on the officers' body cams, forcing Turner's resignation from the Port Authority after the video was placed on you tube.

Turner's answer to what happened-that the officers needed to be trained in "de-escalation," the exact word used in the 2016 Democratic Party platform, is proof that every layer of Democratic party advisers, strategists, elected officials and leaders have been appropriately read in on the party's plan to control America's police. This is a necessary step to advance the transformation the Democrats envision.[112]

Had President Obama been fully vetted by the American media and any effort extended to truly understand his background, we might have been more prepared for what followed. With his fundamental transformation, President Obama unleashed the ideology and instability of the 1960s and 1970s on Americans who thought their votes for him would move us forward as a united country.

Instead, Americans were fooled into installing a government which took us backwards-to the "Days of Rage." The divisive issues that de-

---

[112] "NJ Politics Digest: Ex-Port Authority Commish Now Says Cops Need to Work on 'Tone,' by Steve Cronin, 4/26/2018, *Observer.*

fined the early years of the baby boomer generation- the free speech movement and violent communist minded domestic revolutionaries calling for revolution was back in full bloom after the 2008 election cycle.

The police are the "thin blue line" that stand between anarchy and domestic tranquility in America 24 hours a day, 7 days a week. In Eric Holder's Justice Department, they were the enemy, justifying any technique, regardless of severity, to control them.

The city of New Orleans had a first -hand view of the Holder Justice Department in action. Justice wasn't blind when it came to the police, as the next story proves.

"In a shocking case of 'grotesque' misconduct by federal prosecutors, a federal judge in Louisiana has ordered a new trial for five New Orleans police officers convicted for a shooting on the Danziger Bridge on September 4, 2005 — in the aftermath of Hurricane Katrina — and for a subsequent cover-up. This is another black eye for the Holder Justice Department that the media have barely covered...

"Participating in the misconduct... was Karla Dobinski, a lawyer in the Criminal Section of the Civil Rights Division of the Justice Department and the former deputy chief of the section... Judge Kurt Engelhardt... investigation of the matter provides an intensive inside look at the unprofessionalism of some of the lawyers at the Holder Justice Department, and also at the department's attempts to obscure its misdeeds...

"...lawyers for the defendants had filed a motion for a new trial. They claimed that the prosecutors had leaked secret grand-jury proceedings and engaged in a public-relations campaign to inflame public opinion and sway the jury through anonymous postings on nola.com, the website run by the Times-Picayune... the defendants' lawyers were correct..."

"...the judge detailed his findings that two senior prosecutors in the office of the U.S. attorney in New Orleans were responsible for many of the anonymous postings. These writings 'mocked the defense, attacked the defendants and their attorneys, were approbatory of the

United States Department of Justice, declared the defendants obviously guilty, and discussed the jury's deliberations...'

"...As a result of the judge's findings... two senior prosecutors, Assistant U.S. Attorney Salvador Perricone and First Assistant U.S. Attorney Jan Mann, the chief assistant to U.S. Attorney Jim Letten, resigned...

"...Judge Engelhardt's latest order, issued last month, indicates that Letten may have had knowledge of Mann's blogging much earlier than first reported but didn't inform the judge about it... trying to figure out what the prosecutors had done sent the court 'on a legal odyssey unlike any other...'

"...according to Judge Engelhardt, that federal 'prosecutors acting with anonymity used social media to circumvent ethical obligations, professional responsibilities, and even to commit violations of the Code of Federal Regulations.'

"The 129-page order... details the misbehavior of the Louisiana DOJ lawyers and the Civil Rights Division's Dobinski... She also encouraged other anonymous bloggers, who 'repeatedly posted vigorous pro-prosecution statements strongly condemning the defendants, their witnesses, and their entire defense....'

"Dobinski was the supervising 'taint' attorney assigned to the New Orleans case... a 'taint' lawyer is charged with making sure that the other Justice Department lawyers prosecuting the case do not use such privileged information or evidence. In other words, Dobinski was there in the Louisiana case to ensure that the constitutional rights of the defendants were protected...

"...The fact that Dobinski remains employed at the Department of Justice despite her unethical conduct is deplorable. It's also an extraordinarily sad comment on the behavior that the Holder Justice Department seems to find acceptable in its prosecutors...

"...Judge Engelhardt obviously believes that the DOJ attempted to hide the identity of Dobinski as the third anonymous blogger... Judge Engelhardt seems to believe the Justice Department dragged its feet in conducting this investigation because DOJ officials did not really want to find out who the leakers were...

"Moreover, in what the judge called a 'truly disappointing and unsettling crucial development,' the DOJ was unable to 'forensically recover computer data evidence from [its] internet portals for years 2010 and 2011 because it did not retain' the data. DOJ prosecutors would never accept such an excuse from a private entity if they were seeking computer records of e-mails and Internet usage "at material times to this inquiry....

"...Judge Engelhardt's indictment of the Justice Department is devastating...Finally, Engelhardt points a finger straight at Eric Holder:

"The indictment in this case was announced with much fanfare, a major press conference presided over by U.S. Attorney General Eric Holder, and widespread media attention... A DOJ representative said that the indictments "are a reminder that the Constitution and the rule of law do not take a holiday — even after a hurricane." While quite true in every respect, the Court must remind the DOJ that the Code of Federal Regulations, and various Rules of Professional Responsibility, and ethics likewise do not take a holiday — even in a high-stakes criminal prosecution, and even in the anonymity of cyberspace...The Court simply cannot allow the integrity of the justice system to become a casualty in a mere prosecutorial game..."[113]

Eric Holder's dust-up with a Federal Judge in the New Orleans case, wasn't the only example during his tenure that ran counter to constant boasting about transparency throughout the Obama era. In December 2010 Border Patrol Officer Brian Terry was found murdered on the Mexico/Arizona border. Several weapons sold and traced through a DOJ operation codenamed *Fast and Furious* were found at the scene.

DOJ officials testified before Congress in 2011 that that none of the guns involved in *Fast and Furious* had been walked back to the U.S. from Mexico. The DOJ later retracted the testimony of officials before

---

[113] "'Grotesque DOJ Misconduct, the Holder DOJ Stopped at Nothing to Convict Five New Orleans Police Officers, by Hans A. Von Spakovsky, 10/3/2013, *National Review.*'"

Congress. Of the 2000 guns sold to straw buyers in *Fast and Furious*, only about 710 had been recovered by ATF as of 2012.

Fast and Furious was an undercover sting operation that was tracking some 2000 guns sold to straw buyers. The operation involved "gunwalking" whereby licensed gun dealers sold the weapons, as the ATF worked to track them to targeted high level Mexican drug cartels, where the gun buyer and cartel members could be arrested.

DOJ gave close to 8000 documents to a Congressional investigating committee trying to determine what had happened in *Fast and Furious*. The Republicans, led by Darrell Issa, chairman of the Oversight and Government Reform Committee wanted additional documents disclosed.[114]

President Obama evoked executive privilege to protect Attorney General Holder, as he fought turning over any more documents to the Oversight Committee. The move prompted Brian Terry's father to say that President Obama was a liar. "It sounds like they're hiding something," Kent Terry said during a televised interview. "They're lying big time and passing the buck. That's how I feel. I just know they're hiding something big. Mr. Terry also said his family had not heard from the White House or DOJ since the discovery that Fast and Furious weapons were used in the murder of his son.[115]

Holder was held in criminal contempt of Congress on June 28, 2012 by a vote of 255-67 for his failure to turn over the requested Department of Justice documents.

This is the history that former Attorney General Eric Holder failed to mention. This is his legacy as President Obama's attorney general. Holder's first loyalty wasn't to the rule of law. It was to the fundamental transformation that his Boss, the President, envisioned for America.

---

[114] "A Review of ATF's Operation Fast and Furious Related Matters (PDF). U.S. Department of Justice Office of the Inspector General. November 2012. Retrieved February 6, 2013

[115] "Slain officer's parents call President Obama a liar," by Scott Held, Jun 26, 2012, *News Herald.*

"I'm still enjoying what I'm doing, there's still work to be done. I'm still the President's wing-man, so I'm there with my boy."[116]

---

[116]   Ibid. *Politico,* 4/4/2013.

AP/WIDE WORLD PHOTOS

CHAPTER FOUR

"I'm going to do everything I can to support the resistance." Hillary Clinton

---

In her concession speech following the loss of the 2016 presidential election to Donald Trump, Hillary Clinton told America, "last night I congratulated Donald Trump and offered to work with him on behalf of our country. I hope that he will be a successful president for all Americans.[117]

Less than six months later, Ms. Clinton proved the accuracy of the psychological adage, the best predictor of future behavior is past behavior. Clinton declared, "I'm back to being an activist citizen and part of the resistance."[118]

Speaking at the Book Expo in New York City, Clinton said, *"I'm going to do everything I can to support the resistance."*[119]

Never in the history of American presidential politics has a losing

---

[117] "Hillary Clinton's 2016 Concession Speech," November 9, 2016, *Washington Post*.

[118] Interview of Hillary Clinton, by Christiane Amanpour, CNN, 5/2/2017.

[119] "Hillary Clinton: 'I'm Going to do Everything I Can to Support the Resistance,'" C-Span, 6/1/2017.

candidate pledged to support a strategy of continuous confrontation with the president elected by the people to serve the best interests of the country. Never has one of the major political parties in the United States been so openly hostile and non-compromising to the party that won the presidency and both houses of Congress in 2016.

Without any doubt, the voters in all fifty states and every county in America had made a clear and conscious decision who they wanted to represent them. But not in Clinton's eyes, and not in the view of her Democratic Party.

The Resistance- from the Weather Underground in the 1970's to the 2016 Democratic Party

Resistance was adopted by the leaders of the Democratic Party as the cornerstone of their strategy to oppose President Trump even before he was inaugurated. It is the Resistance that ties this era in American history and the current Democratic Party to the violent, *"communist-minded men and women"* revolutionaries of the 1970's-the same revolutionaries who sought to topple the U.S. government. The plans those revolutionaries proposed, and the slogans and symbols they used in furtherance of their efforts to overthrow the government, have emerged again today from inside the Democratic Party.

The "resistance" connects today's political revolution to the violent revolution in the streets during the 1960's and 1970's-the days history refers to as the "Days of Rage" This is why it's important to understand the words of the revolution and the significance of words to the revolutionaries of today.

The "resistance" was never about President Trump. The "resistance" is a catastrophic reaction from those who believed Hillary Clinton should have won the 2016 election against Donald Trump.

After all, during one of the Democratic Party debates, Hillary Clinton had referred to the Republicans as the enemy. When Ms. Clinton lost the 2016 election, her Party missed the opportunity to hasten the transformation of America into a socialist state.[120]

Had Hillary Clinton and the Democratic Party succeeded in owning the country for another four to eight years, the United States of America would have faced international aggression from within our own hemisphere. Policies designed to stifle dissent and compromise our Constitution would have created massive division and domestic unrest. Third World demands on our national resources would have intensified.

Even President Trump's now famous campaign slogan, "Make America Great Again," severely agitated Democratic Party strategists because it confronted head- on the Party's current premise that America was never great to begin with-and slowed their march to change history and alter perceptions that America will ever be exceptional again.

In 1922 Ludwig von Mises said, "…socialism is not in the least what is pretends to be. It is not the pioneer of a better and finer world, but the spoiler of what thousands of years of civilization have created. It does not build, it destroys. For destruction is the essence of it. It produces nothing, it only consumes what the social order based on private ownership in the means production has created ... Each step leading towards socialism must exhaust itself in the destruction of what already exists."[121]

---

[120]   "How Political Opponents Became Enemies in the U.S.," with Jeff Greenfield, 4/1/2018, *PBS NewsHour Weekend,*

[121]   "What is Socialism? - Collectivism & Statism," Capitalism.org. Ludwig von Mises was an Austrian school economist, historian and sociologist. Mises wrote a number of books, one of the most significant titled, *Socialism,* concluding that "the only viable economic policy for the human race was a policy of unrestricted laissez-faire, of free markets and the unhampered exercise of the right of private property, with government strictly limited to the defense of person and property within its territorial area." Because of his anti-socialist economic views, von Mises had difficulty finding work at any European or American universities, but nonetheless attracted a huge following with his radical opinions and support for free economies. One of his followers won a Nobel Prize for his work in elaborating Mises's business cycle theory during

The strategies and words of the Democratic Party today are in unison with Marxist ideology and the push to embrace socialism as a step towards the purity and utopia promised by communism. The leftist movement in America has long embraced the ideology of communism touted by the Communist Party of the USA, the Black Panther Party, the Students for a Democratic Society and the Weather Underground. All of them are connected by their embrace of the ideology of communism.

The "resistance" on display in today's America is being fueled by Democratic Party politicians for the purpose of votes and power. The "resistance" is about creating permanent and undisputed power, vested in the hands of an elitist few. The Democratic Party of today is about unbridled power. It is about one party rule in America. It does not represent compromise, confronting tyranny, or the rule of law. It represents transformation, socialism, and authoritarian power.

Today's Democratic Party is not the party of President John F. Kennedy. He used his inaugural address in 1961 to tell the world Americans would pay any price and bear any burden "in order to assure the survival and the success of liberty." He encouraged Americans to reach for the moon, to sign up for the *Alliance for Progress* and volunteer their time to help others in need. He kept government in check as a means to control its power over individual freedom.[122]

When Kennedy was still only a candidate for President, he made a campaign stop at the Southern Pacific Railroad Station in Richmond, California. But Kennedy's words on that whistle stop were relevant and prescient in today's political environment- "...there are those who know we can do better, who believe it is a great country but know it can be a

---

the later 1920s and 1930s. Another founded the Mises Institute in Auburn, Alabama, in 1982, which grew considerably in popularity following the collapse of the former Soviet Union. Mises was "a libertarian who championed reason and individual liberty in personal as well as economic matters. As a rationalist and an opponent of statism in all its forms, Mises would never call himself a "conservative," but rather a liberal in the nineteenth-century sense."

[122]   Transcript of President John F. Kennedy's Inaugural Address, 1961.

greater one."[123]

On January 20, 1961, John F. Kennedy was sworn in as the 35th President of the United States. Youthful, energetic, and projecting unending optimism for the future, he was speaking to every one of us when he declared, "and so, my fellow Americans: ask not what your country can do for you-ask what you can do for your country."[124]

Candidate Kennedy's words at the Southern Pacific Railroad Depot parallel "make America great again," the phrase that every contemporary Democrat in 2019 loves to hate. Could there be any better proof that John F. Kennedy's Democratic Party doesn't exist today. The Democratic Party has become a divisive force in American politics and society, because it's been the victim of a hostile takeover by "communist minded men and women. " The party of John F. Kennedy has become the party of the next revolution.

The ideology of communism *is* the influence in today's Democratic Party. Its communist minded revolutionaries are encouraging Americans to be takers. The cost of taking free things from the government, is more control of the individual by the government.

The Weather Underground of the 1970's viewed violent resistance as the strategy that could topple the U.S. Government. They did not believe in American exceptionalism as a cornerstone of America's future. They believed the future of the world belonged to socialism, which would be followed by the utopia of communism.

Infected by the ideology of communism, today's Democratic Party is pursuing political resistance to undermine the Bill of Rights and destroy the rule of law. Their words and actions prove that in 2019 they share the Weather Underground's 1970's philosophy that the American experience is not unique or exceptional.

President Obama, when asked by a French citizen in Strasbourg to offer his thoughts about how America is unique, answered, " I believe in

---

[123]   "Speech of Senator John F. Kennedy, Richmond, California, 8 September,1960," John F. Kennedy Presidential *Library and Museum.*

[124]   Ibid. President John F. Kennedy's Inaugural, 1961.

American exceptionalism, just as I suspect that the Brits believe in British exceptionalism and the Greeks believe in Greek exceptionalism."[125]

Hillary Clinton campaigned for president, ensuring the country that she believed in American exceptionalism, while claiming Donald Trump did not. Hillary Clinton firmly believed she would be the next president. She knew how strongly millions of Americans felt about the country's destiny in the world, but her actions and background seemed in contrast with her steadfast endorsement of American exceptionalism.

As one writer explains it, "to serious conservative advocates of American exceptionalism, there's something crucial missing from her siren song: it's that recognition that America has earned its exceptional role in world affairs by eschewing the socialism and secularism that have crippled Europe."[126]

Neither Hillary Clinton nor Barack Obama, as prominent leaders of the Democratic Party have shown the courage to soundly reject socialism. As Obama's comments in Argentina illustrated, he doesn't see much difference in socialism and capitalism. The problem is that socialism and American exceptionalism are incompatible.

The Democratic Party has to reject exceptionalism to pave the way for the socialist platform it advocates. The party platform is more than consistent with the Weather Underground's *Prairie Fire* assessment of exceptionalism:

"There are two currents of thought and activity that conspire to hold back the power of the movement. They are American exceptionalism and reformism...They are both racist in effect. American exceptionalism is the assumption that for one reason or another-U.S. 'technological superiority,' the 'post-scarcity economy,' the "system of democracy," our 'advanced consciousness...' one is American superiority, a kind of cultural chauvinism...reformism assumes the essential goodness of

---

[125] "How Has American Exceptionalism Fared Under Obama?" by Michael Barone, *National Review*, 1/15/2016.

[126] "Hillary Clinton's 'American Exceptionalism' Won't Win Many Republican Votes," by Ed Kilgore, New *York Magazine*, 8/31/2016.

U.S. society, in conflict with the revolutionary view that the system is rotten to the core and must be overthrown."[127]

The ultimate goal of the resistance is a world without today's America. The Weather Underground's *Prairie Fire* recommends that the resistance include: "guerrilla organization...communist women and men," forging an underground organization inside the United States, dedicated to revolutionary war, and intent on creating a protracted effort to "disrupt the empire."[128]

Their vision for the coming war includes both peaceful and violent mass struggle, clandestine struggle, political, economic, cultural and military upheaval.

Prairie Fire describes the "many faces to militant resistance and fighting...sabotage in the military, on the job, in government, and attacks on the police; mass demonstrations...Marches on the Pentagon... African Liberation Day rallies, International Women's Day marches, Chicano Moratorium marches; demands for control and power through seizures of institutions...community control of hospitals and schools, occupations of land such as Wounded Knee, or symbols such as the Statue of Liberty, People's Park, prison rebellions and takeovers; clandestine propaganda."[129]

The resistance intends to forge an alliance among prisoners, women's groups, collectives, study groups, workers' organizing committees, communes, GI organizers, consciousness-raising groups, veterans, community groups, the Third World and all kinds of revolutionaries, to seize power, destroy imperialism, and create a socialist society.

In *Prairie Fire*, socialism is defined as: "eradication of the social system based on profit...control of the productive forces for the good of the whole community instead of the few who live on hilltops and in

---

[127] Prairie Fire: The Politics of Revolutionary Anti-Imperialism, The Political Statement of the Weather Underground.

[128] Ibid. *Prairie Fire.*

[129] Ibid. *Prairie Fire.*

mansions...priorities based on human need instead of corporate greed...a decent and creative quality of life for all." The socialist revolution, as the resistance sees it, "is a fight for who runs things...for control by the people of...the means of production-the means by which people eat, work, protect themselves from the cold and the rain, get around, raise children and build."[130]

Or, as Hillary Clinton might explain it, "it takes a village." Longing to become a member of that village, Ms. Clinton appeared on the scene of the 2017 Book Expo in New York City to tell Americans that, "I'm going to do everything I can to support the resistance"

Towards that end she announced the establishment of an organization called Onward Together to collect donations and cultivate an organized political resistance to President Trump and the Republicans. Onward Together is described as, "dedicated to advancing the vision that earned nearly 66 million votes in the last election... by encouraging people to organize, get involved and run for office... Onward Together will advance progressive values."[131]

Hillary Clinton is just one of many highly placed Democratic Party leaders endorsing the resistance. In May 2017, Nancy Pelosi, the Democratic Speaker of the House of Representatives, showed up in Dallas, Texas at a CWA Union Hall rally to kick off the *Resistance Summer*. She warned the attendees of the dangers posed to America by President Trump's agenda. "There's so much at stake for the people... this resistance summer is so important. There are so many things happening."[132]

Encouraging activism and mass marches, Pelosi and her party targeted women's groups, climate science and the environment to grow

---

[130]   Ibid. *Prairie Fire.*

[131]   "Failed Candidate Hillary Clinton Launches New Political Organization, 5/16/2017, *The Political Insider.*

[132]   "House Minority Leader Pelosi Calls Sanctuary Cities Law an 'Act of Cowardice," by Anna M. Tinsley, 5/31/2017, *Fort Worth Star-Telegram.*

their base. Tom Perez, the leader of the Democratic National Committee (DNC), told a gathering of followers after the election of President Trump that, "millions of Americans led by women came out and said... Donald Trump, you did not win this election...Donald Trump, you did not win the popular vote...we will continue to resist and resist you have done."[133]

Using the tone and class of a Third World dictator, Perez did his best to delegitimize President Trump's election, while stoking anger and rage in his audience. The video of his embittered performance is available online for all to see.[134]

Bernie Sanders, who was married and honeymooned in the former Union of Soviet Socialist Republics (U.S.S.R.) actually authored a book in 2018 titled, *Where We Go from Here: Two Years in the Resistance.* The book lays out his blueprint for the 2020 presidential election.[135]

"...chronicling the day-by-day struggles that he and his progressive colleagues have waged over the last two years in the fight against Donald Trump's reactionary agenda and for a government that works for all, not just wealthy campaign contributors. ...At home, Sanders has helped lead the fight for Medicare for all, fought for workers desperate for higher wages, and supported immigrants in the DACA program and children affected by gun violence. He has stood with the people of Puerto Rico devastated by Hurricane Maria, as well as veterans, teachers, the incarcerated, the persecuted, and all those who are too often ignored by Washington. Abroad, his voice has been clear that we need a foreign policy that strives for peace—not war—and international cooperation

---

[133] "Come Together Fight Back Tour-Portland, ME," 4/17/2017, *YouTube.*

[134] Ibid. *YouTube*

[135] *Where We Go from Here: Two Years in the Resistance*, Bernie Sanders, Thomas Dunne Books, 11/27/2018.

to address the crisis of climate change."[136]

Since the days of President Jimmy Carter, there has been a steady attack on freedom at home and an erosion of democratic values abroad. This is true despite the collapse of the former Soviet Union and its loss of control over the nations of Eastern Europe. President Carter's emphasis on human rights led to the tyrannical regime that still runs Iran today.

When President Obama and his Secretary of State Hillary Clinton came into office in 2009, the people of Iran were practicing resistance of their own. The penalty for resistance in Iran is death. But that didn't stop hundreds of thousands of Iranians from taking to the streets and launching Iran's Green Revolution.

President Ronald Reagan implored the former Soviet Union's Mikhail Gorbachev to "tear down this wall," as he stood facing the people of Germany with the Berlin Wall over his shoulder, Barack Obama ignored Iranians pleading for freedom. The Green Revolution failed. And the mullahs of Iran set out to develop nuclear weapons.

"What if the president had done more to help the protesters when the regime appeared to be teetering?... When he finally did speak out, he couldn't bring himself to say the election was stolen: 'The world is watching and inspired by their participation, regardless of what the ultimate outcome of the election was.'...

"Behind the scenes, Obama overruled advisers who wanted to do what America had done at similar transitions from dictatorship to democracy, and signal America's support...Obama ordered the CIA to sever contacts it had with the green movement's supporters...Obama from the beginning of his presidency tried to turn the country's ruling clerics from foes to friends...Obama ended U.S. programs to document Iranian human rights abuses. He wrote personal letters to Iranian Supreme Leader Ayatollah Ali Khamenei assuring him the U.S. was not trying to overthrow him. Obama repeatedly stressed his respect for the

---

[136]   Ibid.

regime..."[137]

Hillary Clinton and John Kerry did little during their time as Secretaries of State to advance freedom for the people of the world. John Kerry, who followed Clinton and negotiated Obama's nuclear deal with Iran, said, "war is the failure of diplomacy." However, the nuclear deal Obama and Kerry accepted from Iran was a complete failure as well when it came to protecting America's safety and interests.

"... in 2013, the U.S. position was for Iran to dismantle much of its nuclear infrastructure. By the end of the talks in 2015, Secretary of State John Kerry and his team 'agreed that Iran would then be allowed to build an industrial-scale nuclear program, with hundreds of thousands of machines after a ten- year period of restraint.'"

"...there was a chance for a better outcome. There is no guarantee that an Obama intervention would have been able to topple Khamenei back in 2009, when his people flooded the streets to protest an election the American president wouldn't say was stolen. But it was worth a try. Imagine if that uprising had succeeded. Perhaps then a nuclear deal could have brought about a real peace. Instead, Obama spent his presidency misunderstanding Iran's dictator, assuring the supreme leader America wouldn't aid his citizens when they tried to change the regime that oppresses them to this day."[138]

When President Obama had an opportunity to support the Green Revolution, he looked the other way. When President Bill Clinton had an opportunity to kill Osama bin Laden, he looked the other way. When Hillary Clinton could have told the truth about Benghazi and Libya, she touted the White House lie about a videotape.

Barack Obama's world tour to apologize for America's past actions, while holding the U.S. military budget hostage to bigger government and increased social spending for eight years, solidified the control of the Democratic Party by the communist minded men and

---

[137] "Why Obama Let Iran's Green Revolution Fail," by Eli Lake, 8/24/2016, *Bloomberg Opinion*.

[138] Ibid. *Bloomberg*.

women within in. International solidarity was more important to the White House and Hillary Clinton's State Department than American interests.

Russia's Vladimir Putin is busy trying to recreate the glory days of the Soviet empire. Iran and Syria have allied themselves with Russia, helping it become a player again in the Middle East. North Korea is days away from having its own nuclear arsenal. China is completing new islands it has been building in the South China Sea.

President Obama spent eight years watching the development and growth of ISIS, while normalizing relations with Cuba. The leader of the free world patted the knee of former Russian President Dmitri Medvedev while saying, "'…this is my last election … After my election I have more flexibility…'"[139]

Obama's words came after he urged Medvedev to give him more time to resolve issues of interest to the Russians here in America. No one should be surprised. The victims of loan sharks often beg for more time to pay their debts as well.

Barack Obama ushered in his presidency by criticizing past American attitudes towards foreign partners. He told the French in 2009 "there have been times where America has shown arrogance and been dismissive, even derisive."[140]

A few days later he told the Turks, "the United States is still working through some of our own darker periods in our history." In a 2009 Summit of the Americas, Obama seemingly apologized for past American treatment of Latin American countries, saying, "while the United States has done much to promote peace and prosperity in the hemisphere, we have at times been disengaged, and at times we sought to

---

[139]   "Obama Tells Russia's Medvedev More Flexibility After Election," *Reuters*, 3/26/2012.

[140]   "Barack Obama: 'Arrogant US Has Been Dismissive' to its Allies," by Toby Harnden, 4/3/2009, *The Telegraph*.

dictate our terms."[141]

Even more egregious, in the waning days of his eight years in office, Obama told a group of students in Argentina:

"So often in the past there's been a sharp division between left and right, between capitalist and communist or socialist. And especially in the Americas, that's been a big debate, right? Oh, you know, you're a capitalist Yankee dog, and oh, you know, you're some crazy communist that's going to take away everybody's property. And I mean, those are interesting intellectual arguments, but I think for your generation, you should be practical and just choose from what works. You don't have to worry about whether it neatly fits into socialist theory or capitalist theory -- you should just decide what works."[142]

President Obama's Secretary of State John Kerry told conference attendees at a World Climate Change conference in Indonesia in 2014 that climate change posed, "the greatest challenge of our generation."

President Obama, Secretary of State Clinton and Secretary of State Kerry are bound together by actions which show a rejection of American exceptionalism in favor of an acceptance of worldwide socialism. They even seem to believe it is workable in America. Most Americans are unaware of the extensive influence socialism and socialist mentors had on Hillary Clinton early in her lifetime.

Saul Alinsky: Hillary Clinton's Mentor in the Rules for Radicals

The vast majority of Americans had never heard of Saul Alinsky until former presidential candidate Ben Carson mentioned his name at the Republican National Convention in 2016. Saul Alinsky was the fa-

---

[141]   "Obama Tells Leaders of Americas the US Is Too Disengaged, Dictatorial," by Andrew Malcolm, 4/18/2009, *Los Angeles Times.*

[142]   "Barack Obama: The Last Communist Sympathizer," 3/28/2016, *Investor's Business Daily.*

ther of community organizing. He trained and mentored future community organizers.

Alinsky was a revolutionary whose main and only interest was taking power away from the those who had it. In Alinsky's view, any tactic was fair game, and civil disobedience was on the table. And Alinsky's game had enemies. The people who held power were the enemy. The people who didn't agree with him were the enemy. There was no common ground. Unlike the members of the Weather Underground, Alinsky never thought of himself as a communist.

However, Alinsky and the Weather Underground (WU) both wanted to bring about a socialist revolution in America. The WU recognized that to be successful they would need to form an alliance with an "anti-racist" white movement. Alinsky wrote that community organizing needed to redirect its emphasis to, "America's white middle class. That is where the power is."[143]

Alinsky set forth his revolutionary ideology in the books he wrote, the most significant being *Rules for Radicals*, mentioned by Ben Carson in his speech that night in 2016. Carson's target was none other than Hillary Clinton, the Democratic candidate for president. Despite her constant identification with the pain and unfair suffering of the working class, Ms. Clinton seemed to have an august beginning in life.

She attended Wellesley College in the late 1960s, making her way to Berkeley and Oakland, California after graduation. For those who aren't familiar with Wellesley, it is a "private women's liberal arts college in Wellesley, Massachusetts. As of 2019, Wellesley was ranked the third best liberal arts college in the United States by U.S. News and World Report of 2018, Wellesley is the highest endowed women's college in the world, with an endowment of $2.1 billion. In the United States, Wellesley has the 50th largest endowment among institutions of higher education."[144]

---

[143]   Ibid. *Prairie Fire*. "Want to Understand Hillary Clinton? Read Saul Alinsky," by Roger Kimball, 9/18/2016, *Washington Examiner.*

[144]   "Wellesley College Rankings". *U.S. News & World Report. 2018.*

It was at Wellesley that a young Hillary Rodham became interested in the writings and theories of community organizing of Saul Alinsky. After meeting Alinsky in 1968, she became so influenced by his ideology that she wrote her senior thesis on his community organizing tactics. Alinsky became so interested in her that he offered her a job in 1969.

She declined the offer, moving to Berkeley instead and "'interning at the left-wing law firm Treuhaft, Walker and Burnstein, known for its radical politics and a client roster that included Black Panthers and other militants.'"[145]

The two kept in touch, despite Rodham's belief that she could work within the system to advance the revolutionary cause of taking power from those who held it to do good in the world. In 1971, she wrote a letter to Alinsky, which his secretary responded to within a few days of receiving it.

"Dear Saul:

"When is that new book coming out-or has it come, and I somehow missed the fulfillment of Revelation? I have just had my one-thousandth conversation about Reveille and need some new material to throw at people. You are being rediscovered again as the New Left - type politicos are finally beginning to think seriously about the hard work and mechanics of organizing. I seemed to have survived law school slightly bruised with my belief in and zest for organizing intact. If I never thanked you for the encouraging words of last spring in the midst of the Yale-Cambodia madness, I do so now. The more I've seen of places like Yale Law School and the people who haunt them, the more convinced I am that we have the serious business and joy of much work ahead, if the commitment to a free and open society is ever going to mean more than eloquence and frustration."

"I miss our biennial conversations. Do you ever make it out to

---

[145]   "The Hillary Letters Hillary Clinton, Saul Alinsky correspondence revealed," by Alana Goodman, 9/21/2014, *The Washington Free Beacon*.

California? I am living in Berkeley and working in Oakland for the summer and would love to see you. Let me know if there is any chance of our getting together.

"There were rumors of your going to SE Asia to recruit organizers. Is the lack of imagination among my peers really so rampant as that suggests or did you get yourself a CIA-sponsored junket to exotica?

...Hopefully we can have a good argument sometime in the future."[146]

Alinsky's Thirteen Rules for Radicals

When Alinsky's secretary responded to Hillary Rodham's inquiry, she mentioned Alinsky's new book, *Rules for Radicals.* Here are Alinsky's 13 "Rules."

1. "Power is not only what you have, but what the enemy thinks you have." Power is derived from Main sources – money and people. "Have-Nots" must build power from flesh and blood.

2. "Never go outside the expertise of your people." It results in confusion, fear and retreat. Feeling secure adds to the backbone of anyone.

3. "Whenever possible, go outside the expertise of the enemy." Look for ways to increase insecurity, anxiety and uncertainty.

4. "Make the enemy live up to its own book of rules." If the rule is that every letter gets a reply, send 30,000 letters. You can kill them with this because no one can possibly obey all of their own rules.

5. "Ridicule is man's most potent weapon." There is no defense. It's irrational. It's infuriating. It also works as a key pressure point to force the enemy into concessions.

---

[146]   Ibid.

6. "A good tactic is one your people enjoy." They'll keep doing it without urging and come back to do more. They're doing their thing and will even suggest better ones.

7. "A tactic that drags on too long becomes a drag." Don't become old news.

8. "Keep the pressure on. Never let up." Keep trying new things to keep the opposition off balance. As the opposition masters one approach, hit them from the flank with something new.

9. "The threat is usually more terrifying than the thing itself." Imagination and ego can dream up many more consequences than any activist.

10. "The major premise for tactics is the development of operations that will maintain a constant pressure upon the opposition." It is this unceasing pressure that results in the reactions from the opposition that are essential for the success of the campaign.

11. "If you push a negative hard enough, it will push through and become a positive." Violence from the other side can win the public to your side because the public sympathizes with the underdog.

12. "The price of a successful attack is a constructive alternative." Never let the enemy score points because you're caught without a solution to the problem.

13. "Pick the target, freeze it, personalize it, and polarize it." Cut off the support network and isolate the target from sympathy. Go after people and not institutions; people hurt faster than institutions."[147]

---

[147] "Saul Alinsky's 13 Tried-and-True Rules for Creating Meaningful Social Change," 2/21/2017, *Open Culture.*

It seems clear that Hillary Rodham was influenced by Alinsky's *Rules for Radicals*, his ideas and the political transformation of America at a young age. Living and working in the Grand Central Station of the "Days of Rage-" the San Francisco Bay Area, had to have a compounding effect on her thinking. One writer captured Alinsky's own thinking and intentions in these words. "He (Alinsky) might employ the soothing rhetoric of individual freedom, but his unwavering goal was the acquisition and deployment of power..."[148]

According to Alinsky, "we will start with the system because there is no other place to start except political lunacy... my aim here is how to organize for power: how to get it and to use it" for the sake of revolution.[149]

The same writer went on to emphasize that, "the prime Alinskyite supposition is that 'all life is partisan. There is no dispassionate objectivity.' One might — in fact, one should — mouth various nostrums about the welfare of children, access to healthcare, etc.; one might rail against inequality, sexism, racism, homophobia, etc., but at the end of the day, politics was all about the acquisition of power and life was all about politics."[150]

Not only was life all about politics, Alinsky stood for the notion that the use of any means was justified as long as it brought the desired results. Alinsky, "admiringly cites Lenin's observation that the Bolsheviks 'stood for getting power through the ballot but would reconsider after they got the guns.'"[151]

Saul Alinsky wanted to rid the world of America's constitutional Republic. His *Rules for Radicals* illustrated the importance of deception in building the mass movement necessary to achieve his goals.

---

[148]   Ibid.

[149]   Ibid.

[150]   (Ibid)

[151]   (Ibid)

Hillary Clinton viewed Saul Alinsky as an early mentor. Alinsky's *Rules for Radicals* provides the context for her political growth and evolution as part of today's resistance.

CHAPTER FIVE

---

*"I was involved in a movement that I thought
made a lot of sense, and it began, and the
reason I got involved, was because of United
States foreign policy."* Mayor Bill DeBlasio

As the mayor of New York City, Bill De Blasio is an influential leader in the Democratic Party. In just sixteen years, De Blasio has climbed from city councilman to candidate for president. De Blasio's connections to Cuba, the Nicaraguan Sandinistas, the ideology of communism, and the philosophy of the violent Weather Underground of the 1970's, are the best indication of where his policies and judgment will take America.

The Weather Underground, Black Panther Party and Mayor DeBlasio-They All Love Cuba

After the first Democratic Party primary debate of 2019, De Blasio went to Miami Dade County Airport to address a protest rally sponsored by the Service Employees International Union (SEIU). He wrapped up his speech to the assembled group saying, *"Hasta la victo-*

ria siempre!"[152]

The words roughly translate into "ever onward to victory." These are the same words that were used by Che Guevara, the self-described "cold killing machine," as he murdered thousands in South America under the guise of people's revolutions. Cubans in the crowd who had fled the tyranny of Guevara and Fidel Castro were offended at De Blasio's words.[153]

Attempting damage control, De Blasio apologized on Twitter, "I did not know the phrase I used in Miami today was associated with Che Guevara and I did not mean to offend anyone who heard it that way…I certainly apologize for not understanding that history."[154]

A supporter of the Nicaraguan Sandinistas in 1988 and an advocate of ending the United States ban on travel to Cuba, De Blasio knows more about Cuban history than he wants people to believe.

Several years prior to the Miami incident, De Blasio was running for his first term as New York City mayor. He and his wife were married in Cuba in 1990 when travel to the island was prohibited. He did a radio interview with a Cuban host who had escaped Fidel Castro's communist Cuba in 1970.

The host asked De Blasio, "What did you see in Cuba? What is your impression going on a honeymoon in a country that hasn't had free elections in the last 50 years? What did you get from that trip?"

De Blasio answered, "I didn't go on a trip to study the country. I don't pretend to have full perspective of the country… have a huge

---

[152] "In Miami, DeBlasio Said Four Words in Spanish. Slight Problem: They Were Che's Words," by Taylor Dolven, David Smiley and Samantha Gross, 6/27/2019, *Miami Herald.*

[153] Spanish to English Dictionary Online. "The Killing Machine: Che Guevara, from Communist Firebrand to Capitalist Brand," by Alvaro Vargas Llosa, 7/11/2005, *Independent Institute.*

[154] "DeBlasio Apologizes After Quoting Che Guevara at South Florida Rally," by Allan Smith, 6/27/2019, *NBC News.*

critique of the current government there because it's undemocratic, and it doesn't allow freedom of the press, and I think there's a huge number of problems. I also think it's well known that there's some good things that happened — for example, in health care..."[155]

New Yorker Magazine, in a subsequent interview with De Blasio, gave him the opportunity to explain his Cuban honeymoon travel as a *"youthful indiscretion."* Instead, De Blasio clarified, "No, it's not a youthful indiscretion...I was involved in a movement that I thought made a lot of sense, and it began, and the reason I got involved, was because of United States foreign policy."[156]

The mainstream media has given De Blasio a free pass on questions about his judgment and flirtation with the ideology of communism. His political rise as a champion of progressive causes has gone unchallenged. He seems proud of his activist relationship with the *"movement."* There has never been any attempt to assess his political thinking in the context of historical events that have helped evolve it.

It's fair to ask whether De Blasio was ever a target of recruitment by the Cuban intelligence services. Elected officials take a sworn oath to protect and defend the Constitution of the United States of America against all enemies, foreign and domestic. De Blasio's travel to Cuba and Nicaragua and his attachment to a movement in the 1980's which was diametrically opposed to the foreign policy of President Ronald Reagan, raise serious questions about De Blasio's judgment.

His ideology alone would bring him to the attention of a host of hostile intelligence services, including Cuba. The relationships he established in Cuba and Nicaragua years ago would serve as fruitful avenues through which access could be gained to Mayor DeBlasio.

Reagan's foreign policies destroyed Soviet communism, brought down the Berlin Wall and freed millions of people from the iron rule of

---

[155]   "Host Raps DeBlasio Over Cuban Honeymoon," by Sally Goldenberg, 9/27/2013, *New York Post.*

[156]   "DeBlasio: I'll be a Different Type of Mayor," by John Cassidy, 9/26/2013, The New Yorker.

communism in Eastern Europe. How could anyone oppose that? Instead, De Blasio's comments, political positions and wielding of political power as a New York City councilman and then as mayor, are reflective of Cuban style communism; the radical strategy positions of the communist-inspired Weather Underground, and the main themes of the *Ten Point Program* of the Black Panther Party for Self Defense.

The Black Panther Party's own leaders described it as a communist organization dedicated to the overthrown of the U.S. government. There was a lot happening inside the United States during the time frame De Blasio developed his radical political views. The 1980's were an interesting period in the history of U.S./ Cuban relations when it came to the spy business.

One of the co-authors was working in the FBI's New York City Office during the 1980's, assigned to the Soviet Foreign Counterintelligence Division. There were connections between the work of FBI agents responsible for the intelligence operations of the Soviets, and agents who specialized in Cuba.

The word on the street was that the CIA had successfully penetrated the Cuban services, neutralizing not just their intelligence efforts, but also gleaning information which could assist FBI agents countering the Soviet target. One criteria of success in the spy business is measured in terms of the number of counterintelligence assets developed to cover a particular target. The more information gathered from people and other sources close to an individual of interest, the greater the opportunity to neutralize their hostile actions against America.

The CIA may have thought they had the drop on Cuban intelligence officers and their operations directed at United States. In reality, the Cubans, trained masterfully by their Soviet counterparts, had turned the tables on the Agency. Cuban intelligence had compromised major CIA operations, while effectively penetrating U.S. Government agencies and the American political establishment.

The tiny island of Cuba, just 90 miles from the southern tip of Florida, has long enjoyed the stature of a giant in the eyes of the world's socialist, intellectual elite. The Cuban revolution continues today to be an inspiration for those who still believe that mankind's future will be carved in the image of Marx and Lenin and their vision of communist utopia.

Cuba, Che Guevara, Fidel and Raul Castro are heroes to the American Resistance. The leftist revolutionaries of the 1970's who co-authored *Prairie Fire*, express their adoration of Che and Fidel Castro throughout its pages.

The lengthy strategy document for the revolution leads off with a 1971 quote from Fidel Castro, "... that is good, because revolutionary spirit must always be present, revolutionary spirit must reveal itself. We must arm our spirit. When the spirit is armed, the people are strong."[157]

Cuba, and the heroes of its revolution, were major influences in the development of the philosophical underpinnings of the Weather Underground. Cuba became a safe haven for Weather Underground and Black Panther Party fugitives escaping the United States to avoid arrest for crimes they committed in furtherance of their attempts to overthrow the U.S. Government.

Obama/Democrats Normalize Relations with Cuba -Cuba Continues Harboring Terrorist Joanne Chesimard

Upwards of seventy American fugitives may have fled to Cuba since the early days of the 1970's. This included the likes of Black Power fugitive, Joanne Chesimard. As Bill De Blasio was getting married in Cuba in 1990, the family of New Jersey State Trooper Werner Foerster was still waiting for justice after 17 years. Foerster was slain by Chesimard in 1973.

Chesimard, who now goes by the name Assata Shakur, was convicted, sent to prison, escaped and has been harbored by Cuba since the mid-1970's. When Barack Obama normalized relations with Cuba in

---

[157]   *Prairie Fire*: The Politics of Revolutionary Anti-Imperialism, The Political Statement of the Weather Underground.

2016, he left Chesimard and three other American fugitives in Cuba's hands- a slap in the face to America's law enforcement profession and the rule of law by Democratic Party leaders.

Cuba, the Cuban Intelligence Services, the Weather Underground and the Black Panther Party were a natural fit as comrades in arms. Through its solid connections with Cuba, and their common love affair with socialism and communism, the Soviet Union and even the People's Republic of China, gained direct access to some of America's leftist revolutionaries of the 1970's.

Before his death in 2005, writer John Barron was a recognized expert on the KGB in America. He described the nature of the relationship between the intelligence services of Cuba and the Soviet Union:

"...the service with the greatest potential for furthering Soviet ambitions may be La Direccion General de Inteligencia, or DGI of Cuba... the Cubans possess a glamour which gives them an entree to Latin America and the Third World that no other Soviet-bloc nation enjoys...

"In August 1968, while foreign communist leaders the world over...denounced the invasion of Czechoslovakia, Fidel Castro defended it. The Soviet Union was justified, he said, in preventing the breakdown of a socialist country...And since the 1968 Cuban capitulation, Castro's brother has served as the strongest link between Moscow and Havana...Slowly but firmly, the Soviet Union took possession of...the DGI," transmitting, "basic orders governing policy, reorganization, and new operations through Raul Castro.

"...Raul returned from Moscow in the spring of 1970 with a host of orders that resulted in fundamental reorganization of the DGI...The DGI in late 1970 established an Illegals center to train staff officers for sabotage and espionage missions in the United States...

"Whereas Soviet representatives are nowhere regarded as romantic and heroic, Cubans are still heroes to young people throughout the world. Youthful demonstrators in the United States parade with placards of Che...and girls swoon over Fidel."[158]

---

[158]   *KGB, The Secret Works of Soviet Secret Agents*, by John Barron, Bantam

Despite the undeniable history of collaboration between Cuban and Soviet intelligence operations directed at the U.S. government and Cuba's continuing sanctuary status for dangerous members of the radical left, President Obama made it a priority in 2016 to re-open America's front door to Cuba's diplomats during the final year of his presidency. America received little in return.

However, modern day Russia regained the help of Cuba, its partner inside the United States, as a force multiplier for Russian spying efforts. The Cubans are especially adept at targeting emigres and recruiting politicians who use their influence to alter perceptions of the reality of socialism and communism.

High profile American politicians like Bernie Sanders, Barack Obama and Bill De Blasio, who define their political leanings in terms of democratic socialism and social democracy make these ideologies sound kind. In fact, they are wittingly aiding the cause of America's most dangerous foes. Their words influence people inside U.S. Government agencies who may already have made up their minds to help the Russian and Cuban intelligence services. The officers in those hostile services have cast a wide net to identify and recruit spies based on their ideology.

Their purpose is to further espionage and *"active measures"* campaigns designed to undermine the American political system, while compromising and weakening the structure of that system at every turn. When most people hear the word spy, they think of espionage and the theft of critical military or classified science and technical information. That type of espionage does happen. But the major goal of the Russian and Cuban services, executed through their sprawling and unique political intelligence branches is to alter our thinking that they are an enemy.

An extreme example of how political intelligence operations can potentially work involves President Donald Trump. Under the auspices of a Russian *"collusion"* investigation, fueled by the political rhetoric of the left, it's becoming increasingly clear that U.S. Government intel-

Books, January 1974, pages 200-208.

ligence agencies were weaponized under the Obama Administration. They targeted the newly elected President as part of a hostile intelligence operation to remove him from office. The trail of money, lawyers, cutouts, corruption, and foreign agents identified in the Russian collusion investigation of the Special Counsel leads back to the Democratic Party.

Despite a major investigation that found no evidence of any connection between Russia and President Trump, left wing activists who took over the House of Representatives in the 2018 general election continue to use their positions of power to resist the president, call for his impeachment, and otherwise block his initiatives to fight the imposition of socialism on unsuspecting Americans.

Mayor DeBlasio's Anti-Capitalist Agenda of Racism, Reparations, and International Solidarity

Democratic Party politicians like De Blasio and other Democratic Party candidates for president in 2020 now work from inside the government, promoting policies and initiatives taken directly from the pages of the 1970's communist revolutionary movement to overthrow the American government. Today's Democratic Party has become America's Trojan Horse.

By using Che Guevara's words, De Blasio joined the Weather Underground's worship of Che as a hero and a martyr. Praise for Che Guevara is infused throughout the Weather Underground's communist manifesto, *Prairie Fire.*

De Blasio's words and actions have shown a consistent adherence to the ideology, strategy, and tactics of the Black Panther Party and the Weather Underground.

One of the Black Panther Party demands was reparations for slavery, "we want an end to the robbery by the capitalists of our black community...We believe that this racist government has robbed us, and now we are demanding the overdue debt of forty acres and two mules. Forty acres and two mules were promised 100 years ago as restitution for slave labor and mass murder of Black people. We will accept the payment in currency which will be distributed to our many communities."[159]

Asked his thoughts on reparations at an event sponsored by the immigrant advocacy group, *Make the Road,* "De Blasio responded, "there's no question that the issue of reparations has to be taken seriously...I think we're going to need something bigger even in a way, broader even in a way, then some of the ideas that have been put out there... bigger discussion about income inequality and oppression of other groups including Latinos, Native Americans, Asian and women...".[160]

Mayor DeBlasio's position on reparations is consistent with the Black Panther Party demands of the 1960's and 1970's. The Mayor's answer to the question posed to him about reparations, also confirmed his solidarity with the ideology of the communist -minded women and men of the Weather Underground (WU) on the composition of the masses.

As the WU wrote in the *Prairie Fire* manifesto, "this defined our international responsibility and our duty as white revolutionaries inside the oppressor nation...a system which includes unprecedented slaughter...continuous wars, genocide, the violent suppression of Black, Puerto, Chicano, and Indian people, the subjugation of women."[161]

The Democratic Party platform from 2016, long before the party gave a thought to losing the election to Donald Trump, also echoed the strategy of the Weather Underground, identifying the target group they would need to appeal to with their political message of racism and division, "we have been inspired by the movements... that... address the

---

[159] Black Panther Party *Ten Point Program*, written by Huey Newton and Bobby Seale, October 1966.

[160] "Bill DeBlasio Goes Full Blown Socialist, Says America Needs 'Actual Redistribution' of Wealth," by Chris Enloe, 4/8/2019, *The Blaze*.

[161] *Prairie Fire:* The Politics of Revolutionary Anti-Imperialism, The Political Statement of the Weather Underground.

discriminatory treatment of African Americans, Latinos, Asian Americans…Pacific Islanders, and American Indians…"[162]

Another Black Panther Party demand was "decent housing fit for the shelter of human beings… if white landlords will not give decent housing to our black community, then the housing and the land should be made into cooperatives so that our community, with government aid, can build and make decent housing for its people.""[163]

Early in 2019, Mayor De Blasio gave his state of New York City address. He went after landlords in the city who he claimed push people out of their buildings so that they can raise the rent. De Blasio declared, "the city's worst landlords will have a new sheriff to fear – The Mayor's Office to Protect Tenants…we'll use every tool we have. We'll fine the landlords. We'll penalize the landlords. But if the fines and the penalties don't cut it, we will seize their buildings. And we will put them in the hands of a community non-profit that will treat tenants with the respect they deserve."[164]

A state assembly member, Nicole Malliotakis, saw parallels with what happened to her family members in Cuba prior to them coming to the United States- "I can say that as a daughter of Cuban refugees who fled Castro's Cuba in 1959, this is what happened to her family, she had her home taken, my grandfather had his gas station taken…this is extreme even for Mayor de Blasio, because we know that he has socialist leanings, but this is straight communism and I think it's very scary to America-loving, democracy-loving people."[165]

Mayor De Blasio is also pushing a plan to change the entry criteria

---

[162] Democratic Party 2016 Platform.

[163] Black Panther Party *Ten Point Program*, written by Huey Newton and Bobby Seale, October 1966.

[164] "Transcript: Mayor de Blasio Presents 2019 State of the City," 1/10/2019, *NYC*, the Official Website of the City of New York.

[165] "NYC Mayor Proposes Communist Plan to Seize Property from Landlords," by Carbine Sabia, 1/16/2019, *The Federalist Papers*.

for students entering New York City's top public high schools. He wants to replace standardized testing as the means by which students compete to get into the schools with a system that looks at middle school ranking and state test scores.

In a 2018 op-ed in the New York Daily News, the mayor's son, Dante, who is black, wrote that he was a victim of racism in public schools. In the op-ed, Dante De Blasio said that "racism is all too common." He related that Asian students told him he'd been accepted to Yale University "probably...because of affirmative action or my last name."[166]

In addition to changing the testing requirements for the most prestigious high schools, Mayor De Blasio wants twenty percent of the seats in the schools to be reserved for low income students. Commenting on his son's editorial he said, "It's heartfelt and well-written and it makes me very proud of him, but it also makes me sad that he had to write it...I think, like many students, he often felt isolated and he often felt judged unfairly."

Mayor De Blasio and his son, Dante, have been vocal in claiming racism colors decisions in America's schools. The Mayor believes racism is a factor in admissions tests and standards. Dante attributed the lack of black and brown students attending New York City High Schools on racism.

Mayor De Blasio's solution to racism in the public education system is government action to increase the diversity of the student body. The Black Panther Party blamed racism for an educational system that failed to meet the needs of black students, but offered a different solution, "...it is their right, it is their duty, to throw off such government, and to provide new guards for their future security."[167]

The Weather Underground envisioned racism as their primary

---

[166] "Mayor de Blasio's son Dante says the SHSAT, the Elite High School Admissions Test Fostered Racism at Brooklyn Tech, by Dante de Blasio, 6/14/2018, *The New York Daily News.*

[167] Black Panther Party *Ten Point Program.*

weapon in the coming revolution. They would deploy it to incite the masses. The masses would use it as justification to attack the institutions of the United States Government, the corporations that grew from capitalism, and the police who maintained order. They devoted sections of the *Prairie Fire* communist manifesto to the importance and significance of racism:

"Opposition to racism. The spirit of resistance inside the US was rekindled by Black people. The power and strategy of the civil rights movement, SNCC, Malcolm X, and the Black Panther Party affected all other rebellion. They created a form of struggle "called direct action; awoke a common identity, history and dignity for Black people as a colonized and oppressed people within the US; drew out and revealed the enemy through a series of just and undeniable demands such as the vote, equal education, the right to self-defense, and an end to Jim Crow."

"The police, the troops, the sheriffs, the mass arrests and assassinations were the official response. The Black movement was pushed forward into a revolutionary movement for political power, open rebellion and confrontation with the racism of white people and the racism of institutions..."[168]

Mayor De Blasio's constant attacks on the New York City Police Department and his allegations that American law enforcement is institutionally racist, illustrates his willingness to use the main weapon of the Weather Underground in toppling the U.S. Government-the weapon of racism. Convincing Americans that law enforcement is racist weakens their trust in the police and erodes their confidence in the rule of law.

De Blasio's dishonest attacks on the police have been unrelenting. In July 2014, a New York City police officer attempted to arrest Eric Garner, a black male, who was selling loose, untaxed cigarettes on a street corner. Garner had previously come to the attention of the police. He decided to resist arrest. He engaged in a struggle, was placed in a chokehold by the officer, and subsequently died. A New York Grand

---

[168] Ibid. *Prairie Fire.*

Jury heard the evidence in the case and decided there should be no criminal indictment of the officer.

In an interview with George Stephanopoulos of ABC News, De Blasio said, "we have to have an honest conversation in this country about the history of racism…about the problem that has caused parents to feel their children may be in danger in their dynamics with police." De Blasio went on to say he had spoken with his own biracial son, Dante about the importance of obeying officer's commands if he was ever stopped.[169]

When De Blasio ran for mayor in 2013, he used Dante in an ad pledging to put an end to police stop and frisk practices, which he said were used far more often against blacks and Latinos than against whites. He also advocated the opening of police racial bias investigations predicated simply on the use of bias sounding language in arrest situations or other encounters between police and black Americans.

By 2016, De Blasio decided that New York City's 35,000 police officers should have special training in "implicit bias." The Mayor fell in line with the Obama Administration's Department of Justice thinking that policing in America was so institutionally racist that officers did not even know or realize they suffered from the disease. Legions of psychologists and academicians jumped on the bandwagon to lend their expertise to the media in explaining to the public that the U.S. government had to become more involved in local policing to erase such powerful implicit hate from the minds of police officers everywhere.

The 2016 Democratic Party platform explains how and why Democratic Party politicians plan to insert themselves into policing decisions:

"We will work with police chiefs to invest in training for officers on issues such as de-escalation and the creation of national guidelines for the appropriate use of force. We will encourage better police-community relations, require the use of body cameras, and stop the use of

---

[169]   "Hundreds of Cops Turn Their Backs on New York Mayor During Slain Officer's Funeral," by Keegan Hamilton, 12?27/2014, *Vice.*

weapons of war that have no place in our communities...

"We will end racial profiling that targets individuals solely on the basis of race, religion, ethnicity, or national origin, which is un-American and counterproductive. We should report national data on policing strategies and provide greater transparency and accountability...

"We will require the Department of Justice to investigate all questionable or suspicious police-involved shootings, and we will support states and localities who help make those investigations and prosecutions more transparent, including through reforming the grand jury process..."[170]

In July 2016, New York Police Department Officer Miosotis Familia was sitting inside a police vehicle doing some paperwork, when she was shot in the head by a gunman with a history of mental illness. New York City police jumped into action. Officer Familia's friends and family mourned.

Mayor De Blasio boarded an airplane while his police department mourned the loss of one of their own. He flew to Hamburg, Germany. His purpose-to give the keynote address in support of a mass rally and progressive event called *Hamburg Shows Attitude*- "a demonstration for 'human rights and humanity,' for a policy of communion and peaceful coexistence..." Mayor De Blasio chose solidarity with the masses in pushing the progressive agenda, over the heroic men and women of the New York City Police Department.

Should any of this be a surprise? The answer is no. From almost the first day he stepped into office, De Blasio, like President Obama, reintroduced racism to America. A country that thought it was healing and moving on, was being held back by its own leaders. These are De Blasio's own words:

"This is now a national moment of grief, a national moment of pain, and searching for a solution . . . We're not just dealing with a problem in 2014, we're not dealing with years of racism leading up to it, or decades of racism — we are dealing with centuries of racism that have

---

[170]   Democratic Party 2016 Platform.

brought us to this day."[171]

Despite Mayor De Blasio preaching about decades of institutional racism involving actions by New York police, an independent research study determined:

"...the city's Department of Investigation released a report on Wednesday showing that the New York Police Department hadn't substantiated a single one of the public's 2,495 complaints of biased policing since 2014, when it started specifically tracking such complaints."[172]

Mayor De Blasio's words appear to reflect the Black Panther Party demands- "...we will protect ourselves from the force and violence of the racist police...defending our Black community from racist police oppression and brutality."

De Blasio's political tactics and positioning as New City Mayor with a love affair for communist Cuba, make him an ideal candidate to fulfill the strategy of the Weather Underground:

"We need a revolutionary communist party in order to lead the struggle, give coherence and direction to the fight, seize power and build the new society...

"Our intention is to engage the enemy . . . to wear away at him, to harass him, to isolate him, to expose every weakness, to pounce, to reveal his vulnerability...

"Che Guevara urged that we "create two, three, many Vietnams," to destroy US imperialism by cutting it off in the Third World tentacle by tentacle and opening another front within the US itself. At home, the struggle and insurrection of the Black liberation movement heightened our commitment to fight alongside the determined enemies of the empire...

"We live inside the oppressor nation...The cities will be a major battleground, for the overwhelming majority of people live in the cities;

---

[171]   "N.Y. Mayor Bill de Blasio Spoke Bluntly On Race, Policing, in Ways Harder for Obama," by Vanessa Williams, 12/5/2014, *Washington Post.*

[172]   "De Blasio's Tough Talk on Police Reform Rings Hollow," by the Editorial Board, 6/27/2019, *The New York Times.*

the cities are our terrain."[173]

The leaders of the Black Panther Party were heavily influenced by Fidel Castro and Che Guevara. Many black power fugitives fled to Cuba and were given sanctuary during the 1970's. Cuban intelligence services played an important role in subverting other governments in South and Central America, with the goal of assisting the Soviet Union in the furtherance of its foreign interests.

President Ronald Reagan challenged those interests across the globe, confronting the Soviets and their allies and labeling them as the "axis of evil." Standing in front of the Berlin Wall in June 1987, President Reagan forcefully declared, "Mr. Gorbachev, tear down this wall."[174]

Two years later Germans destroyed the Berlin Wall and rejected communist rule. Eastern Europe was no longer the Soviet Union's loyal communist ally-it disintegrated in front of the entire world. Two years later the Union of Soviet Socialists Republics, cracking under the pressure President Reagan had applied, totally collapsed. Communism was dead.

When Mayor Bill De Blasio proudly states that he didn't agree with U.S. foreign policy at the time and was a part of the movement against it, he is also confirming that he was on the wrong side of history and freedom. But Mayor De Blasio's political education throughout the 1980s, during a time of intense showdowns between America and the Soviet Union, and his ideological connections to Cuba and Nicaragua, shed light on the origin of his political positions.

Mayor De Blasio quotes the mass murdering revolutionary Che Guevara. He travels to Nicaragua to support the Sandinistas and protest the Reagan foreign policy that toppled European communism and the former Soviet Union. He pushes for reparations to compensate for Black slavery. He threatens to seize private property as a means to pro-

---

[173] *Prairie Fire:* The Politics of Revolutionary Anti-Imperialism, The Political Statement of the Weather Underground.

[174] Reagan's Berlin Speech, by John P Rafferty, *Encyclopedia Britannica*

mote housing equality. He attacks the New York City educational system as racist. He accuses America's police of decades of racial bias. In so doing, Mayor DeBlasio is using his power base to promote the communist minded ideology of the Black Panther Party and the Weather Underground.

The price of free health care, education, and Democratic Party enforced equality, will be individual freedom.

CHAPTER SIX

---

*"A nation will not survive morally or
economically when so few have so much and
so many have so little." Bernie Sanders*

It's likely that Senator Bernie Sanders knows the history of the former Soviet Union better than he understands the history of the United States. If he knew anything at all about American history, he would not have said what is quoted at the beginning of this chapter.

The United States of America was founded by very moral people who believed in helping one another and taking full responsibility for their own lives. They worked hard. They believed in an almighty God. More than once throughout America's history, they made the decision to risk everything, so that others might throw off the chains of tyrannical and authoritarian government rulers, who wanted to control every aspect of their lives.

Americans have always been willing to leave the comfort of their own lives behind, to stand alongside citizens of other countries who were fighting for their own freedom. In the early days of America's birth as a new country, fellow Americans stood together to expand the nation's borders to the west. Some became legends.

One of the most enduring of those legends was Daniel Boone, who was born in 1734 and died in 1820, at the age of 85. As a frontiersman and pioneer, Boone was 41 when he paved the way for thousands of people to move west of the Appalachian Mountains, using his *Wilderness Road* that allowed travel between North Carolina and Tennessee to Kentucky through the *Cumberland Gap.* Two hundred thousand (200,000) Americans would migrate west using Boone's route by the end of the 18th century.[175]

Boone spent his life earning a living from trapping furs, as a soldier, militia officer, sheriff, tavern keeper, surveyor, land speculator, and merchant. He even won three elections to the Virginia State Assembly. Boone fought in the Revolutionary War and several other wars during his lifetime. He enjoyed a reputation as a fair and honest man.

Boone has been quoted as saying, "may the same Almighty Goodness banish the accursed monster, war, from all lands, with her hated associates, rapine and insatiable ambition!" (Rapine means "pillage" or "plunder." It's interesting that Boone associates the word rapine with "insatiable ambition." Insatiable means "incapable of being satisfied.)"[176]

Two hundred and forty years after the true events that inspired Daniel Boone's life and contributions to the growth of a free nation, Senator Bernie Sanders of Vermont is advocating democratic socialism for the United States, proclaiming, "the future of our country... (is) dependent upon our ability to make a political revolution."

Nothing could be further from the truth. When Daniel Boone and America's pioneers moved west, they took what little they possessed in search of land and liberty to raise their families, and along the way, built a nation. They relied on each other. They built churches, towns, and schools, while creating thriving local economies.

Daniel Boone's prescient quote connecting rapine and insatiable ambition describes Sanders' lifelong ambition to use the U.S. Government as a weapon to plunder and pillage freedom because of his own outsized ambitions. Today, an entire mainstream political party (the

---

[175] *Wikipedia.*

[176] Merriam Webster Dictionary.

Democrats) believes the same, as it races to increase the power of government, while depriving American citizens of the freedoms guaranteed them through the Bill of Rights.

The uniquely American westward pioneer movement stands as overwhelming proof that Sanders' quote lacks any credibility. The only truth about the Democratic Party of today, is that the progressive ideology of Senator Sanders conceals his true purpose- a "political revolution" that pillages and plunders, to feed the insatiable appetite for power of those who believe in the ideology of communism.

The insatiable Senator Bernie Sanders of Vermont has written five books and run for President twice. In 2018 Sanders wrote, *Where We Go from Here, My Two Years in the Resistance.* The chapter titles of Sanders's book are clear illustrations of what's written on the pages.

"The Most Progressive Political Platform in U.S. History;"

"Our Revolution is Formally Launched;"

"A Progressive Foreign Policy;"

"The Political Revolution is Looking Great."

Sanders wants a progressive revolution. He will stop at nothing to attain it. That includes destruction of the present- day Democratic Party, the Constitution of the United States and the Bill of Rights.

Sanders' vehicle to the democratic socialism he wants for America is the Democratic Party. Sanders' methods come directly from the strategy of the Weather Underground, the Black Panther Party of the 1970's, and the Communist Party of the United States (CPUSA)- which has a long history of collaboration and collusion with the hostile intelligence services of Russia.

These are Sanders' own words:

"The future of our country... dependent upon our ability to make a political revolution....no real change in American history-not the labor movement, the civil rights movement, the women's movement, the gay rights' movement, the environmental movement, nor any other movement for social justice-has ever succeeded without grassroots activism, without millions of people engaged in the struggle for justice...

"We're making progress...when millions of people... take to the streets for the Women's march in opposition to Trump's reactionary agenda...Our job, for the sake of our kids and grandkids, is to bring our people together around a progressive agenda...We must build a nation that leads the world in the struggle for peace, and for economic, social, racial, and environmental justice...The struggle continues."[177]

Sanders Clenched Fist, International Solidarity and the Ideology of Communism

On the cover of his book, Sanders displays the clenched fist of the communist revolutionaries of the 1960's and 1970's. The Black Panther Party made the closed fist a symbol of international solidarity with the worldwide Communist movement and Black Power.

In 1979 Cuba's Fidel Castro raised the clenched fist while speaking to the General Assembly of the United Nations.

On posters, websites, in articles and at countless protests, the clenched fist is held high in the air by Black Lives Matter, the New Black Panther Party, the Communist Party of the United States, and the Revolutionary Communist Party. Sanders is not alone. Elizabeth Warren raises her clenched fist often-in solidarity with a symbol of authoritarianism. And yes, the Democratic Socialists of America, of which a number of current United States Congressmen and women are members, flies the red flag with the clenched fist. It's all about the "struggle."

Comparing Sander's Agenda with the Words of "Communist Men and Women" of the 1970's Resistance

Prairie Fire, the manifesto of self- described communist men and women, explains:

---

[177]   *Where We Go from Here, My Two Years in the Resistance* by Bernie Sanders, Thomas Dunne Books, 11/27/2018

"PRAIRIE FIRE is written to communist-minded people, independent organizers...those who carry the traditions and lessons of the struggles of the last decade, those who join in the struggles of today. PRAIRIE FIRE is written to all... to prisoners, women's groups, collectives, study groups, workers' organizing committees, communes, GI organizers, consciousness-raising groups, veterans, community groups and revolutionaries of all kinds...It is written as an argument against those who oppose action and hold back the struggle...

"...the duty of a revolutionary is to make the revolution...organize the masses of people and build the fight...PRAIRIE FIRE is offered as a contribution to this unity of action and purpose. Now it is in your hands."[178]

The Communist Party of the United States (CPUSA) puts it this way:

"...We need real solutions to real problems, not the empty promises of politicians and corporate bosses. We need peace, justice, and equality. We need socialism. The United States has a proud history of radical and revolutionary struggles, of mass movements demanding and winning economic and social programs to meet the basic needs of the people, of protecting and expanding democracy, and of uniting to overcome obstacles with initiative, energy, and innovation....

"...We believe that the millions of working people have the power, if organized and united, to run this country... The people of our country have the right and responsibility, faced with an exploitative, oppressive economic system, to alter or abolish it. We can eject the fat-cat financial donors from the election process, throw the scavengers out of the banks, eject the CEOs from their golden parachutes, and elect regular, honest working people to represent us in government instead of corporate lawyers and multi-millionaires...

"The struggles for the immediate demands and reforms needed by working people today are essential steps toward our ultimate goals of

---

[178] *Prairie Fire: The Politics of Revolutionary Anti-Imperialism, The Political Statement of the Weather Underground.*

the revolutionary transformation of society and the economy, toward socialism and then communism...."[179]

The only distinction between what Bernie Sanders wants for America, and what the Communist Party of the United States wants for America, is that the Communist Party has revealed its true intention, "...our ultimate goals of the revolutionary transformation of society and the economy, toward socialism and then communism...."[180]

There it is again, "...revolutionary transformation of society and the economy" is the way the Communist Party says it. But the meaning is the same as Barack Obama's "fundamental transformation of America," and Huey Newton's "total transformation of society."

Bernie Sanders hasn't told the American public the truth about his vision for the United States. But his own words, and the words of his own movement, expose the facade that he hides behind. Sanders speaks these words from an indoctrination in the ideology of communism.

When Sanders says that, "the future of our country... dependent upon our ability to make a political revolution," he is aligned with the Weather Underground's Prairie Fire, "...the duty of a revolutionary is to make the revolution."

When Sanders calls for grassroots activism, as a United States Senator from inside the Government, and reminds people they cannot succeed in the revolution, "without millions of people engaged in the struggle for justice...," he is one with the Communist Party of the United States, when it declares, "we believe that the millions of working people have the power, if organized and united, to run this country."

When Sanders espouses, "peace... economic, social, racial, and environmental justice...," he is in line with the Communist Party's push for, "peace, justice, and equality. We need socialism."

When Sanders tells his followers to, "take to the streets for the Women's march in opposition to Trump's reactionary agenda," as part

---

[179]   "Road to Socialism USA: Unity for Peace, Jobs, Equality," by CP Program Collective, Communist Party of the USA, 3/2/2019

[180]   Ibid. CPUSA

of the resistance, he is in step with the Weather Underground in Prairie Fire, "there are many faces to militant resistance and fighting... An examination of recent history points to mass demonstrations . . . Marches on the Pentagon, Stop the Draft Week, African Liberation Day rallies. International Women's Day marches..."

Sanders acknowledges to his followers that they are engaged in a "struggle for justice," and that, "the struggle continues." The Weather Underground Prairie Fire Manifesto is written for, "those who carry the traditions and lessons of the struggles of the last decade, those who join in the struggles of today..." while attacking "those who hold back the struggle."

The Communist Party of the United States recognizes that, "the United States has a proud history of radical and revolutionary struggles...the struggles for the immediate demands and reforms needed by working people..."

Sanders realizes that Americans will never knowingly vote for a candidate espousing communism in America. Instead, he markets social democracy and democratic socialism as a cover for what he is really selling-big government, harsh government, repressive government.

In another of his books, Bernie Sanders, Guide to Political Revolution, he writes, "the word 'government' refers to the way people organize authority to perform essential functions. It usually describes who does what, who has what power...There are many ways to get and hold power."[181]

In the same book, Sanders defines communism as, "everyone is considered equal and private ownership of property or wealth is forbidden. Communism's aim is a classless society."[182]

On his campaign 2020 website, Sanders lists of policy issues is replete with positions such as "health care for all, college for all, jobs for all, justice and safety for all..." His call to the American people is,

---

[181] *Bernie Sanders Guide to Political Revolution,* Henry Holt and Company, 8/29/2017

[182] Ibid. *Bernie Sanders Guide to Political Revolution,* page 202

"the movement we build together can achieve economic, racial, social and environmental justice for all."[183]

Sanders pledges cancellation of all student debt, passage of a Green New Deal to combat climate change, and to get big money out of politics to restore democracy. All of this is aimed at specific groups of people Sanders is fighting for, "fight for working families...fight for women's rights...fight for disability rights...fight for LGBTQ +equality...fight for fair trade and workers..."[184]

The list has a specific category for "empowering the people of Puerto Rico, racial justice... empower tribal nations...and reinvesting in public education and teachers."[185]

Finally, Sanders rails at the wealthy, "demand that the wealthy, large corporations and Wall Street pay their fair share in taxes... real Wall Street reform..."[186]

The words could be organized differently. The phrases are not exactly in the same order. The types of people who define the masses has been updated. But the evidence is clear. The Weather Underground call for political and violent revolution through the resistance of organized masses of people, is the same plan Bernie Sanders is pushing for America, without the open call for violence. That will be the natural consequence of his ideology.

Nonetheless, the resistance is designed to divide the American public by race, and a long list of social justice issues involving women, wealth and wage inequalities. The aim is to establish a democratic socialist form of government to pave the way to communism. This is precisely what the Communist Party of the United States advocates in its own writings. It is what Huey Newton, the co-founder of the Black

---

[183]   *Bernie Sanders' Official Campaign Website*

[184]   *Bernie Sanders' Official Campaign Website*

[185]   *Bernie Sanders' Official Campaign Website*

[186]   *Bernie Sanders' Official Campaign Website*

Panther Party expressed in his speech at Boston College in 1970.

It is what the Democratic Party platform of 2016 was built upon.

"We believe that today's extreme level of income and wealth inequality—where the majority of the economic gains go to the top one percent and the richest 20 people in our country own more wealth than the bottom 150 million—makes our economy weaker, our communities poorer, and our politics poisonous."[187]

The American republic was founded on the premise that "all men are created equal, that they are endowed by their Creator with certain inalienable rights, that among those are life, liberty and the pursuit of happiness."[188]

Daniel Boone, war hero, trailblazer and pioneer, would have serious disagreements with Senator Bernie Sanders, on just about every political issue facing America today. Sanders, professional politician, Russian traveler, and socialist, believes in equality, built around government redistribution of wealth.

Boone lost most of his wealth several times during his life. He was constantly in debt over land speculation. And he had this to say about his own pursuit of happiness- "all you need for happiness is a good gun, a good horse, and a good wife."[189]

Today's Democrats and Sanders would buy back Boone's gun because it represents violence. They would take his horse because the waste it produces impacts the climate. They would accuse him of sexism since he equates his wife with property-and places her third behind his good gun and good horse.

The Democratic Party resistance, the Communist Party of the United States, and Senator Bernie Sanders have taken the phrase, "all men are created equal," and replaced equal with all men and women

---

[187] *2016 Democratic Platform* by Democratic National Committee, CreateSpace Independent Publishing Platform, July 28, 2016.

[188] *Declaration of Independence,* by Thomas Jefferson, 1776.

[189] *Brainy Quotes*-Daniel Boone.

deserve equality. In one of his own books, Sanders defines communism as a classless society where everyone is equal. In a communist society, people do not have property rights, they cannot question government authority, and their equality is bestowed upon them by the grace of government-not God. Daniel Boone took Americans West. Bernie Sanders wants to take Americans Left.

Bernie Sanders- Targeted for Recruitment and Agent of Influence by the Former Soviet Union

Sanders' writings and current political positions need to be assessed in the context of his political evolution during the 1980's-a time forever framed in history as the "decade of the spy." In particular, 1985 is known throughout intelligence circles as the "year of the spy," when America and the Soviet Union stood eyeball to eyeball, both heavily laden with nuclear weapons that could end life on our planet as we knew it.

The FBI's "flagship" New York Office Foreign Counterintelligence program from the late 1970's to the mid-1980's was on the front lines of the spy war. One of the New York Office counterintelligence squads consisted of approximately 20 FBI agents assigned to combat the work of a branch of the Soviet KGB called Line PR. Line PR stood for the Political Branch of the KGB-by far the largest of the several lines that comprised the Soviet Union's intelligence services.

Line PR officers were concentrated in New York City at the Soviet Mission to the United Nations, and at Soviet Consulates in Washington, D.C. and San Francisco. Line PR officers were also sent to America under the cover of correspondents of official Soviet media agencies, such as Pravda. These were Soviet propaganda machines that spun fake news on a daily basis about the greatness of the Soviet Union. In essence, they were a 24/7 cycle of lies, deception and marketing on behalf of communism.

Line PR was aggressive in its collection of political and economic information about the United States. It gathered personality and behavioral information on American leaders, inside and outside government. Specific individuals were targeted for development as potential Soviet agents inside America. Line PR designed "active measures" campaigns to influence and sway public opinions on the Soviet Union and promote its foreign policy interests over that of America.

For years, Line PR officers also traveled to New York City annually, to clandestinely provide the Communist Party of the United States with one million dollars to fund its subversive work. To complement its efforts at undermining the United States, KGB officers worked closely at times and shared information with colleagues from the Cuban Intelligence Services.

The Soviets constantly challenged American Presidents. President Ronald Reagan turned the tables and challenged Soviet President Mikhail Gorbachev to tear down the Berlin Wall. Reagan had surprised the world by defeating Democratic President Jimmy Carter. Reagan would go on to win a landslide re-election in 1984 against the Democratic Party presidential candidate Michael Dukakis, taking all fifty states.

His challenge surprised Gorbachev and the Soviet Union as well. When citizens of West and East Germany tore the Berlin Wall down with their own hands and the Soviet Union collapsed from the weight of its own communist ideology in 1991, it seemed as if socialism and all its dangerous forms had perished from the earth. But that wasn't going to happen.

There were too many others still standing who carried the socialist virus. The entire world understood what was happening during this historic period. But what did small town Mayor Bernie Sanders of Vermont have to say as history was being remade? What was he doing? What was he learning from one of the major cataclysmic events of our generation's lifetime?

In 1988, then Mayor Bernie Sanders of Burlington, Vermont, traveled to Yaroslavl in the former Soviet Union. He desired to establish a sister city relationship between that town and Burlington. During his remaining ten days in the former Soviet Union, Sanders traveled the countryside and celebrated his honeymoon. *Politico Magazine* recently viewed several hours of tapes from Sanders' trip.[190]

From sitting shirtless in a sauna with Soviet officials and drinking vodka, visits to Moscow and St. Petersburg, in addition to the time Sanders spent in Yaroslavl, Sanders, his wife, Jane, and his delegation were treated very well by the Russians. Following his trip, Sanders was quoted, "they were just as friendly as they could possibly be... the truth of the matter is, they like Americans, and they respect Americans, and they admire Americans.'"[191]

The television studio is not releasing much of the video they have archived as a result of Sanders' trip. However, Politico observed, "... the hours of footage include a scene of Sanders sitting with his delegation at a table under a portrait of Vladimir Lenin. Sanders can also be heard extolling the virtues of Soviet life and culture, even as he acknowledges some of their shortcomings."

A political internist who travelled with Sanders summarized the "effect" the visit had on the future United States Senator.

"'He was delighted...he met people he cared about and cared about him. He got very curious about life in Russia, and I think it became part of his life. He was interested in the way they organized health care, education, street life, families . . . It opened up a new world for me and, I expect, for him, too.'"[192]

An individual who accompanied Sanders on the trip was upset by

---

[190] "Bernie's Mystery Soviet Tapes Revealed," by Holly Otterbein, *Politico*, 5/17/2019. Chittenden County, Vermont's television Channel 17, (CCTV 17) has in its archives 3 ½ hours of videotapes of Mayor Bernie Sanders visiting the former Soviet Union in 1988. A reporter from *Politico* was able to view the videos in their entirety, however, CCTV 17 has decided not to air the videos publicly. They can only be viewed inside the station's archives.

[191] Ibid. Politico.

[192] "Inside Bernie Sanders' 1988 10-Day 'Honeymoon' in the Soviet Union," by Michael Kranish, *The Washington Post*, 5/3/2019.

how he roundly criticized America in meetings attended by Soviet officials and citizens.

"'I got really upset and walked out,' said David F. Kelley, who had helped arrange the trip and was the only Republican in Sanders's entourage. 'When you are a critic of your country, you can say anything you want on home soil. At that point, the Cold War wasn't over, the arms race wasn't over, and I just wasn't comfortable with it.'"[193]

After returning from his trip to the Soviet Union, Sanders' staff began planning a trip to Cuba for the next year. He had visited Nicaragua in 1985 to show support for Daniel Ortega, who was actively trying to turn the country into a Cuban/Soviet satellite in Central America, only to be blocked by the foreign policy of President Ronald Reagan.

Following Sanders' 1985 travel to Cuba, he was effusive in his praise of the Cuban Revolution:

"Under Castro, enormous progress has been made in improving the lives of poor people...I did not see a hungry child. I did not see any homeless people...not only has free health care but very high-quality health care...the revolution there is far deeper and more profound than I understood it to be. It really is a revolution in terms of values."[194]

Sanders' Membership in the Socialist Worker's Party (SWP)

Sanders' comments and conclusions from his travels to the Soviet Union and Cuba shouldn't be surprising. He had been referring to himself as a socialist for many years. What he wasn't telling people during those same years is that he had been an ardent supporter of the *Socialist Workers' Party*, a group designated by the FBI as a communist/Marxist organization desiring the overthrow of the United States government.

The FBI had a Full Field investigation on the *Socialist Worker's*

---

[193]   Ibid. *The Washington Post.*

[194]   Ibid. *The Washington Post.*

Party (SWP) (COINTELPRO/Socialist Workers' Party, 100-436291). The *SWP* had split from the Communist Party of the United States, and at the time was one of the most influential communist organizations in the United States. It's membership today has been drastically reduced. But its goals remain the same.[195]

"The *Socialist Workers Party (SWP)* is a communist party in the United States. Originally a group in the Communist Party USA that supported Leon Trotsky against Soviet leader Joseph Stalin, it places a priority on "solidarity work" to aid strikes and is strongly supportive of Cuba. The *SWP* publishes *The Militant,* a weekly newspaper that dates back to 1928."[196]

During the 1980s, as Americans read espionage novels, watched spy movies, and tuned into nightly television shows, real Soviet KGB officers worked passionately to place "moles" inside United States Government agencies. Real FBI agents worked tirelessly across the nation to stop them. America's politicians have long been targets of the former Soviet Union and now Russia. John Barron, one of the most noted scholars and experts on the inner workings of the KGB during the timeframe explained how the intelligence services operated:

"…the Soviet Union has for years sponsored grand deceptions calculated to mislead, confound, or inflame foreign opinion…Soviet rulers have shown no disposition to abandon organized deception as an instrument of national policy…Lenin…extolled the 'poison weapons of deceit, duplicity and slander…The practical part of communist policy is to incite one against another…We communists must use one country against another…My words were calculated to evoke hatred, aversion, and contempt…not to convince but to break up the ranks of the opponent, not to correct an opponent's mistake but to destroy him, to wipe his organization off the face of the earth. This formulation is indeed of such a nature as to evoke the worst thoughts, the worst suspicions about the opponent…"

---

[195] "FBI Records: The Vault, Socialist Workers' Party."

[196] "Socialist Workers' Party (United States)," Wikipedia.

"…The Russians define disinformation as the 'dissemination of false and provocative information.' As practiced by the KGB, disinformation…entails the distribution of forged or fabricated documents, letters, manuscripts, and photographs; the propagation of misleading or malicious rumors and erroneous intelligence by agents; the duping of visitors to the Soviet Union; and physical acts committed for psychological effects."[197]

Although Sanders sells himself as a socialist or democratic/socialist, he continues to support the themes, objectives, and issues supported by Russia and its allies. He and his presidential campaigns use the same words, slogans and strategy of communist ideology-driven organizations like the Weather Underground, Black Panther Party and Communist Party of the United States.

Sanders has never stopped criticizing America. Even as the mainstream news media has downplayed or failed to educate the public on his past extensive connections with the former Soviet Union, and his support for the revolutions in Cuba and Nicaragua, Sanders has been allowed to dodge the only relevant question-what is it about his judgment that prevents him from seeing the tyrannical and dubious nature of socialism and communism up close?

Perhaps John Barron's book, KGB, holds the answer to the question:

"Visiting politicians, scholars, journalists, clergymen, and other professionals whose opinions are influential are the most common targets of concerned disinformation efforts. Typically, the KGB strives to control what the foreigner sees while persuading him that he is freely seeing what he wishes. It tries to shape his conclusions while making him think that he is reaching them on his own…The record reveals many illustrious victims of its manipulations."[198].

Sanders continued to compare and contrast American and Soviet

---

[197] *KGB: The Secret Works of Soviet Secret Agents,* by John Barron, Bantam Books, pages 224-225.

[198] Ibid. *KGB*

life, even before his trip to the Soviet Union had ended:

"As he stood on Soviet soil, Sanders, then 46 years old, criticized the cost of housing and health care in the United States, while lauding the lower prices — but not the quality — of that available in the Soviet Union...Returning to Vermont, Sanders held an hour-long news conference in which he extolled Russian policies on housing and health care, while criticizing the cost of both in the United States — and boasted that he was willing to criticize his homeland."[199]

John Barron explained the negative impact of Soviet disinformation campaigns. In the mid-1970s the Soviet housing shortage was 'acute" and housing was "grossly inadequate." The Soviet Union's own political leadership acknowledged they had an acute housing problem.

Years before Sanders was extolling the virtue of Soviet housing, the KGB disinformation campaign had reached into the office of A. Allan Bates, then the Director of the Office of Standards Policy of the Commerce Department. Bates wrote a report in 1969, concluding that "'they (the Soviets) had solved the problem of the people living there... the Soviet Union is the first and thus the only nation which has solved the problem of providing acceptable low-cost housing for its masses of citizens.'"[200]

Bates' report was quoted by other U.S. government agencies as an authoritative look at Soviet housing solutions, and yet when challenged as to the accuracy of his facts, numbers, and information, Bates said he hadn't read any Soviet data on housing, studied or had access to any "official" housing reports, or first- hand information as to the relevancy and accuracy of his conclusions.[201]

Instead, Bates is quoted as saying, "I have been in over 100 cities and communities in the Soviet Union, and I know what is going on. My contacts? Well, I don't have time to tell you the dozens and dozens of

---

[199]   Ibid. *The Washington Post.*

[200]   Ibid. *KGB.* Pages 231-232.

[201]   Ibid. *KGB.* Pages 231-232.

high authorities I have talked to."[202]

And yet, based on Bates' report, an American Under Secretary of Commerce said, "the Soviet Union has far surpassed the United States in solving the low-cost housing needs of its people and may well be on its way to becoming the first large nation in the world to eliminate the blight of slums."[203]

There's little doubt that both Bates and Bernie Sanders are the very definition of Russian intelligence services disinformation campaigns. Now, Bernie Sanders himself is running a presidential disinformation campaign against the American public. Pretending to be a democratic socialist, his words, slogans, strategies and life experiences, all reveal a candidate who desires to lead America towards the ideology of communism.

---

[202]   Ibid. *KGB*. Pages 231-232.

[203]   Ibid. *KGB*. Pages 231-232.

CHAPTER SEVEN

"They even came to my house to interview me,
which of course I refused..." Barbara Lee

California Congresswoman Barbara Lee believes that America has an *"antiquated"* way of thinking about Cuba. Ms. Lee, whose Congressional District includes the cities of Oakland and Berkeley, has spent over two decades educating Americans as to the appropriate way to think about the communist run island, 90 miles off the Florida coast.

Congresswoman Lee has the insider credentials to act as a tourist agent on behalf of Cuba and its tyrannical leaders. Former Cuban President Fidel Castro referred to her as "Dear Comrade" in a 2009 letter. His brother Raul, who has ruled Cuba since Fidel's death in 2016, also has a longstanding relationship with Lee. She's taken other United States Congressmen and influential Americans to Cuba. On at least one occasion, Lee and her delegation engaged in secret meetings with Cuban leaders and officials, unaccompanied by representatives of the U.S. State Department.

Lee's never-ending work to change U.S. policy towards Cuba was boosted by President Obama's election. In the new president, she found a sympathetic voice who believed in normalizing relations with Cuba. Lee wasted little time after Obama's election, traveling to Cuba with five members of the Congressional Black Caucus in April 2009- Emanuel Cleaver of Missouri, Marcia Fudge of Ohio, Laura Richardson and Melvin Watt from California, and Bobby Rush from Illinois.

The group was accompanied by Patrice Willoughby, the executive assistant to the Congressional Black Caucus. Lee's small delegation held a secret meeting with Raul for 4-1/2 hours.

When she came out of the meeting, Lee had nothing but good things to say about Castro,

"All of us are convinced that President Castro would like normal relations and would see normalization, ending the embargo, as beneficial to both countries..."[204]

Congresswoman Lee could be considered a bridge throughout the ages. She was involved in the Black Panther Party in Oakland, California when Huey Newton became a fugitive, escaping America to Cuba in the 1960's and protected by Fidel Castro for three years before returning to the United States.

By the time Barack Obama became President, Congresswoman Lee appeared to trust President Castro far more than she ever trusted any member of the Republican opposition party. Lee played a major role in President Obama's decision to lift sanctions on Cuba in 2016.

Lee has a Master's in Social Work from the University of California at Berkeley. She was active in the Shirley Chisholm Presidential campaign. She worked as a secretary for the Black Panther Party during its early days in Oakland.

Lee was an office intern to former Democratic Congressman Ronald Dellums. Dellums was a radical progressive advocate for socialism in America. Eventually, Lee became Dellums' Chief of Staff.

In 1997, Lee was elected to replace Dellums in Congress. In her capacity as a member of the United States Congress, Lee played a significant role in changing America's foreign policy with respect to Cuba. When President Obama decided to lift sanctions on Cuba in 2016, he rewarded Ms. Lee's efforts. At the same time, President Obama fulfilled

---

[204] "Fidel Castro Energetic in Meeting with U.S. Lawmakers," by Jeff Franks and Thomas Ferraro, *Reuters*, 4/7/2009

a key foreign policy goal of Vladimir Putin's Russia.

Congresswoman Barbara Lee's Early Connections to the Black Panther Party

Congresswoman Lee started working for the Black Panther Party for Self Defense in 1971. She stood in awe of co-founder Huey Newton's intellectual prowess and co-founder Bobby Seale's charisma.

Looking back on her days in the Black Panther Party, she believes that time and history have contributed to create an image of the party that is anything but accurate. Instead of being the violent, arms laden gang roaming the streets of Oakland and wreaking havoc with the police, Lee feels the black community benefited from the Panther's community involvement, food, medical, educational and outreach programs.

She blames racist police tactics and the FBI's COINTELPRO program for the party's violent image. Lee's assessment of Newton, Seale, and the Black Panther Party are interesting, given her close involvement with its leaders and some of the events that occurred while she was an active member. For example, despite Newton's growing use of drugs like cocaine, Congresswoman Lee never saw him using drugs, and always regarded him as a gentleman who was extremely protective of her.

It was Newton who told Congresswoman Lee of the murder of Alex Rackley, a 24 year- old Black Panther Party (BPP) member in New York. Bobby Seale and another party member were charged with the murder. The word had spread in the community that Rackley had become a law enforcement informant. Rackley was actively working with the party when its bookkeeper, Betty Van Tanner, disappeared in the midst of an internal inquiry into missing Black Panther Party funds. Van Tanner was found by police two months after she disappeared. She had been murdered from apparent blows to the head. Congresswoman Lee relates Van Tanner's death to COINTELPRO tactics.

Referred to inside the BPP as Comrade Barbara, Congresswoman

Lee found it easy to justify a march and armed incursion into the California State Capitol in Sacramento in 1967 by the Black Panther Party. She believed the Panthers were justified in carrying weapons to protect the black community from the police in Oakland.

Congresswoman Lee has even rationalized Black Panther Party extortion of local businesses, under the auspices of collecting contributions towards the Panther's community survival programs. To this day, Congresswoman Lee believes that the Black Panther Party for Self-Defense represented and fought for justice, community survival and self-defense against racist police.

She remains friends with Bobby Seale and Elaine Brown, the party's first female chairperson in 1974. Lee blames the FBI's COINTEL-PRO for the destruction of the Black Panthers. She is convinced that the Bureau's efforts directed against the Panthers constituted illegal surveillance and spying on U.S. citizens. Lee wrote a book and told the story of an FBI visit to her house. She refused to speak to the agents.

"They even came to my house to interview me, which of course I refused. I requested my FBI files under the Freedom of Information Act for that period...they had spied on me...it was surreal, and I felt violated."[205]

If Congresswoman Barbara Lee refused to be interviewed by the FBI about her involvement with the Black Panther Party then, what is the nature of her relationship with the FBI today? Her frequent travels to Cuba and exposure of other U.S. Congress men and women to the brutal regime, kept afloat by the work of its own hostile intelligence service, are troubling. For the sake of America's national security, she should be keeping the FBI fully advised of who she is meeting when she travels to Cuba, and who is meeting her.

Events in Grenada during the Presidency of Ronald Reagan explain why Ms. Lee should have a revolving door policy when it comes to talking to the FBI. There is significant documentation that during the

---

[205] *Renegade for Peace and Justice, A Memoir of Personal and Political Courage,* by Barbara Lee, Rowman and Littlefield, 9/26/2008

1980's Congresswoman Lee, while an assistant in the office of Congressman Ronald Dellums, was actively working to undermine the foreign policy of President Reagan during the invasion of Grenada.

On May 14, 1980, while working for Dellums, Lee received material in the mail from someone inside Grenada Prime Minister Maurice Bishop's office. The information was critical of the newly installed Marxist government of Grenada and appeared to indicate opposition to Marxist Prime Minister Bishop from inside his own office.

Lee called Dessima Williams, Bishop's ambassador to the Organization of American States (O.A.S.), to tip her off about the anti-government information Dellums' office received.

Williams then wrote a letter to Prime Minister Bishop asking, "how is it possible for such vicious anti-government propaganda to be mailed and stamped from the Prime Minister's Office to a friendly Congressional Office?"[206]

Despite the intensive efforts of Congressman Ron Dellums and his staff to influence the U.S. Congress that an airstrip in Grenada was for tourists and not of any military significance, President Ronald Reagan launched an invasion of Grenada in 1983. Reagan's goal was to prevent the island from falling into the hands of Cuban and Soviet backed Marxists.

As the U.S. Army and American intelligence agencies searched the offices of Grenada's government officials, they found correspondence between Dessima Williams, Grenada's representative to the O.A.S and the office of Prime Minister Maurice Bishop, confirming that Barbara Lee and Dellums' office, were working on behalf of Grenada. Not America

---

[206] "Barbara Lee (D-CA-13)- Key Wiki Progressive/Marxist Profiles," by Trevor Loudon, 4/17/2014.

Cuban Intelligence Services and the American Target-the Story of Ana Montes

The 1980's was a critical time in the history of U.S./ Cuban relations when it came to the spy business. FBI agents working Soviet Counterintelligence matters knew there were connections between the operations and work they did, directed against the former Soviet Union and the work being done by colleagues, who specialized in Cuba. The word on the street at the time was that the CIA had successfully penetrated the Cuban services, neutralizing not just the intelligence efforts of the Cubans, but also gleaning information which could assist against the Soviet target.

As most agents working counterintelligence understand, the intelligence services of Russia, Cuba and the People's Republic of China can be very patient when they are recruiting individuals to penetrate U.S. Government agencies. In the case of ongoing espionage between Cuba and the United States, successful Cuban moles recruited in the 1980's were still at work inside the U.S. government decades later. One of the most notable examples is the case of an American spy, Ana Montes, recruited by Cuba's intelligence service.

America was still reeling from the 9/11 international terrorist attacks on the World Trade Center and Pentagon, when FBI agents arrested Ana Montes on September 21, 2001. The daughter of a U.S. Army physician, Montes was a research analyst in the Defense Intelligence Agency at the time of her arrest. Her specialty was Cuba.

And she was good at what she did. Montes began working at the Defense Intelligence Agency in 1985, and by 1992 was chosen for the Exceptional Analyst Program. Her key judgments on Cuba made their way to the President of the United States, where they factored into foreign policy decisions.

The story of Ana Montes is a story of treason and dishonor. It is also a story of the never-ending quest of hostile nations to harm our national security through the recruitment of U.S. citizens who are willing to sell out their country to its enemies. Montes had grown up in the

Washington, D.C. area, attended the University of Virginia and Johns Hopkins University, and went to work for the Department of Justice in 1984.

While she was at the Department of Justice, people became aware of her favorable view of Cuba and the Cuban government. Montes was an active and vocal supporter of the Cuban revolution and Fidel Castro. Montes subsequently traveled to New York City, where she was introduced to Cuban intelligence officers.

During the next year, Montes decided to seek employment with the Defense Intelligence Agency. She passed the background investigation, appropriate polygraphs and was granted a U.S. government clearance that allowed her to have access to highly classified intelligence community reporting on Cuba.

When Montes walked into the Defense Intelligence Agency facility to start her first day as an intelligence analyst in 1985, she was already a fully recruited "mole" for the Cuban intelligence services. Over the next several years, Montes wrote research reports, conducted analysis of Cuba's foreign policy approach to dealings with the U.S. government, and reached conclusions that were shared with U.S. policy makers. She became aware of American intelligence assets inside Cuba from her growing access to information from their reporting. She worked diligently to identify these critical intelligence sources.

Montes' ideology paved the way for her identification and eventual recruitment as a Cuban intelligence agent. President Obama's decision to normalize relations with Cuba set the stage for the successful recruitment of other Cuban moles like Ana Montes.

Congresswoman Barbara Lee- a Study in International Solidarity and the Ideology of Communism

Obama's follow-up orders requiring federal law enforcement agencies to share information with Cuba's Interior Ministry had every potential to become a national security nightmare. Whether it involves Americans traveling to Cuba aboard cruise ships; airline flights to the island; increased trips by politicians and businessmen; the enhanced presence of Cuban diplomats inside the United States; or contacts between American law enforcement agencies and the Cubans, Obama's short -lived détente with Cuba facilitated the work of Cuban intelligence in the United States against American targets.

When Obama decided to lift sanctions on Cuba without any commitment from the Cuban government to return American fugitive and cop killer Joanne Chesimard to the United States, Congresswoman Lee stood by his side.

After taking office, President Trump reversed Obama's Cuban course, but the damage had already been done. Cuban intelligence officers will use any newly found access they developed through the Obama open window to target Cuban emigres, infiltrate U.S. government agencies, and increase the number of intelligence operations they run against America.

The FBI is already overloaded in its national security responsibilities, with a strained Counterintelligence Division that must deal with countless active Russian and Chinese operations directed against the United States, while addressing terrorism at home and around the world.

Congresswoman Barbara Lee spent two decades trying to open the door to Cuba. It earned her the deepest respect from the murderous Castro brothers, who honored her as their "Dear Comrade."

When Fidel Castro died in November 2016, Lee eulogized his leadership, "My deepest condolences to Fidel Castro's family and the Cuban people during this time. While there are many disagreements between our countries, President Castro was a recognized world leader who was dedicated to the Cuban people."[207]

Congresswoman Lee also tweeted, "My thoughts & prayers are with the Cuban people. We must continue to build on the progress

---

[207] "Congresswomen Lee Releases Statement on the Passing of Fidel Castro," Congresswoman Barbara Lee Website, 11/28/2016.

we've made strengthening ties between our nations."[208]

Neither of California's U.S. Senators, Diane Feinstein and Barbara Boxer, released any statements upon Castro's death.

Conversely, Congresswoman Nancy Pelosi said, "generations of Cuban political prisoners, democracy activists and families suffered under Fidel Castro's rule... in their name, we will continue to press the Cuban regime to embrace the political, social and economic dreams of the Cuban people."[209]

On her website, Congresswoman Lee devotes one of her "issues" to "Caribbean, Haiti and Cuba." It says, "Congresswoman Lee has worked for decades to normalize relations with Cuba. She has visited the island more than two dozen times and is working in Congress to lift the trade embargo and end the travel ban."[210]

Lee uses the site to continue her advocacy for the foreign policy objectives of Cuba and Russia:

"While President Obama made immeasurable strides towards repairing and normalizing U.S.-Cuba relations, President Trump has prioritized rolling back our progress. We must act quickly to end the travel ban and the embargo and repair this relationship before the window of opportunity closes. For years, efforts to improve relations between our two nations have been an Executive Branch-led endeavor. If Congress is serious about repairing U.S.-Cuban ties and improving the well-being of the Cuban people, we must take action to reset relations and ensure the next 60 years are not filled with the same outdated, unproductive, and shortsighted rhetoric and policies of generations past."[211]

---

[208] Representative Barbara Lee Tweet, 11/26/2016.

[209] "Pelosi Statement on Death of Fidel Castro," Congresswoman Nancy Pelosi Website, 11/28/2016, Press Release

[210] Caribbean, Haiti and Cuba," Issues, Congresswoman Barbara Lee Website.

[211] Ibid.

With respect to the **"Economy and Jobs,"** Lee calls for, "a thriving economy...good-paying jobs... the right to organize." Her website calls her a leader in, "the fight to end the wage gap, raise the minimum wage, establish a living wage and address growing income inequality."[212]

The right to organize is a subtle reference to the importance of community organizers, and union organizing of public and private employes, the vital ingredients in any revolution to swing the country towards the ideology of communism. Congresswoman Lee emphasizes income inequality because she has to- it is a longstanding lynchpin of the socialist revolution.

In her issues list, the Congresswoman comments on a variety of topics. Congresswoman Lee's positions on the following issues are consistent with the positions of the Democratic Party, Weather Underground, Black Panther Party and Communist Party of the United States.

Energy and Environment- "...we must *demand* environmental justice... ensure that... good-paying jobs created by the growing green energy sector are open to all, especially people of color, women and veterans."[213]

Gun Violence- "...Gun violence is a national public health crisis... background checks, close loopholes, and get weapons of war off the street. No family in America should have to live in fear of gun violence."[214]

The Communist Party of the United States endorses the Democratic Party's position on guns and gun control. While they propose background checks, and getting weapons of war off the streets, their primary goal is to incrementally do away with the right to bear arms. The same

---

[212]   Economy and Jobs," Issues, Congresswoman Barbara Lee Website.

[213]   Energy and Environment," Issues, Congresswoman Barbara Lee Website.

[214]   "Gun Violence," Issues, Congresswoman Barbara Lee Website.

political party that has advocated for nuclear disarmament has little regard for a citizen's right to bear arms.

LGBT- "...Congresswoman Lee has fought to ensure equality for all... While marriage equality is now a reality across the U.S., Congresswoman Lee is committed to the unfinished work of advancing equality for all, including preventing employment discrimination and combatting homophobia and transphobia."[215]

Women- "... full and lasting equality for women remains elusive... structural sexism is even worse for women of color. Congresswoman Lee... is the author of the EACH Woman Act which would repeal the discriminatory Hyde Amendment that has restricted many women's access to reproductive healthcare."[216]

The Democratic Party, its 2016 Platform, the Communist Party of the USA, the Weather Underground and the Democratic Socialists of America view the LGBT and Women's issues as victim classes that can join illegal immigration and race to build the mass movement that will use systemic racism as a weapon to transform, restructure and/or install a socialist government in the United States. Along the way, the same forces will show international solidarity with terrorist supporting countries and nations that believe in the ideology of communism. Diversity is already becoming a more significant factor in managing major U.S. Government agencies than demonstrated competency and skills.

Global Peace and Security- "...Congresswoman Lee...served as a representative to the 68th and 70th United Nations General Assemblies... Following the horrific events on September 11th, Congresswoman Lee cast the lone vote against the overly broad authorization for the use of military force...Congresswoman Lee is dedicated to increasing effective foreign assistance and reshaping Pentagon spending to meet the nation's real and pressing 21st century national security

---

[215] "LGBT," Issues, Congresswoman Barbara Lee Website.

[216] "Women," Issues, Congresswoman Barbara Lee Website.

needs."[217]

The Democratic Party, its 2016 Platform, the Communist Party of the USA, and the Democratic Socialists of America, would like to see the Pentagon driven by climate change, disarmament, and diversity. International solidarity with America's enemies will negate the need for defense of the United States and its interests in the world.

Poverty- "…As chair of the Democratic Whip Task Force on Poverty, Income Inequality and Opportunity, she continues fighting to protect bridges over troubled water for struggling families… Congresswoman Lee has long championed global poverty eradication efforts."[218]

Lee's words and actions are an indicator of her own indoctrination in the ideology of communism. Her long history of support and involvement with the Black Panther Party has shaped her views of America and how she believes it should be restructured. She has used race and Third World loyalties throughout her career in politics, seldom advancing America's interest, but rather her radical revolutionary ideology and the goals of hostile intelligence services of nations like Cuba, and its ally, Russia.

One of Lee's key mentors on the road to a seat in Congress, Ronald Dellums, had this to say about his own activist, socialist roots, "…If it's radical to oppose racism and sexism and all other forms of oppression, if it's radical to want to alleviate poverty, hunger, disease, homelessness, and other forms of human misery, then I'm proud to be called a radical…"[219]

An article in Common Dreams, named Dellums as, "…the first self-described socialist in Congress since Victor L. Berger. In the 1970's

---

[217] "Global Peace and Security," Issues, Congresswoman Barbara Lee Website.

[218] "Poverty," Issues, Congresswoman Barbara Lee Website.

[219] Ron Dellums, Radical Antiwar Activist, Unlikely House Armed Services Chairman, Dead at 82," by staff of *Common Dreams*, 7/31/2018.

Dellums was a member of the Democratic Socialist Organizing Committee...an offshoot of the Socialist Party of America. He later became Vice Chair of the Democratic Socialists of America...which works within and outside the Democratic Party."[220]

When Dellums died, Congresswoman Lee released a statement expressing her condolences, "I feel blessed to have called Congressman Dellums my dear friend, predecessor, and mentor...I will hold dear to my heart the many lessons I have learned from this great public servant."[221]

It's no surprise that the Democratic Socialists of America supported Congresswoman Lee when she ran for Congress in 2001. She was merely continuing the long history of support for socialist causes in the footsteps of her mentor, Ron Dellums.

In 2002, Joelle Fishman, current Chair of the Communist Party, USA, Political Action Committee, and a district organizer for the Communist Party of Connecticut, supported Lee for her congressional seat.

Today, Fishman is preparing the Communist Party plan to elect progressive Democrats across the country in an effort to chase Republicans from the House, Senate, local and state political offices. Here's why, in Fishman's own words:

"This is an extraordinary election year. There is horror and there is hope. These elections will mark either a step toward or a step back from growth of fascism in our county...

"The CPUSA National Committee is charged with adopting a strategic plan that will engage the entire Party in the 2018 elections and in movement building. We lay out our plans as an outpouring of protests and actions across the country, usher in the year — from Martin Luther King Jr.'s birthday marches to the Women's March featuring many first-time grassroots women candidates, to nationwide protests of the tax scam and the budget deal which failed to fund community health cen-

---

[220]   Ibid.

[221]   "Rep. Barbara Lee: Statement on Passing of Congressman Ron Dellums," Congresswoman Barbara Lee Website, 7/30/2018.

ters, protect the Dreamers or provide relief for Puerto Rico. Such expressions of unity and solidarity are key to defeating the policies of the Trump administration and Republican Congress which are rooted in racism, division and bigotry. They are looting our economy to benefit the .1% and the Military-Prison-Industrial complex, limiting democratic rights and hurting millions of people...

"When people see their common interests, these policies can be successfully challenged, as was shown when the Muslim ban and repeal of the Affordable Care Act were blocked last year...

"There is an urgent danger that the extremist right-wing section of capital is using the Trump presidency, which is based on white supremacy and America First, to consolidate a mass fascist movement organizationally, financially and politically in our country...

"We have a responsibility to adapt and employ the united front strategy in today's conditions while at the same time organizing onto the offensive for a radical restructuring of our economy and society to the benefit of all...

"At the fore is raising class consciousness and rejecting race baiting, union hating, misogyny, anti-immigrant bigotry and national chauvinism...

"Rep. Keith Ellison says: "human solidarity is the best weapon against Trump." It is good to hear the deputy chair of the DNC calling for door-to-door organizing, listening to people's concerns and sticking with them year- round...

"In today's fight to defeat the billionaires, generals and demagogues we also realize the need for fundamental change because racism, exploitation and war are embedded into capitalism...

"A widespread, determined movement is emerging in 2018 aimed at ending extremist right-wing Republican control of the House and Senate, and electing progressives to state houses and local offices across the country. Thousands of people, horrified by Trumpism, and buoyed by the growing resistance, including many young women, African American and Latino, union members, and LGBTQ, have been inspired to get involved in politics and run for office."[222]

There is little doubt that the current day Democratic Party, people like Congresswoman Lee, and former Deputy Chair of the Democratic Party Keith Ellison, have adopted the ideology of communism-and are actively and aggressively promoting democratic socialism as a cover for their real intensions should they seize the power of the presidency.

Eagerly joining the Democratic Party's resistance against President Trump, Fishman, a key leader of the Communist Party of the United States of America, sounds the words, issues, and strategies her organization will use in 2020 to unseat the president. They are identical to the 2016 Democratic Party platform, and the positions of the current crop of Democratic Party candidates for President in 2020.

The Democratic Party is moving the new "political revolution" forward, using the same strategies and methodologies validated by the Weather Underground of the 1970's, the Black Panther Party of the 1960's and the Communist Party of the United States, in 2019.

Congresswoman Lee is one of the most aggressive and longstanding voices for the ideology of communism inside America. Her warm relationship with the Castro brothers and Cuba for fifty years has served totalitarian Cuba very well. Unfortunately, the same cannot be said for her service to protect the interests of America.

---

[222] "All in for Unity, Solidarity and Get Out the Vote," by Joelle Fishman, Communist Party of the USA Website, 2/28/2018.

CHAPTER EIGHT

"African American students can talk to people who actually were in that movement, and they can take from that movement." Keith Ellison

---

Former United States Congressman and current Attorney General for the state of Minnesota, Keith Ellison, was selected as the Deputy Chairman of the Democratic National Committee in 2017. The position qualifies Ellison as one of the most influential leaders in the Democratic Party today. Democrat Howard Dean and Republican George H.W. Bush served in similar positions in their respective parties. Bush moved on to become Ronald Reagan's Vice President for eight years and was eventually elected President of the United States. Dean ran unsuccessfully for his party's nomination for president.

Keith Ellison- An Anti-Police Activist Since College

Ellison pursued his law degree at the University of Minnesota, where he was a "student activist." He was also the President of the Black Law Student Association while at the University. In 1989, Ellison and another student were interviewed for an article that appeared in *Forward Motion* magazine published by the Freedom Road socialist organization. The article was motivated by a series of incidents involving the Minneapolis Police Department and minorities.

"...The people have been subjected to too much police brutality, and they just got sick of it. Having said that, nationally, during the Reagan era, the unemployment rate for Blacks has increased, and the unemployment rate for whites has decreased. The life expectancy rate for white males has increased, while the life expectancy rate for Black males has decreased...

"These changes aggravated the contradictions such that people are coming face to-face with their own oppression.... Eight years of mean-spiritedness of the Reagan era have encouraged fascist and racist forces to come out again...

"The more the right attacks, the more we have to respond, and that is essentially what has happened... in the same way that the racists were cut loose, we're noticing a reaffirmation of what it means to be an African person, and a working- class person."[223]

Forward *Motion (FM)* is self-described as:

"a magazine of socialist opinion and advocacy. We say socialist opinion because each FM presents analyses of important organizing work and reviews of political and cultural trends. We say socialist advocacy because FM is dedicated to a new left-wing presence in U.S. politics and to making Marxism an essential component of that presence. We share these purposes with other journals, but we seek for FM a practical vantage point from within the unions, the Black and other freedom struggles, the women's movement, the student, anti-war, and gay liberation movements, and other struggles...

"We also emphasize building working people's unity as a political force for social change, particularly through challenging the historical pattern of white supremacy and national oppression in the capitalist domination of this country.[224]

---

[223]   "Students and Community Ally in Minneapolis, Battling the Rise in Police Brutality," by Geoff Hahn, *Forward Motion, A Socialist Magazine*, June 1989

[224]   Ibid. *Forward Motion, A Socialist Magazine*, June 1989

Ellison used the interview in *Forward Motion* to present a list of demands to local government officials and the police department. Until his demands were met, Ellison saw nothing to be gained from talking with the police. Ellison's "demands," were a stark reminder of the demands issued by the Black Panther Party for Self-Defense in their *Ten Point Program* twenty -two years earlier.

Years later, Congressman Ellison would say this about policing activities inside Black communities, "I know a lot of police officers who are on the force to do the right thing to protect people. But how can you deny this pattern, this disturbing pattern, Alton Sterling, Mr. Castile in my own community, Philando Castile, but then Tamir Rice, Mike Brown, Eric Garner, Sandra Bland?"[225]

Ellison referenced a number of high -profile citizen confrontations with police in several American cities in an attempt to validate revolutionary left claims of systemic racism and police brutality. The revolutionary left has always believed that America's police are more apt to use deadly force against Black Americans solely because of their race.

But the true purpose of the revolutionary left, who believe in the ideology of communism, is to drive a wedge between police and the communities they serve. Ellison's examples do not illustrate systemic police brutality. They are specific to the situations police officers find themselves in every day across America-requiring split second decisions that could spell life or death for the officers involved or any other citizens who happen to be nearby as a situation erupts.

Independent investigations of the incidents Ellison cited, ended in a jury finding police officers not guilty, grand juries failing to deliver an indictment, or prosecutors deciding not to file any charges. In several cases he used as examples, the FBI concluded the officers involved were justified in using lethal force.

- Tamir Rice was twelve years old in 2014, when he was killed by a Cleveland, Ohio police officer. The officer was responding to a complaint that a black male, "keeps pulling a gun out of his

---

[225] "The Lead with Jake Tapper," CNN, July 7, 2016.

pants and pointing it at people." A grand jury heard the facts of the case and declined to indict the police officer. A video surveillance of the incident showed the black male was drawing a gun from his waist when the police arrived. A former FBI agent also reviewed the investigation and concluded the officer's, "response was a reasonable one".

- Following the officer involved shooting of Michael Brown in Ferguson, Missouri in 2014, a witness reported that Brown's hands had been raised in the air, and he told the officer, *"don't shoot."* Immediately, protesters shouting police brutality, including people such as the Reverend Al Sharpton, coaxing the mainstream news media, proclaimed "hands up, don't shoot" as their rallying cry.

- Several nights of protests erupted in Ferguson. Attorney General Eric Holder ordered an FBI investigation into Brown's shooting. Holder also launched a civil rights investigation of the Ferguson Police Department.

- St. Louis County prosecutor, Robert McCulloch convened a grand jury and presented extensive evidence of the incident. On November 24, 2014, several months prior to the Department of Justice decision that the officer acted in self-defense, McCullough told the public that the grand jury decided not to return an indictment against the police officer.

- The FBI investigation found forensic evidence that supported the officer's account. The Bureau also determined that the witnesses who corroborated the officer's account of the incident were credible. To the contrary, witnesses who had incriminated the police officer with their accounts of the event were not credible. Some even admitted to the FBI that they had not even seen the incident. The FBI concluded the witness who initially reported that Brown had his hands raised in the air and was shouting, "don't shoot," had been lying.

- On March 4, 2015, following completion of the FBI's investigation, the Department of Justice concluded the officer was not in violation of any civil rights statutes and that the Ferguson police officer shot Brown in self-defense.

- In 2015, a resident of Texas, Sandra Bland, was arrested following a traffic stop, subsequently committing suicide in her jail cell. The circumstances of the arrest were recorded on the police officer's dash cam, on the cell phone of an onlooker and on Bland's phone. A grand jury looked at the evidence and declined to indict the officer or the county sheriff and jail staff in connection with Bland's death.

- In 2016, prosecutors in Ramsey County, Ohio, charged an officer with several felony counts, including manslaughter, as a result of Philando Castile's death during a traffic stop. The officer was acquitted of all of the charges against him by a Ramsey County trial jury.

- In 2017, the Department of Justice concluded that no charges would be filed against officers involved in an altercation with Alton Sterling during an attempt to arrest him. The Louisiana Attorney General declined to file any charges against the officers, concluding they acted in a "reasonable and justifiable manner."

- Eric Garner was selling individual cigarettes on the street in New York City in July, 2017, when police officers stopped to question him. When Garner became belligerent and resisted, an officer applied a chokehold, which resulted in Garner's death. Nationwide demonstrations, rallies and public protests accusing the NYPD and the officer of police brutality and the misappropriation of lethal force followed the release of a video of the incident. However, a Grand Jury decided against indicting the police officer involved. Five years after Garner's death, the Department of Justice declined to bring any federal criminal and/ or civil rights charges against him. At the five -year mark in the Garner incident, the officer was fired.

Contrary to Keith Ellison's statements of excessive use of police force against minorities, none of the police officers involved in the incidents he cited, were found to be guilty of any such charges. The FBI and Department of Justice, grand juries in multiple venues, and in some cases, trial juries, independently heard the facts of the incidents in their entirety. None of them concluded that any of the officers involved had committed any civil rights violations against black citizens by the unlawful use of force. And yet, several of the officers lost their jobs and municipalities paid millions in settlements to the families of those involved.

Ellison's History with the Weather Underground, Black Panther Party, and Nation of Islam

Congressman Keith Ellison has excelled at concealing his past history of pushing the ideology of communism and revolution as espoused by the Black Panther Party, Weather Underground, and other communist connected organizations identifiable with the "movement" of the 1960's and 1970's. In his 1989 interview with *Forward Motion,* Ellison was explicit about the movement:

"A lot of students who have been active in this thing grew up or were born in the sixties and did get a taste of the radicalism of the later sixties and early seventies. And the difference between this era and that era is that in the forties and fifties there was no comparable movement that people could relate to on a personal basis. These days African American students can talk to people who actually were in that movement, and they can take from that movement."

Ellison's own words reflect his familiarity with the ideology of the

Black Panther Party for Self-Defense. His past relationships with the Council on Islamic Relations (CAIR), a group with ties to international terrorist organizations, and his connections to anti-Semite Louis Farrakhan, are other clear examples of the ideology of political revolution he takes to his role as an elected official in the United States-who is sworn to uphold the rule of law and protect and preserve the United States Constitution.

Ellison is one of several Democratic Congressmen who can be tied to Louis Farrakhan. Other Democrats connected to Farrakhan have included; Congressmen Danny Davis of Illinois, Andre Carson of Indiana, Gregory Meeks and Al Green of Texas, and Congresswomen Maxine Waters and Barbara Lee of California.

President Barack Obama had his photograph taken with Farrakhan before he became President. The photo was concealed from the public until after Obama left the White House. All of this is relevant to any discussion of racism and white supremacy, since Farrakhan and his radical revolutionary friends and followers use racism to divide Americans and promote the goals and objectives of Black Power advocates.

It's no coincidence that the Nation of Islam was a significant influence on the leaders and co-founders of the Black Panther Party of Self-Defense in the late 1960's and early 1970's. Louis Farrakhan is the current religious leader of the Nation of Islam. On its website, the Southern Poverty Law Center characterizes the Nation of Islam:

"Since its founding in 1930, the Nation of Islam (NOI) has grown into one of the wealthiest and best-known organizations in black America, offering numerous programs and events designed to uplift African Americans. Nonetheless, its bizarre theology of innate black superiority over whites – a belief system vehemently and consistently rejected by mainstream Muslims – and the deeply racist, antisemitic and anti-gay rhetoric of its leaders, including top minister Louis Farrakhan, have earned the NOI a prominent position in the ranks of organized hate."[226]

The *Southern Poverty Law Center* website also features a short his-

---

[226] "Nation of Islam," *Southern Poverty Law Center* Website, page 1.

tory of the Nation of Islam using the words of its own leaders with respect to its anti-Semite views of the Jewish race. Called, "In Its Own Words," the ideology of the Nation of Islam speaks for itself:

"These same Jews that are attacking the Minister are the blood relatives of the slave ship owners." (Nuri Muhammad, "Countering the Conspiracy to Destroy the Black Family," November 2018).

"Also pushing the federal government are the wicked members of the Jewish community, who have opposed every good deed and all of the good works of a good man." (Richard B. Muhammad, "Straight Words," Final Call, Volume 37 Number 35, Aug. 14, 2018).

"These false Jews promote the filth of Hollywood that is seeding the American people and the people of the world and bringing you down in moral strength. ... It's the wicked Jews, the false Jews, that are promoting lesbianism, homosexuality. It's the wicked Jews, false Jews, that make it a crime for you to preach the word of God, then they call you homophobic!" (Louis Farrakhan speech, Feb. 26, 2006).

"Who are the slumlords in the Black community? The so-called Jews. ... Who is it sucking our blood in the Black community? A white imposter Arab and a white imposter Jew." (Speech by NOI national official Khalid Muhammad, Nov. 29, 1993).

"Jews have been conclusively linked to the greatest criminal endeavor ever undertaken against an entire race of people ... the black African Holocaust. ... The effects of this unspeakable tragedy are still being felt among the peoples of the world at this very hour." (The Secret Relationship Between Blacks and Jews (NOI book), 1991).

"The Jews don't like Farrakhan, so they call me Hitler. Well, that's a good name. Hitler was a very great man. He wasn't a great man for me as a black person, but he was a great German. Now, I'm not proud of Hitler's evils against Jewish people, but that's a matter of record. He raised Germany up from nothing. Well, in a sense you could say there's a similarity in that we are raising our people up from nothing." (Louis Farrakhan, radio interview, March 11, 1984).

"Integration is against the Desire and Will of God Who Wants and must Do that which is written He Will Come and Do: Restore the earth to its rightful owner (Black Man)." (Elijah Muhammad, "Our Savior Has Arrived," 1974).[227]

The Nation of Islam was founded in the 1930's. It was led for many years by Elijah Mohammed. Another of its more infamous leaders was Malcolm X. Over the years the Nation of Islam has advocated that equality for blacks will only come from the creation of a separate and independent state where black citizens control their own social, economic, and political power. Attempts at integrating blacks into American society, according to the Black Power extremism adopted by the Nation of Islam and its leaders, would only lead to a perpetuation of institutional racism.

The only solution in the eyes of the Nation of Islam is a separate state for blacks. A major spokesperson for this point of view in the late 1960's and early 1970's was Black Power advocate Stokely Carmichael. Stokely Carmichael, who later changed his name to Kwame Turre, was a student, socialist activist and organizer while attending Howard University.

Carmichael is largely credited with creating the Black Power movement, eventually leading the Student Non -Violent Coordinating Committee, serving as an honorary "Prime Minister" for the Black Panther Party, and a leader for the All African People's Revolutionary Party.

Carmichael drew inspiration from Malcolm X and believed that the Black Power movement needed to endorse the idea of Black Independence from whites. He carried this philosophy into his leadership of the Student Non- Violent Coordinating Committee taking the place of John Lewis who was elected to Congress in 1996. He actively encouraged Dr. Martin Luther King to take an active stand in the name of Black Power and to reject the notion that Blacks should become integrated into the white middle class.

"Now, several people have been upset because we've said that integration was irrelevant when initiated by blacks, and that in fact it was

---

[227]   Ibid. Pages 1-2.

a subterfuge, an insidious subterfuge, for the maintenance of white supremacy.

"Now we maintain that in the past six years or so, this country has been feeding us a 'thalidomide drug of integration," and that some Negroes have been walking down a dream street talking about sitting next to white people; and that that does not begin to solve the problem; that when we went to Mississippi we did not go to sit next to Ross Barnett; we did not go to sit next to Jim Clark; we went to get them out of our way; and that people ought to understand that; that we were never fighting for the right to integrate, we were fighting against white supremacy.

"Now then, in order to understand white supremacy, we must dismiss the fallacious notion that white people can give anybody their freedom. No man can give anybody his freedom. A man is born free. You may enslave a man after he is born free, and that is in fact what this country does. It enslaves black people after they're born, so that the only acts that white people can do is to stop denying black people their freedom; that is, they must stop denying freedom. They never give it to anyone."[228]

In 1967 Carmichael, in his capacity as the leader of the Student Non-Violent Coordinating Committee, pushed coalition building with organizations such as the Students for a Democratic Society and Saul Alinsky's *Industrial Areas Foundation*. During the same year Carmichael left his leadership position, replaced by another Black Power advocate, H. Rap Brown.

Carmichael became affiliated with the Black Panther Party, conducting international liaison and solidarity building on the Panthers' behalf. Since co-founders Huey Newton and Bobby Seale made no secrets of the Marxist/Leninist leanings of the party, they were under close scrutiny by the FBI due to their relationships with nations that supported hostile intelligence operations inside America-Cuba, China, Russia among them.

---

[228]   Black Power" by Stokely Carmichael, *Social Justice Speeches,* 1966.

Stokely Carmichael was in awe of Che Guevara and Fidel Castro. When Che Guevara died, Carmichael paid tribute, "the death of Che Guevara places a responsibility on all revolutionaries of the World to redouble their decision to fight on to the final defeat of imperialism. That is why in essence Che Guevara is not dead, his ideas are with us..."[229]

Carmichael established a friendship with Cuban President Fidel Castro over the years, expressing his admiration for the Cuban leader in a letter, "it was Fidel Castro who before the OLAS (Organization of Latin American States) Conference said 'if imperialism touches one grain of hair on his head, we shall not let the fact pass without retaliation. It was he, who on his own behalf, asked them all to stay in contact with me when I returned to the United States to offer me protection."[230]

Carmichael left the United States in the late 1960's and established the All African People's Revolutionary Party in Guinea. He subsequently worked to intensify connections between the Revolutionary Party and other revolutionary and progressive groups. Examples include the American Indian Movement, National Joint Action Committee in Trinidad, Palestine Liberation Organization, Pan Africanist Congress, and the Irish Republican Socialist Party.

The history of the rise of Stokely Carmichael is important in any discussion of Keith Ellison, who hasn't altered his revolutionary beliefs. He is the same Keith Ellison from the 1989 interview with *Forward Motion*-the Socialist Magazine. Ellison clearly adopted the Black Power and revolutionary language of the 1960's and 1970's, reflecting the ideology of communism.

By 1989, he was repeating all of it as a student activist. Ellison understood in great detail how the mass movement would need to be organized in America and which groups would need to align to be successful. He explained himself during the 1989 interview:

---

[229] "Stokely Carmichael Interview, Part I," by Kwame Ture, aka Stokely Carmichael

[230] Ibid.

"At this stage I can honestly say that the white progressives who have sought to join forces with the African community, the Asian community, and the Native American community, have been very respectful of African leadership, and have been very careful to make sure actions they want to take have been discussed with people in the communities of color. I hope that those communities will continue to do that...

"The theories that the people have been working with are sound ones. For instance, some groups work under the premise that Malcolm X set forth for the white progressive-that is, if you want to defeat white supremacy, you need to work with your own people. You can convince them that white supremacy is an evil system far better than an African person can. Because the African person is its victim. While white progressives have taken that charge, they also have wanted to join in coalition when that was appropriate too...

"Many of the white progressives we've joined with-not all, but many-come from the progressive student movement. What we've yet to do, I think I'm safe to say, is bridge the gap with organized labor. That may cause serious difficulties in terms of the movement. I hope it doesn't. And it's my expectation that no white supremacist problem will arise. But that will be the true test...

"I'd also like to engage in some serious mutual uplift with the Native American community, the natural ally of the African American community. That coalition has never really been solidified the way we know that it can be. That's an important thing we hope will come out of this struggle."[231]

Keith Ellison and his Democratic Party strategists have worked to separate him from comments he has made and articles he has written, since his political profile has become more visible.

By 2016, Ellison was forced to address his past relationship with Louis Farrakhan and the Nation of Islam:

"Man, I'm telling you back in 2006 and before, I disavowed them. That's the ridiculous thing about this, that we keep on having to answer

---

[231] Ibid

this kind of stuff."[232]

A spokesperson for Ellison independently confirmed that Ellison had rejected Farrakhan and his ideology, releasing a statement that Ellison "had no additional involvement with March (referring to the Million Man March on Washington, D.C. in 1995) organizer Louis Farrakhan or his organizations, has long since denounced him, and rejects all forms of anti-Semitism."[233]

Ellison first renounced his association with Farrakhan in 2006, when he ran for Congress, however, was forced to confront the issue again when he sought the post of Democratic National Committee chairman. He told the Washington Post, "these men organize by sowing hatred and division, including anti-Semitism, homophobia and a chauvinistic model of manhood. I disavowed them long ago, condemned their views and apologized."[234]

The *Washington Post* concluded that Ellison continues to have some sort of relationship with Farrakhan, despite his denials to the contrary:

"Ellison is seen chatting with a group of men that includes Farrakhan during a function at the Dar Al-Hijrah Islamic Center in Falls Church, Virginia…The date of the event is unclear, but it was between 2010 and 2013…

"Ellison attended a dinner for Iranian President Hassan Rouhani on Sept. 23 (2013) with at least 30 other U.S. Muslim leaders, including Farrakhan. 'The Wall Street Journal' first drew attention to this dinner, which is documented on the websites of the Nation of Islam and the Islamic House of Wisdom…

"Ellison met privately with Farrakhan … Farrakhan…said that Ellison and Rep. Andre Carson (D-Ind.), the only other Muslim member

---

[232] MSNBC, *Morning Joe*, 12/14/2016

[233] "DNC vice chair Keith Ellison and Louis Farrakhan: 'No relationship'?" by Glenn Kessler, *The Washington Post*, 3/9/2018

[234] Ibid

of Congress, had recently met with him and had a private chat. 'Both of them, when I was in Washington, visited my suite and we sat down talking like you and I are talking.' Farrakhan told his interviewer, Munir Muhammad. 'But evidently, the enemy has made me the litmus test for all black people who want to rise in their world.'"[235]

Congressman Andre Carson confirmed the 2016 meeting with Farrakhan, "As a Member of Congress, I have met with a diverse array of community leaders, including Minister Farrakhan, to discuss critical issues that are important to my constituents and all Americans...As public officials, we must all recommit ourselves to simultaneously advocating for our communities while fostering a more inclusive, tolerant society."[236]

After several months of failing to address questions from the *Washington Post* regarding the exact state of his relationship with Farrakhan and whether he had a meeting in a hotel room in 2016 with the Nation of Islam leader, Ellison appeared on Jake Tapper on CNN, and the *Washington Post* reports his comments as follows:

"Update, June 26: In a somewhat defensive appearance on CNN's 'The Lead with Jake Tapper Ellison denied he had met with Farrakhan in his hotel suite in 2016: 'That is a false — that did not happen.... That is untrue. I'm not – I don't know if he's lying or not. I could tell you I was in no such meeting. I was in no such meeting.'"[237]

The *Washington Post* didn't buy Ellison's denial and has given him a rating of four Pinocchio's.

Despite Ellison's aggressive attempts to convince Americans that he is a different person from the 1989 radical student activist at the University of Minnesota Law School, Ellison advocates causes intended to divide Americans, while pushing positions that are more in the interests of America's most dangerous world foes.

---

[235] Ibid

[236] Ibid

[237] Ibid

As recently as 2018, Ellison was pushing the 1960's-1970's revolutionary tirade of racism, bigotry, and white supremacy-accusing President Donald Trump of fanning the flames of hate:

"The point is that Donald Trump has a long history of racism. And whether he said shithole or shithouse, he has deprecated people and people of color, people who are Muslim people who are Mexican. He has done it for literally years. And so, the real question for me is not house or hole. The question is what are we going to do about it? The chief executive of the United States, the commander in chief, has racist ideas about America and this country, and the American people, all 320 million of us, better figure out what to do about it. Because if somebody is just some regular person who holds his attitudes, maybe it doesn't make that much of a difference. But this guy is a commander in chief. He controls the largest military economy and surveillance in the world. And so, his racism is dangerous to people. And we've all got to step up and deal with that."

Although he has claimed to reject the ideology of revolutionary communism, Ellison uses the same words today, he did then. His weapon is the same now as it was at the University of Minnesota- use racism as a weapon to create anger and division in America.

Through his own words, Ellison has connected himself to the ideology of communism and the revolutionaries who wanted to overthrow the United States government in the era of Vietnam. Now he sits as a highly placed Democratic Party official, a potential candidate for President himself, one day in the future.

CHAPTER NINE

*I now have a lot of responsibility… and a lot
of power." Congressman Jerry Nadler*

Congressman Jerry Nadler, Democrat from New York, is one of the best examples of the threat posed to America by the ideology of communism. While attending Columbia University in New York City, he organized students into a group that became known as the *West End Kids*. They were enamored by the Presidential campaign of Eugene McCarthy, and swept up in the anti-Vietnam war protest movement of the 1960's.

From founding the *West End Kids* at Columbia, to becoming Chairman of the House Judiciary Committee, Nadler has held elective office almost his entire life- forty-two years. He never fought in a war. He never policed a street in America. He never created a job for another American.

"My original motive in politics, from the time I was probably 12 years old, was civil rights and civil liberties and due process… I have always concentrated on them, and that has never changed…I now have a lot of responsibility, which I didn't have, and a lot of **power**…"[238]

---

[238] "Man of the Moment," by invreporter@strausnews.com, StrausMedia, 4/10/2019

Nadler's political rise coincides with his passionate devotion to the same issues as the Weather Underground, the Black Panther Party of Self-Defense, the Democratic Socialists of America, and the Communist party of the United States.

On the way to becoming Chairman of the House Judiciary Committee, where he has oversight of the Department of Justice and the FBI, Nadler has formed alliances with the Democratic Socialists of America and union leaders sympathetic to the ideology of communism. He has accepted hundreds of thousands of dollars from those unions.

From advancing the cause of public employee unions populating U.S. Government agencies with people who are loyal to unions and the Democratic Party, to securing presidential pardons for cop killing revolutionaries, Congressman Nadler has been on the front lines of fulfilling the ideology of communism-incrementally but absolutely.

He considers himself the man of the hour, as our Constitutional Republic faces an unprecedented crisis, precipitated by power, "I'm in the right place at the right time. And it's a place I wanted, it's a place I think I'm well trained for, it's a place I think I'm well suited for..."[239]

Nadler has no self-doubts about the road he is traveling with America and Americans, "I'm in the middle of a lot of things I care very deeply about as chairman of the Judiciary Committee, and people look to me for leadership and guidance by virtue of this position..."[240]

Every American should have a clear understanding of how Chairman Nadler's political ideology developed. Chairman Nadler has had a long career as a progressive in the Democratic Party. According to his Congressional website Nadler is, "a veteran member of the Congressional Progressive Caucus, Jerry Nadler has been a champion of progressive causes both in New York and throughout the country."[241]

---

[239] "Man of the Moment," NY Press, invreporter@strausnews.com, 4/10/2019

[240] Ibid. "Man of the Moment"

[241] https://nadler.house.gov/about-jerry/

Nadler has spent years as a "champion of progressive causes" pursuing freedom for convicted terrorists who played a major role in crimes in which police officers were murdered. He has used his position of "power" as a United States Congressman who took an oath of office to protect and defend the U.S. Constitution, to free from prison terrorists who fought for the revolutionary overthrow of the United States Government. Nadler used his position of "power" as an elected official to fight for people who had declared war on the United States of America and desired to replace our constitutional Republic with socialism- followed by communism.

Nadler's Role in the Pardon of Weather Underground Terrorist Susan Rosenburg

Jerry Nadler is very familiar with the domestic revolutionaries of the 1970's. At Nadler's urging, President Bill Clinton pardoned Susan Rosenburg, a member of the May 19 Communist organization, and former member of the Weather Underground, for her role in committing terrorist acts of violence in the 1980's, in an effort to overthrow the U.S. Government.

In a brazen 1981 military style assault on a Brink's armored car in the town of Nyack, New York, members of the Weather Underground and individuals connected to the Black Liberation Army, ambushed and murdered Brinks' guard, Peter Paige, during an armed robbery attempt. Another Brinks' guard was wounded. As Nyack police officers arrived at the scene of the robbery and gave chase to the getaway cars, two Nyack officers, Edward O'Grady and Waverly Brown, were killed in the ensuing shootouts.

The FBI and police investigation identified six Black Liberation Army (Jeral Wayne Williams, Donald Weems, Samuel Brown, Samuel Smith, Edward Ferguson, Cecilio Ferguson) and four Weather Underground members (David Gilbert, Judith Clarke, Kathy Boudin and Marilyn Buck) involved in the Brink's robbery and murders. Federal investigators also established that Susan Rosenburg was a driver of a getaway car and acted as a lookout during the robbery. Following the Brinks' robbery, Rosenburg became a wanted fugitive.

In 1984 Rosenburg and Timothy Blunk were apprehended in New Jersey while unloading almost 650 pounds of explosives from a U-Haul truck into a storage unit. They were in possession of weapons, false identification and terrorism manuals. Rosenburg and Blunk admitted they were part of a domestic terror network planning additional terrorist bombings inside the United States.

"Blunk and Rosenberg acted as their own attorneys during the trial. Rosenberg screamed revolutionary slogans in court and demanded the maximum sentence. 'The truth,' Rosenberg pronounced, was that 'revolutionary resistance fighters were defending the world-wide anti-colonial and anti-imperialist peoples and nations.' 'The system,' she thought, would not last as long as her sentence. A federal jury, the majority of whom were women, found her guilty, and she was sentenced to 58 years in prison."[242]

A few days before he left office in January 2001, President Bill Clinton pardoned Rosenburg. The New York Times captured the outrage of the moment, "Mayor Rudolph W. Giuliani, a Republican, and United States Senator Charles E. Schumer, a Democrat, were among those who criticized the pardon, as did Bernard B. Kerik, New York City's police commissioner, and David Trois, a Rockland County police union official." [243]

Jerry Nadler used his Congressional office to play an untiring role over several years in pressing forward with efforts to have Rosenburg pardoned. Rosenburg's parents were long time Democratic Party supporters. While Rosenburg was incarcerated in a Lexington, Kentucky prison, an organized campaign was mounted to secure her freedom.

Nadler's synagogue social action committee showed a documenta-

---

[242] "Jerry Nadler's Family Values," by Mary Grabar, Real Clear Politics, 5/22/2019

[243] "Officials Criticize Clinton's Pardon of an Ex Terrorist," by Eric Lipton, The New York Times, 1/22/2001

ry on prison conditions where she was incarcerated. A story line developed that Rosenburg and Blunk "were not convicted for their connection with explosives or attempted prison breakouts or bank robberies or seditious conspiracy, but because they happened to be attending a rally in Central Park."

Marshall Meyer, Nadler's rabbi subsequently ended up on a discussion panel where Rosenburg's father delivered the same dual messages about Rosenburg's unfair sentence and conditions at the Lexington, Kentucky prison where she was sent to serve her sentence on the explosive possession charges. Rabbi Meyer accepted the newest narrative about Rosenburg's imprisonment. He enlisted the help of a friend, Rabbi Rolando Matalon to get Rosenburg freed from prison.

In 1993, Matalon and Rosenburg's mother had a meeting with Nadler to seek a commutation of her sentence so that she could visit her dying father. Nadler held a meeting with the head of the Bureau of Prisons on her behalf.

In 1994, Nadler wrote a letter to the parole board, seeking a pardon for Rosenburg. He cited her work on AIDS, creative writing classes, and her status as a model prisoner in support of his request. Rabbi Matalon was also involved in the pardon efforts. By this time, Nadler and the other activists trying to get Rosenburg out of jail stressed she was never charged in the 1981 Brink's robbery.

However, U.S. Attorney for New York City, Mary Jo White, responded that "compelling evidence pointed to her complicity." Due to the letter, Rosenburg's attorneys waived any further requests for consideration of parole.[244]

Following Blunk's release from prison in 1997, Rosenburg's lawyers again asked for, and received, Nadler's help in securing a pardon for her. Continuing work was being done on several fronts by a number of people, including Nadler, to get the pardon. Rosenburg had a meeting with, and told her story to, a senior producer at CBS' 60 Minutes.

---

[244]   "Jerry Nadler's Family Values," by Mary Grabar, Real Clear Politics, 5/22/2019

A CBS segment on Rosenburg with host Morley Safer aired in late 2000, minimizing her criminal culpability and involvement with the Weather Underground. A few weeks later President Clinton received yet another letter from an "important congressman" urging Rosenburg's pardon. Clinton commuted her sentence and credited her with time served. This led to her immediate release, just a day before Bill Clinton left the White House, in January 2001.

In 2011, Nadler was interviewed about the Brinks robbery and Susan Rosenburg. His response- "a couple of cops were killed...she proclaimed that she was innocent of that...she was sentenced to 58 years in jail, which is a hell of a sentence, you know, 59 months for this stick of dynamite..." [245]

But in 2017, prosecutor Andrew McCarthy had this to say about Rosenburg:

"Rosenberg turned her New Jersey terrorism trial into a circus, posturing as a political prisoner. At her sentencing, she urged her supporters to continue their war against the United States. ("When we were first captured, we said, we're caught, we're not defeated, long live the armed struggle. We'd like to take this moment to rededicate ourselves to our revolutionary principles, to our commitment to continue to fight for the defeat of U.S. imperialism.") She expressed remorse about only one thing: she hadn't had the courage to shoot it out with the police who'd apprehended her...

"Her brazen barbarism moved a highly respected federal judge not only to impose the 58-year sentence but to recommend against parole (within the limits of then existing law, under which convicts "maxed out" after two thirds of their jail terms). Southern District U.S. Attorney Rudy Giuliani then dismissed the Brinks charges: not because Rosenberg was innocent but because there had already been a grueling trial that Rosenberg didn't deign to attend while she was out plotting murder and mayhem. There was no need for the pandemonium a second Rosenberg trial promised: the New Jersey sentence should have kept her on

---

[245]   Ibid

ice for at least 20 and, more likely, well over 30 years…"[246]

Nadler's Role in Commuting Weather Underground Terrorist Linda Evan's Sentence

Nadler's aid and support for radical revolutionaries didn't end with Rosenburg. He realized President Bill Clinton and Hillary Clinton needed his continuing political support if she was to become the next Senator from New York. Nadler skillfully used his influence to intervene with Clinton on behalf of Linda Evans, another Weather Underground terrorist seeking early release from prison. Like Rosenburg, Evans was caught possessing explosives to further the revolution.

"In the late spring of 1985, she was arrested, charged and then convicted for acquiring deadly weapons. Specifically, she was planning to target the United States Capitol Building, the National War College, the Navy Yard Computer Center, the Navy Yard Officers Club, the Israeli Aircraft Industries, the FBI, and the New York Patrolman's Benevolent Association. Her plans were ambitious, but she was well armed. In her possession were well over 700 pounds of dynamite."[247]

Again, Nadler succeeded with President Clinton. Linda Evans was released from prison, 24 years early, her sentence commuted by the White House. It was only 8 months before America would suffer a devastating international terrorist attack killing over 3,000 people on 9/11. And following the 9/11 terror attacks and election of Barack Obama in 2008, Nadler became a major Congressional supporter of Obama's arms deal with Iran.

In the meantime, Linda Evans reprised her role in the political revolution, remarkably and unabashedly lacking any remorse.

---

[246] "Eleventh Hour Terrorist Pardons," Andrew C. McCarthy, National Review, 1/18/2017

[247] "Adams: Jerry Nadler is a Dishonorable Traitor," by Mike Adams, Daily Wire, 10/22/2018

"Along with her partner, Eve Goldberg, Evans travels around the United States advocating for lesbian and female inmates' rights. [248] Evans is involved with the activist organization the *Center for Third World Organizing*.[249] In March 2002 she helped convene a conference with other formerly incarcerated people, entitled *Tear Down the Walls*, in an attempt to gain support for giving amnesty to people she identified as political prisoners, claiming that, 'These political prisoners of war are women and men incarcerated because of their involvement in political activities which challenged the unjust nature of the U.S socioeconomic system.'" [250]

"In 2003 Evans gave an interview in which she identified her sexuality as an influence for her political activities, stating that 'Being a lesbian has always been an important part of the reasons why I am a revolutionary – even before I was self-conscious about how important this is to me' and 'because I experience real oppression as a lesbian and as a women, I am personally committed from the very core of being to winning liberation for women, lesbians, and all oppressed people.'" [251]

Nadler's Role in Clemency for Weather Underground Terrorist Judith Clark

Nadler signed his name on an April 2, 2019 letter to the New York State Board of Parole, along with other Democratic Congressional Rep-

---

[248]   "Linda Evans (Radical)," Life Since Prison, Wikipedia, retrieved 12/15/2019

[249]   John Perazzo. Front Magazine (August 26, 2003)

[250]   "Prisoners of War." David Horowitz, Front Magazine (September 5, 2001)

[251]   "Linda Evans, Susan Rosenberg, and Laura Whitehorn, Biographies." In Imprisoned Intellectuals: America's Political Prisoners Write on Life, Liberation, and Rebellion, by Joy James. (Lanham, 2003)

resentatives, seeking the early prison release of Judith Clark, another driver of a getaway car in the Brink's armed car robbery.

"Ms. Clark participated in an unspeakable tragedy. Three people were killed, including two police officers. Although Ms. Clark was the "getaway" driver and did not fire any weapon, she does not minimize her role or in any way try to absolve herself from guilt. Judith Clark is painfully aware of the irrevocable harm she caused, and for more than three decades has done everything a human being could do to repair, repent and express remorse. She again forthrightly acknowledged her role, accepted responsibility, and expressed her contrition to the Parole Board at her initial appearance before the Board in April 2017…

"At age 69 and after 37 years in prison, Judith Clark is among the oldest and longest serving women in New York State prison (only one woman among the almost 2,400 currently incarcerated in New York has served longer than Ms. Clark.

'We ask that you consider who she is today in 2019, not who she was in 1981, and implore you to grant her release…" [252]

The letter was also signed by Representatives Yvette Clarke, Adriano Espaillat, Hakeem Jeffries, Carolyn Maloney, Gregory Meeks, Alexandria Ocasio-Cortez, Jose Serrano, Nydia Velazquez, Tom Suozzi.

Like Rosenburg in 2001, Clark apparently worked on behalf of AIDS causes, had been a model prisoner, and began writing poetry while in prison. By a vote of 2-1, the New York State Parole Board released Judith Clark from prison. Although it took him several years of effort, Nadler was successful again, securing the release of yet another terrorist.

The New York Times and many hundreds of advocates for Clark's release from prison stressed that she had become a changed person inside the gates-writing poetry, working as an AIDS activist and behaving as a model prisoner.

---

[252] Letter dated April 2, 2019 to the New York State Board of Parole Requesting the Prison Release of Judith Clark, https://www.manhattanbp.nyc.gov/wp-content/uploads/2019/04/Elected-Officials-and-Civil-Rights-Groups-Letter-4-2-19-FINAL.pdf

However, Tina Trent, in *"No, Judith Clark Isn't A 'Reformed Prisoner.' Yes, Her Victims Are Still Dead. And Guess Which Congressional Freshman Supported Her Parole,"* sees it differently:

"...Her demand that prisoners receive better education wasn't about readily available GEDs but about institutionalizing limitless, taxpayer-funded access to a plethora of fake university and graduate programs taught by tenured radicals, intent on fomenting violence and resentment among the incarcerated.

"All of her activism behind bars was and is no different from the primitive demands for attention and communist revolution she once levied at the end of a gun. Only the tactics changed..." [253]

Decades after self-described "communist women and men" used the anti-Vietnam War movement as their catalyst to build the masses, establish international solidarity with America's enemies and overthrow our Constitutional Republic, mainstream media, books and online references paint a deceptive image of the terrorists liberated from prison by Congressman Jerry Nadler.

Wikipedia leads off an article on Susan Rosenburg, describing her as, "a far-left revolutionary, author and advocate for social justice and prisoners' rights. Rosenberg was active in many radical movements of the 1970s."

The article ends with the words of a *Kirkus* review of Rosenburg's 2011 book, *An American Radical: A Political Prisoner in my Own Country.* "Articulate and clear-eyed, Rosenberg's memoir memorably records the struggles of a woman determined to be the agent of her own life." [254]

Wikipedia calls Linda Evans, "an American radical leftist who was convicted in connection with violent and deadly militant activities committed as part of her goal to free African Americans from white oppres-

---

[253] *"No, Judith Clark Isn't A 'Reformed Prisoner.' Yes, Her Victims Are Still Dead. And Guess Which Congressional Freshman Supported Her Parole,"* by Tina Trent

[254] Susan Rosenburg, Wikipedia

sion." [255]

In a lengthy article appearing in *The New York Times* in 2012, five years before Judith Clark was released from prison for her role in the Brink's 1981 murders and robbery, the author describes her "radical transformation," and by the third paragraph points out that, "No one ever accused Clark of holding or firing a gun that deadly afternoon." The author is Tom Robbins, described then as teaching, "investigative reporting at CUNY's Graduate School of Journalism." [256]

Nadler's Defense of Clemency for the FALN

The FALN (Fuerzas Armadas de Liberación Nacional) (Armed Forces of National Liberation) is described by the FBI as "an extremist organization advocating for Puerto Rican independence through acts of violence. The group, active in the 1970s and early 1980s, is credited with committing more than 100 bombings that caused several deaths, multiple injuries, and millions of dollars in damage."[257] The bombings occurred in Puerto Rico and New York.

In August 1999, President Bill Clinton offered clemency to twelve imprisoned FALN members if they would sign a statement of remorse for their terrorist activities. Clinton's motivation appeared to be related to his wife Hillary, her upcoming run for Senator from New York state, and the Puerto Rican vote in New York.

Both the Senate and House were outraged with Clinton, given the FALN's history of violence and terror. A vote was scheduled for September 9, 1999, to pass resolutions condemning Clinton's actions. In debate before the vote, Congressman Jerry Nadler defended Clinton's

---

[255]   Linda Evans, Wikipedia

[256]   "Judith Clark's Radical Transformation," by Tom Robbins, The New York Times Magazine, 1/12/2012

[257]   FBI Most Wanted, William "Guillermo" Morales, fbi.gov

clemency decision, calling it a matter of the "rule of law." [258]

"What is relevant…is the rule of law…this resolution frankly is an outrage…this Bill makes many questionable statements of fact…these people were not condemned as terrorists. They were condemned for the crimes of seditious conspiracy and weapons possession…They were not convicted of bombing anybody, planning to bomb anybody, murdering anybody…If the President believed that the interest of justice called for clemency because they had been sentenced far in excess of the normal sentence…that's his privilege as President to make that decision. It's all our privileges to agree or disagree or criticize him severely as individuals." [259]

The House and Senate resolutions passed despite Nadler's plea based on the "rule of law." As Clinton left office, sixteen FALN members were granted commutations of their sentences. From Wikipedia:

"The commutation was opposed by the U.S. Attorney's Office, the FBI and the Federal Bureau of Prisons, and was criticized by many, including former victims of FALN terrorist activities and the Fraternal Order of Police. Hillary Clinton, then campaigning for her first term in the Senate, initially supported the commutation,[8] but withdrew her support three days later.

"The U.S. House Committee on Government Reform held an investigation on the matter, but the Justice Department prevented FBI officials from testifying. President Clinton cited executive privilege for his refusal to turn over some documents to Congress related to his decision to offer clemency to members of the FALN terrorist group."[260]

Like so many other terrorist acts of the past, the FALN still haunts law enforcement. The FBI continues to look for fugitive William Guill-

---

[258]   Floor Debate, Nadler/FALN, C-SPAN, 9/9/1999 House Session

[259]   Floor Debate, Nadler/FALN, C-SPAN, 9/9/1999 House Session

[260]   "Bill Clinton Pardon Controversy," FALN Commutation of 1999, Wikipedia, (from Black, Chris (September 5, 1999). "First lady opposes presidential clemency for Puerto Rican Nationalists". CNN. Retrieved July 23, 2017)

ermo Morales, for Unlawful Flight to Avoid Prosecution and Escape. Born in 1950 in New York, Morales vanished in 1988. He is likely being granted sanctuary by the Cuban Government.

"'William "Guillermo' Morales was an explosives expert/bomb maker for the FALN..., an extremist organization advocating for Puerto Rican independence through acts of violence. The group, active in the 1970s and early 1980s, is credited with committing more than 100 bombings that caused several deaths, multiple injuries, and millions of dollars in damage.

"On July 12, 1978, Morales was working on a bomb at a house in East Elmhurst, New York, when it exploded prematurely. Morales was severely injured, taken to a hospital, and arrested. Due to his injuries, Morales was held at the Bellevue Hospital prison ward in New York City until his potential transfer to federal prison. Morales escaped from Bellevue Hospital and fled to Mexico, where he was captured in May of 1983. He was imprisoned in Mexico, but eventually handed over to Cuban authorities and is believed to still be in that country."[261]

Nadler's propensity to intervene in some of the most significant terrorism investigations of the 1980's to secure the release from prison of convicted terrorists is horrifying. His cavalier attitude on the pardon of Susan Rosenburg ("a couple of cops were killed") is appalling.

But his words and actions are a clear illustration of solidarity with the violent revolutionaries who comprised the Weather Underground (WU) during the 1970's. The revolutionaries described themselves as "communist women and men." Their goal was toppling our constitutional Republic. Since Rosenburg, Evans and Clark never pulled the trigger of a gun, Nadler believed they deserved to be released from prison. He was well aware of their history, and more importantly, the history of the violent revolutionary organizations they represented.

Most Americans do not understand or are unaware of the intensive efforts made during the 1970's to topple the United States Government. America's determined domestic enemies were supported by communist

---

[261]   FBI Most Wanted, William "Guillermo" Morales, fbi.gov

governments worldwide-the Soviet Union, People's Republic of China, and Cuba. The same voices, words and slogans active then are active now-from inside the Democratic Party.

The Democratic Party does understand the violent history of the 1970's. Revolutionary terrorists joined with committed anarchists to form the masses that wanted to terminate the American experience and replace it with the Marx/Lenin version of communist utopia. The FBI stopped the revolution then. It is helpless to stop the same voices inside the Democratic Party today.

Here is the rest of the story on the history Congressman Jerry Nadler ignored, as he used his position of power as a United States Congressman to free convicted terrorists from prison.

Ten years before the Brink's robbery, Kathy Boudin and fellow domestic terrorist Cathy Wilkerson, were in a terrorist safe house in Greenwich Village in New York City when a deadly explosion rocked the structure. Three members of the Weather Underground were killed in the blast. A witness saw Cathy Wilkerson run from the building. The terrorists inside had been preparing for a bombing attack directed at Fort Dix, New Jersey, when the explosion happened.

Boudin, Wilkerson, and several other members of the Weather Underground terror cell fled New York City, becoming FBI fugitives as a result of the Greenwich Village explosion. As the FBI fugitive investigation to locate Boudin, Wilkerson and the others gathered steam, information pointed to the San Francisco Bay Area as a possible hiding spot.

San Francisco was also seeing increasing terrorist attacks in the greater Bay Area and suspected the Weather Underground or Black Panther Party might be involved. In February,1970, a San Francisco police officer was murdered in a brazen terror attack on the city's Ingleside Station.

Less than a month after the Greenwich Village explosions, FBI Special Agent Donald Max Noel was assigned to work a San Francisco FBI "office special," directed at the Weather Underground. One of the investigative projects involved the examination of deceased infant identities, and then comparison of the identities to various public records and Department of Motor Vehicle information.

DMV agencies were asked to provide the FBI with Driver's License photos, as agents checked other records ranging from library cards to Pacific Gas and Electric utility bills. The FBI hoped to identify Weather Underground fugitives using deceased infant identities and thereafter trace them to their safe house addresses. As information rapidly developed, the FBI became more confident that some Weather Underground fugitives had taken up residence in San Francisco.

Agents combined neighborhood investigations, surveillances and other techniques, combined with the deceased infant project, to locate the fugitive terrorists. Weather Underground members became aware that the FBI was on their trail and developed a plan to escape from the Bay Area. In need of money to implement their escape plan, they turned to the National Lawyers Guild in Chicago.

The National Lawyers Guild arranged to send funding to the fugitives through Western Union. The FBI became aware of the time, location, and name of the person who was supposed to pick up the money. FBI agents assigned to criminal squads teamed up with agents assigned to counterintelligence squads to conduct surveillances of the local Western Union office.

In the ensuing investigation, the criminal squad agents would collect evidence related to the Weather Underground bombings. The counterintelligence agents would analyze information to determine any connection between the Weather Underground and the foreign intelligence services of Cuba and the Soviet Union. The immediate plan was to follow whoever picked up the money at Western Union.

Agents discreetly observed the entrance to Western Union from their vantage points on the adjacent streets as an old Volvo sedan, with a man and a woman inside, appeared on the scene. While the woman waited in the car, the man went into the Western Union office to pick up the money wired by the National Lawyers Guild.

The unidentified man passed close by one of the surveilling agents, who let others know that the man looked like Jeff Jones (a highly sought

Weather Underground fugitive). Another agent, who got a good look at the female who stayed in the car, told his colleagues she looked a lot like Cathy Wilkerson.

When the man cleared the Western Union office and returned to his car, the duo rapidly sped off into a maze of San Francisco streets and were lost by their hunters. A team of agents stayed behind at Western Union to process the documents the man touched for fingerprints, as others rushed to develop surveillance photographs.

The fingerprints and photographs revealed a shocking reality-the man and woman who picked up the money at the Western Union office were the notorious Weather Underground fugitives Jeff Jones and Cathy Wilkerson.

Later the same evening, agents carpooling home spotted the Volvo sedan parked on Golden Gate Avenue near the Federal Building. For several days the agents followed the car and its driver (not Jones or Wilkerson), until losing the vehicle in the vicinity of Pine and Taylor Streets. Teams knocked on doors throughout the neighborhood, left business cards behind, and did everything possible to get a break in their search.

After several days coming up empty handed, the agents got the break they were looking for. The owner of an apartment building called to report that he hadn't seen the tenants in one of his buildings for some time. Dated newspapers had gathered outside the door. The owner felt the people who had rented his apartment matched the information that had been conveyed to him by a neighbor who had been visited by the FBI.

He unlocked the door and let the agents and members of the San Francisco Police Department bomb squad into the apartment. Inside they found an abandoned bomb factory. Anti-personnel devices, wire, various papers, and a trunk loaded with military C4 explosives filled the floor. Communist literature, mostly in praise of China and Mao, filled the apartment. There was ample propaganda strewn about inside about the revolution, but very little about the Vietnam War.

For the FBI and police, the find was highly important. San Francisco had been the sight of numerous terror attacks in 1970 and 1971. The murder of Officer John Young at Ingleside Station in 1971 had been especially tragic, leaving behind a grieving family and stunned police department.

The San Francisco Police Department never gave up pursuing the identities of those who attacked the Ingleside Station in 1970. Detectives assigned to take another look at the case were closing in on those responsible, as President Bill Clinton was entering his final days of office and preparing to commute the sentences of Susan Rosenburg and Linda Evans. Thanks to the determined efforts of Congressman Nadler.

On January 23, 2007, eight individuals were arrested after being charged with the attack on Ingleside Station in 1971. Seven of the men had been members of the Black Liberation Army. Two men were charged with the actual shooting of Sergeant Young and the others with playing various roles in the assault on the police station. Herman Bell, the alleged shooter, already serving time in prison for the murder of two police officers in New York City, pleaded guilty to killing Young, and was placed on probation inside the prison where he is incarcerated.

During the timeframe between 1967 and the mid-1980's, thirty-five (35) police officers in the United States were killed by Black Panther Party members or the Black Liberation Army. They were casualties in the communist revolution to overthrow the United States government.

Nadler's Relationship with the Democratic Socialists of America (DSA)

As early as 1977, Nadler was identified as a member, or former member of the Democratic Socialists of America:

- 1983- Nadler was identified as a member of Democratic Socialists of America in DSA's *Democratic Left*, January 1983 issue, page 14.

- 1990- As part of the *New Democratic Coalition*, Jerry Nadler endorsed the New York mayoral campaign of DSA member David Dinkins. The *New Democratic Coalition* was a "coalition of progressive Democrats" and included New York Democratic Socialists of America, and known members and supporters of the Communist Party, USA.

- 1996-The Democratic Socialists of America Political Action Committee endorsed Jerrold Nadler

- 1995- Nadler chaired the DSA "People's Hearing on Economic Insecurity" on October 28, 1995. He claimed in the meeting, "many economists show that putting more money in the hands of the poor and middle class is more effective, and that one dollar spent by the government has greater impact on the economy than one dollar spent by the private sector."

- Summer, 2004- The *Democratic Left* had an article on New York City DSA's Socialist Scholars Conference. For May Day, the local DSA held an event in Union Square Park with Congressman Nadler and other speakers about the erosion of the rule of law under the Bush administration.

- 2009-Nadler was on a list of speakers at the 2009 *America's Future Now* conference, which was organized by the Institute for Policy Studies, and Democratic Socialists of America.

- 2010- Jerry Nadler, was listed as serving on the advisory board of the Democratic Socialists of America, *National Jobs for All Coalition*.

- 2/ 20/ 2019-Nadler endorsed the Green New Deal, sponsored by Congresswoman Alexandria Ocasio-Cortez, a known member of the Democratic Socialists of America.

Nadler's Connection with the Communist Party of the United States (CPUSA)

- 10/23/1986-Nadler greeted the Great Peace Marchers, after they hiked 3,500 miles to New York City. The following Friday, the Communist Party USA's *People's Daily World* sponsored a reception for the marchers at Unity Auditorium on West 23rd St.

- 8/6/1993- Nadler was one of the speakers at Hiroshima Day, sponsored by Metro New York Peace Action Council. The group would "urge swift and complete nuclear disarmament," by the United States during the gathering.

- 1997- Nadler was one of 33 people to sponsor a Communist Party backed Jobs Bill, H.R. 950. The leaders of the, *Los Angeles Labor Coalition for Public Works Jobs* and its affiliate, *New York Coalition for Public Works Jobs*, were all known supporters or members of the Communist Party USA.

- 2001-Nadler spoke at the Memorial service of Ernesto Jofre, a New York labor activist and Communist Party USA honoree, who was the business manager and secretary/treasurer of the Amalgamated Clothing and Textile Workers Union Local 169. He said that President Bush was "making war on workers," and told people at the service, "don't mourn. Organize."

- 3/ 3/2013-Nadler was one of 59 House members urging President Obama to support travel to Cuba by granting general licenses for all current categories of travel. The purpose of the request-"eliminating the laborious license application process, especially for people-to-people groups, managed by the Office of Foreign Assets Control (OFAC), the majority of the bureaucratic red tape that holds up licensable travel to Cuba would disappear and actually facilitate what the President wanted to see in 2011, liberalized travel regulations."

- 2014- Elizabeth Gurley of the New York chapter of the Communist Party USA Flynn Club wrote, "sometimes, we must be free to disagree with Democrats on selected issues even those whom we have supported, such as Obama on a national level, Jerrold Nadler, a progressive Congressman from Manhattan, and Bill DeBlasio, who is New York City's new progressive mayor."

Nadler, the Congressional Progressive Caucus, and the CPUSA

Congressman Nadler has been a longstanding member of the Congressional Progressive Caucus. In 1999, 2000, and 2003 he was a speaker for the Progressive State of the Union address.

In September 2009, following the lead of Senate colleagues, the House of Representatives voted overwhelmingly to cut off funds to the group, ACORN. The vote was 345-75. The seventy-five votes to continue Federal funding for ACORN were all cast by Democratic progressives, including Congressman Nadler. During a floor speech, Nadler aggressively fought Congressional efforts to cut off funds to ACORN:

"A little while ago, the House passed an amendment to the bill that we were considering that says no contract or federal funds may ever go to ACORN, a named organization, or to any individual or organization affiliated with ACORN. Unfortunately, this was done in the spirit of the moment and nobody had the opportunity to point out that this is a flat violation of the Constitution, constituting a Bill of Attainder. The Constitution says that Congress shall never pass a Bill of Attainder. Bills of Attainder, no matter what their form, apply either to a named individual or to easily ascertainable members of a group, to inflict punishment. That's exactly what this amendment does. It may be that ACORN is guilty of various infractions, and, if so, it ought to be vetted, or maybe sanctioned, by the appropriate administrative agency or by the judiciary. Congress must not be in the business of punishing individual organizations or people without trial."[262]

A report highlighting the CPUSA's connection to the Congressional Progressive Caucus was delivered at the 14th International Meeting of Communist and Workers' Parties, held in Beirut, Lebanon, from Nov. 22 to 25, 2012:

"'The Communist Party USA not only welcomes the reelection of President Barack Obama, but actively engaged in the electoral campaign for his reelection and for the election of many Democratic Party congressional candidates. ... 'In our electoral policy, we seek to cooperate and strengthen our relationship with the more progressive elements in Democratic Party, such as the Progressive Caucus in the U.S. Congress, a group of 76 members of the Congress co-chaired by Raul Grijalva, a Latino from Arizona, and Keith Ellison, an African American Muslim from Minnesota. ... 'In its domestic policy, for example, the Progressive Caucus has put forth a program for using the public sector to deal with unemployment. It has opposed the use of the so called 'war on terror' to incarcerate U.S. citizens indefinitely without criminal charges. In its foreign policy, the Progressive Caucus and the Black Caucus are outspoken in their opposition to U.S. imperialist policies abroad. The Progressive Caucus, now that Obama has been reelected, will be playing an important role in contributing to the mobilization of mass activity on critical issues to bring pressure on the Congress and administration to act on them.'" [263]

Congressman Jerry Nadler likes to remind Americans that he has fought on behalf of the rule of law and civil liberties his entire career. He was one of the most passionate defenders of President Bill Clinton

---

[262] "Nadler: Republican ACORN Amendment is Flatly Unconstitutional and Threatens any Organization Disliked by Congress," Press Release, https://nadler.house.gov/news/documentsingle.aspx?DocumentID=392322, 9/16/2009

[263] Congressional Progressive Caucus Has Extensive Ties to Marxist Organizations, Association of Mature American Citizens, 11/27/2018

during the latter's impeachment process.

Despite Nadler's assertions, he has consistently fought for progressive causes, on behalf of positions supported by America's enemies (i.e.: ending the U.S. ban on travel to and trade with Cuba), and securing the release of imprisoned terrorists.

Congressman Jerry Nadler sits today as the Chairman of the immensely powerful Judiciary Committee, with control over, and power to influence, the FBI and the Department of Justice. He has consumed himself with efforts to impeach President Donald Trump.

Following the tragic mass shootings in El Paso, Texas, where a gunman killed 33 people, Jerry Nadler had this to say about President Trump trying to link immigration reform to gun legislation:

"…These shootings were clearly, in part, a result of his racist rhetoric. That's clear. His divisive and racist rhetoric. People have warned they would lead to violence and now they have…

"And then to come out and say he could go for background checks for gun owners, but only if there's immigration reform? What's the connection between background checks and immigration reform? That we have to keep guns out of the hands of the invading hordes of less-than-human people coming across our borders?...

"That's the implication. That's disgusting. ... It reminds me of the 1930s in Germany."[264]

Pursuing "social justice" and "oppression," House Judiciary Chairman Jerry Nadler did everything he could to see that Susan Rosenburg, Linda Evans and Judith Clark were released from prison for the roles they played in crimes that furthered the communist supported revolution and murder of police officers. He fought aggressively to defend President Bill Clinton's pardon of a dozen FALN terrorists, knowing that the FALN was a Marxist/Leninist group trying to foster a communist revolution in Puerto Rico.

---

[264] "House Judiciary chairman says Trump's call for immigration reform after shootings 'reminds me of the 1930s in Germany'" by Tucker Higgins, cnbc.com 8/5/2019

Yet now he sits as the chairman of a powerful House Committee, sounding the words of the same revolution. In Nadler's words, this is what Americans should find "disgusting."

CHAPTER TEN

"To me, capitalism is irredeemable…"
Alexandria Ocasio-Cortez

In 2018, voters in New York's 14th Congressional District elected Alexandria Ocasio-Cortez to the United States Congress. Despite her status as one of the newest members of Congress, Ocasio-Cortez has captured the attention of voters nationwide and members of her own party, pushing an aggressive agenda of the Green New Deal, and engaging in frequent Twitter battles with President Donald Trump.

She was an early supporter of 2016 Democratic Party presidential candidate Bernie Sanders. She is an ardent advocate of democratic socialism for the United States.

Alexandria Ocasio-Cortez- the Poster Politician for Democratic Socialism and the Green New Deal

Ocasio-Cortez is not shy about telling Americans she is a member of the Democratic Socialists of America. The Democratic Party, regardless of what Speaker Nancy Pelosi has said, seems to have conceded the socialist ground to Ocasio-Cortez and the so-called *"squad"*-Ilhan Omar of Minnesota, Ayanna Pressley from Massachusetts, and Rashida Tlaib of Michigan.

As Ocasio-Cortez sees it, "'when millennials talk about concepts like democratic socialism, we're not talking about these kinds of Red Scare boogeyman…We're talking about countries and systems that already exist that have already been proven to be successful in the modern world… "We're talking about single-payer health care that has already been successful in many different models, from Finland to Canada to the UK." [265]

During an interview at a South by Southwest conference in Texas, Ocasio-Cortez defined "Capitalism… an ideology of capital — the most important thing is the concentration of capital and to seek and maximize profit."[266]

She went on to say, "to me, capitalism is irredeemable…it's just as much a transformation about bringing democracy to the workplace so that we have a say and that we don't check all of our rights at the door every time we cross the threshold into our workplace…Because at the end of the day, as workers and as people in society, we're the ones creating wealth."[267]

Like the majority of socialist elites, Ocasio-Cortez provided a glimpse of her ego and narcissism during an interview with the *New Yorker:*

"…I'm a Democrat. I'm a woman. I'm a young woman. A Latina. And I'm a liberal, a D.S.A. member… I believe health care is a right and people should be paid enough to live. Those are offensive values to them. But this ravenous hysteria—it's really getting to a level that is kind of out of control. It's dangerous and even scary. I have days when it seems some people want to stoke just enough of it to have just enough

---

[265] "Red Tide: Number of Americans Who Embrace Socialism Skyrockets," by Jack Davis, *The Western Journal,* 5/21/2019.

[266] "Ocasio-Cortez: Capitalism is Irredeemable," by Michael Burke, *The Hill,* 3/10/2019.

[267] Ibid. *The Hill.*

plausible deniability if something happens to me."[268]

When Senator Lindsey Graham and Ocasio-Cortez engaged in a Twitter battle, she said,

"According to Lindsey Graham, the President failing to condemn neo-Nazis, forcing thousands of federal workers to go to food pantries, & risking all their credit scores is whatever, but not letting the President march down the House Floor until we pay people first is 'a new low.'"[269]

Graham answered her, "even worse news, AOC... and her new socialist colleagues seem hell-bent on making sure that our last 12 years will be spent as Venezuelan socialists, not Americans."[270]

The Democratic Socialists of America

The Democratic Socialists of America is described on its website as follows:

"The Democratic Socialists of America (DSA) is the largest socialist organization in the United States. DSA's members are building progressive movements for social change while establishing an openly democratic socialist presence in American communities and politics...

"At the root of our socialism is a profound commitment to democracy, as means and end. As we are unlikely to see an immediate end to capitalism tomorrow, DSA fights for reforms today that will weaken the power of corporations and increase the power of working people. For example, we support reforms that...

"-decrease the influence of money in politics...

"-empower ordinary people in workplaces and the economy...

"-restructure gender and cultural relationships to be more equitable...

---

[268] "Ocasio-Cortez: Our Society Can't Stand the Idea of Me Being As 'Powerful as a Man,'" by Julio Rosas, *Media ite* 3/5/2019.

[269] Lindsey Graham: Alexandria-Ocasio Cortez is 'Hell Bent' on Americans Becoming 'Venezuelan Socialists," by Jessica Kwong, *Newsweek*, 1/24/2019.

[270] Ibid. *Newsweek*.

"We are activists committed to democracy as not simply one of our political values but our means of restructuring society. Our vision is of a society in which people have a real voice in the choices and relationships that affect the entirety of our lives. We call this vision democratic socialism-a vision of a more free, democratic and humane society...

"We are socialists because we reject an international economic order sustained by private profit, alienated labor, race and gender discrimination, environmental destruction, and brutality and violence in defense of the status quo...

"We are socialists because we share a vision of a humane international social order based both on democratic planning and market mechanisms to achieve equitable distribution of resources, meaningful work, a healthy environment, sustainable growth, gender and racial equality, and non-oppressive relationships."[271]

Although she identifies with the goals and direction of DSA, pledging support to "decrease the influence of money in politics..." Ocasio-Cortez' own Chief of Staff, Saikat Chakrabarti, was forced into resignation in August 2019 after it was disclosed that he is the target of a federal investigation into allegations that he diverted one million dollars from two Political Action Committees, Brand New Congress and Justice Democrats into two private companies that he controlled and incorporated. The names of those companies were Brand New Congress, LLC and Brand New Campaign, LLC.

When the allegations first surfaced, Chakrabarti and Ocasio-Cortez denied any wrongdoing, but Chakrabarti was so instrumental in pushing the Congresswoman's positions on campaign contributions and how the capitalist system takes advantage of the "workers," that his departure from her staff was inevitable.

The goals of one of the Political Action Committees getting Chakrabarti's attention, Justice Democrats, sound a lot like all the other manifestos, policy statements and platforms now integrated into the Democratic Party' agenda for America-an agenda with a history of con-

---

nection to those who once desired to overthrow the government of the United States by violence, but whose ideology has been modified to expand their strategy-allowing for a political revolution from the inside.

During the 2018 election process, the Justice Democrats supported 79 candidates for national elections. Twenty-six of their candidates won respective primaries and seven won their elections-Raul Grijalva, Ro Khanna, Ayanna Pressley, Rashida Tlaib, Ilhan Omar, Ocasio-Cortez, and Pramila Jayapal. Here's the list of objectives the Justice Democrats envision for America:

> Creating a new infrastructure program called the Green New Deal.
> Ending arms sales to countries that violate human rights such as Saudi Arabia and Egypt.
> Enacting a federal jobs guarantee, which would promise all Americans $15 per hour plus benefits.
> Ending the death penalty.
> Ending the practice of unilaterally waging war, except as a last resort to defend U.S. territory.
> Ending the War on Drugs in favor of legalization, regulation, taxation, and pardoning and treating addicts.
> Ensuring free speech on college campuses and supporting net neutrality.
> Ensuring universal education as a right, including free four-year public college and university education.
> Ensuring universal healthcare as a right.
> Establishing paid maternity leave, paid vacation leave, and free childcare.
> Expanding anti-discrimination laws to apply to LGBT people - see Equality Act.
> Expanding background checks on firearms and banning high capacity magazines and assault weapons.
> Funding Planned Parenthood, other contraceptive and abortion services, recognizing reproductive rights.

Implementing electoral reform and publicly financed campaigns.

Implementing instant run-off nationwide to make third-party and independent candidates more viable.

Implementing the Buffet Rule, ending offshore financing center, changing the capital gains and income taxes, and increasing the estate tax.

Making the minimum wage a living wage and tying it to inflation.

Pardoning Edward Snowden prosecuting CIA torturers and DOD war criminals, shutting down the Guantanamo Bay detention centers and all other extrajudicial prisons, and ending warrantless spying and bulk data collection by the National Security Agency.

Passing the Paycheck Fairness Act.

Abolishing the U.S. Immigration and Customs Enforcement agency (ICE).

Reforming police by mandating body cameras, establishing community oversight boards, eliminating broken window, ending stop and frisk, and appointing special prosecutors to hold police accountable in courts.

Renegotiating other free trade deals CAFTA-DR and NAFTA and opposing the Permanent Normal Trade Relations with China and the World Trade Organization.

Stopping any reductions to Social Security, Medicare, and Medicaid and establishing single-payer universal health care.

Stopping anthropogenic climate change through an ecological revolution and upholding the United States' participation in the Paris Climate Agreement.

Uncompromisingly rejecting President Trump's immigration proposals and policies, particularly Executive Order 13769 and deportation of illegal immigrants, and implementing comprehensive immigration reform which will include giving non-criminal illegal immigrants a path to citizenship.

DSA has a youth section, Young Democratic Socialists of America (YDSA). Made up of students from colleges and high schools, the YDSA works on economic justice, social justice in democracy and prison justice projects. It is a member of the International Union of Socialist Youth, an affiliate of the Socialist International. YDSA meets several times during the year.

John Bachtell, the head of the Communist Party of the United States, considers the Democratic Socialists of America to be an ally in the "struggle" to bring communism to America. In 2018 Bachtell coordinated a webinar involving the Democratic Socialists of America, Freedom Road, and several other socialist organizations. The purpose was to build solidarity in the fight for democratic socialism.

Today, the Democratic Socialists of America more than rival the Communist Party of the United States in the ongoing quest to scrap the United States Constitution and our constitutional Republic. They favor a socialist government based on equality, government control of production and government oversight of police, health care, education, and housing.

The Communist Party USA grew to become the domestic political arm of the international Marxist revolution operating inside America. The Democratic Socialists of America has become the political arm of the ideology of communism envisioned by the Weather Underground as it attempted to overthrow the U. S. Government by force during the late 1960's and early 1970's.

In their 1974 *Prairie Fire* Communist manifesto, the Weather Underground stated, "revolutionary war will be complicated and protracted. It includes mass struggle and clandestine struggle, peaceful and violent, political and economic, cultural and military, where all forms are developed in harmony with the armed struggle…without mass struggle there can be no revolution…without armed struggle there can be no victory…"[272]

In a June 2016 article appearing on the Democratic Socialists of

---

[272] Ibid. *Prairie Fire.*

America website, the title leaves little to the imagination, connecting the era of the first revolutionary attempts to overthrow the United States government to the present day- "Resistance Rising: Socialist Strategy in the Age of Political Revolution…"[273]

The Weather Underground was composed of violent revolutionaries who broke from the SDS in the late 1960's. The Weather Underground "communist minded men and women" wanted a bloody revolution, while the SDS leadership was in favor of a political overthrow of the U.S. government.

The Democratic Socialists of America has replaced the Students for a Democratic Society in today's America. Their goal, however, is the same. Using the cover of socialist democracy, equality, and corporate greed, they're actually selling the end of capitalism to usher in the beginning of communism.

The ties that bind the current Democratic Socialists of America with the Weather Underground and its forerunner, the Students for a Democratic Society don't stop there.

The predecessor of the SDS was called the Student League for Industrial Democracy (SLID), a youth organization for the League of Industrial Democracy, founded by a socialist college professor named Michael Harrington. The SDS was actually a name change to replace SLID, intended to attract a broader band of the "masses" to the cause of socialism. However, after conflict among its leaders as to the direction the new SDS should take, Harrington left his involvement with SLID and SDS behind. He subsequently founded the Democratic Socialists of America.

Today, the Communist Party of the United States, the Democratic Socialists of America, and the 2016 Democratic Party platform express the same goals and objectives. They are not any different than the goals and objectives represented in the Weather Underground *Prairie Fire* manifesto or the Black Panther Party *Ten Point Program*. They are not any different than the policies being introduced by mainstream Demo-

---

[273]   Ibid. DSA.

cratic Party politicians and presidential candidates.

All share the same strategy-domestic and international resistance to President Trump. All share the same aggressive and offensive messaging-America is a country characterized by institutional racism, white supremacy, and inequality. The only means to end the systemic racism and inequality they allege exists, is bigger and more controlling government in the form of democratic socialism.

The Communist Party of the USA (CPUSA), Democratic Socialists of America (DSA), Weather Underground (WU), Black Panther Party (BPP), 2016 Democratic Party platform, and Congresswoman Ocasio-Cortez are linked by the ideology of communism. Their common goal is the installation of socialism in the United States, as a major step in their strategy of incremental communism.

Comparing- CPUSA, DSA, WU, BPP, 2016 Democratic Party Platform, and Ocasio-Cortez

The Goals of the CPUSA

From the "Socialist Bill of Rights," posted on the website of the CPUSA:

"...In a socialist economy, things get turned right side up. The ownership and control of the means of production would be in the hands of those who do the work...We could fully fund public education and health care for all. We could have mass transit, Social Security, free college tuition and childcare...War, racism, sexism, and homophobia would lose their corporate sponsors...

"...Socialism in the United States would be built on the strong foundation of our Constitution's Bill of Rights. This includes making the promises of freedom of speech, freedom of religion, and equality for all real. The rights to a job, to health care, and education must also be guaranteed by the Constitution. The criminal justice, police and prison systems must be overhauled from top to bottom to get rid of racial disparity...

"...A fairer political system goes hand-in-hand with a socialist economy...Ten million undocumented workers are a part of our country's working class. They must be welcomed to participate as citizens in a socialist democracy. By the same token, the voting rights of millions of incarcerated Americans – mostly African Americans and Latinos – must be restored. In place of voter suppression laws, fair election processes are needed. Universal voter participation is the basis of democracy...racial inequality and sexism are built into the structure of our nation's capitalist economy and society...The unity of America's working people – African American and white, Latino, Asian, Indian and Middle Eastern – is critical to our progress. Men and women, LGBTQ and straight, young and old must stand together for each other..."[274]

From the DSA

From "Resistance Rising: Socialist Strategy in the Age of Political Revolution," June 25, 2016, on the website of the Democratic Socialists of America:

"...Our vision entails nothing less than the radical democratization of all areas of life, not least of which is the economy...economic democracy. This simply means that democracy would be expanded beyond the election of political officials to include the democratic management of all businesses by the workers who comprise them and by the communities in which they operate. Very large, strategically important sectors of the economy — such as housing, utilities and heavy industry — would be subject to democratic planning outside the market, while a market sector consisting of worker-owned and -operated firms would be developed for the production and distribution of many consumer goods...investments in renewable energy and efficient technologies would be prioritized to guarantee ecological sustainability and the fu-

---

[274]   https://www.cpusa.org/party_info/socialism-in-the-usa/ "Socialist Bill of Rights, CPUSA

ture existence of life on Earth....

"A democratic socialist society would also guarantee a wide range of social rights in order to ensure equality of citizenship for all. Vital services such as health care, childcare, education (from pre-K through higher education), shelter and transportation would be publicly provided to everyone on demand, free of charge. Further, in order to ensure that the enjoyment of full citizenship was not tied to ups and downs in the labor market, everyone would also receive a universal basic income...

"Our strategy... consists of fighting on a number of interconnected fronts in the short-term, leveraging gains made in these struggles into more structural, offensively oriented changes in the medium-term and ultimately employing the strength of a mass socialist party or coalition of leftist and progressive parties to win political power and begin the process of socialist transformation...the only democratic socialist strategy capable of effective resistance to capitalism is one that links together antiracist, feminist, LGBTQ, labor, anti-ableist... (as well as other) movements by "connecting the dots" between them...

"...It is difficult to imagine how we could achieve any of our objectives in the United States without taking part in the electoral process...The nature of our electoral activism will vary based on local political conditions. But it will include supporting progressive and socialist candidates running for office, usually in Democratic primaries or as Democrats in general elections but also in support of independent socialist and other third-party campaigns outside the Democratic Party..."[275]

From the Weather Underground's *Prairie Fire*

"...Revolution is a fight by the people for power. It is a changing of power in which existing social and economic relations are turned

---

[275] "Resistance Rising: Socialist Strategy in the Age of Political Revolution," June 25, 2016, website of the Democratic Socialists of America

upside down. It is a fight for who run things, in particular, for control by the people of what we communists call the means of production -the means by which people eat, work, protect themselves from the cold and the rain, get around, raise children and build...

"...A system which includes unprecedented slaughter...continuous wars, genocide, the violent suppression of Black, Puerto Chicano, and Indian people, the subjugation of women...

"We live inside the oppressor nation, particularly suited to urban guerrilla warfare...

"We are strategically situated in the nerve centers of the international empire, where the institutions and symbols of imperial power are concentrated. The cities will be a major battleground, for the overwhelming majority of people live in the cities; the cities are our terrain...

"It is the responsibility of mass leaders and organizations to encourage and support revolutionary armed struggle, in open as well as quiet ways. Actions are more powerful when they are explained and defended. The political thrust of each armed intervention can be publicly championed and built on. Parallel mass support will further both the mass and military struggle...."

"...The spirit of resistance inside the US was rekindled by Black people. The power and strategy of the civil rights movement, SNCC, Malcolm X, and the Black Panther Party affected all other rebellion. They created a form of struggle "called direct action; awoke a common identity, history and dignity for Black people as a colonized and oppressed people within the US; drew out and revealed the enemy through a series of just and undeniable demands such as the vote, equal education, the right to self-defense, and an end to Jim Crow. The police, the troops, the sheriffs, the mass arrests and assassinations were the official response. The Black movement was pushed forward into a revolutionary movement for political power, open rebellion and confrontation with the racism of white people and the racism of institutions...

"...Anti-crime legislation mobilizes racist fears in the white population. It has been successful enough to undo many gains of the previous two decades: to initiate preventive detention, undermine the jury system and put into effect new mandatory death penalties...If we do not create an anti-racist left, the masses of white people being bombarded with these measures have little alternative but to resolve these fears and these conflicts the traditional way —in complicity with racism..."

"...Our final goal is the destruction of imperialism, the seizure of power, and the creation of socialism...the total opposite of capitalism/imperialism. It is the rejection of empire and white supremacy. Socialism is the violent overthrow of the bourgeoisie, the establishment of the dictatorship of the proletariat, and the eradication of the social system based on profit. Socialism means control of the productive forces for the good of the whole community... Socialism means priorities based on human need instead of corporate greed. Socialism creates the conditions for a decent and creative quality of life for all. After a long struggle, power will be in the hands of the people... [276]

From the Black Panther Party *Ten Point Program*, 1967

"...We believe that Black people will not be free until we are able to determine our destiny...We believe that the federal government is responsible and obligated to give every man employment or a guaranteed income. We believe that if the White American businessmen will not give full employment, then the means of production should be taken from the businessmen and placed in the community...

"...We believe that this racist government has robbed us, and now we are demanding the overdue debt of forty acres and two mules... promised 100 years ago as restitution for slave labor and mass murder of Black people....

"...We believe that if the White Landlords will not give decent housing to our Black community, then the housing and the land should be made into cooperatives so that our community, with government aid...

---

[276]   Ibid. *Prairie Fire*

"...We believe we can end police brutality in our Black community by organizing Black self-defense groups that are dedicated to defending our Black community from racist police oppression and brutality...

"...We believe that all Black people should be released from the many jails and prisons because they have not received a fair and impartial trial..."

"...whenever any form of government becomes destructive of these ends, it is the right of the people to alter or abolish it, and to institute a new government...and to provide new guards for their future security."[277]

From the Democratic Party Platform, 2016:

"...Every four years, the Democratic Party puts together our party platform, the ideas and beliefs that govern our party as a whole...What follows is our 2016 platform—our most progressive platform in our party's history and a declaration of how we plan to move America forward...

"...Democrats believe that today's extreme level of income and wealth inequality—where the majority of the economic gains go to the top one percent and the richest 20 people in our country own more wealth than the bottom 150 million—makes our economy weaker, our communities poorer...We firmly believe that the greed, recklessness, and illegal behavior on Wall Street must be brought to an end...We believe that Americans should earn at least $15 an hour and have the right to form or join a union and will work in every way we can—in Congress and the federal government, in states and with the private sector—to reach this goal...

"...Corporate profits are at near-record highs, but workers have not shared through rising wages...

"...Democrats will fight to end institutional and systemic racism in our society. We will challenge and dismantle the structures that define

---

[277]   Black Panther Party *Ten Point Program*, 1967.

lasting racial, economic, political, and social inequity. Democrats will promote racial justice through fair, just, and equitable governing of all public-serving institutions and in the formation of public policy...We will push for a societal transformation to make it clear that black lives matter and that there is no place for racism in our country....

"...America's economic inequality problem is even more pronounced when it comes to racial and ethnic disparities in wealth and income...Democrats believe it is long past time to close this racial wealth gap...

"...Democrats are committed to reforming our criminal justice system and ending mass incarceration...We will rebuild the bonds of trust between law enforcement and the communities they serve...We will work with police chiefs to invest in training for officers on issues such as de-escalation and the creation of national guidelines for the appropriate use of force. We will encourage better police community relations, require the use of body cameras, and stop the use of weapons of war that have no place in our communities. We will end racial profiling that targets individuals solely on the basis of race, religion, ethnicity, or national origin, which is un-American and counterproductive. We should report national data on policing strategies and provide greater transparency and accountability. We will require the Department of Justice to investigate all questionable or suspicious police-involved shootings, and we will support states and localities who help make those investigations and prosecutions more transparent, including through reforming the grand jury process...

"...Democrats believe we need to urgently fix our broken immigration system—which tears families apart and keeps workers in the shadows—and create a path to citizenship for law-abiding families who are here, making a better life for their families and contributing to their communities and our country...

"...We will appoint judges who defend the constitutional principles of liberty and equality for all, and will protect a woman's right to safe and legal abortion...low income communities and communities of color are disproportionately home to environmental justice 'hot spots...'

this is environmental racism...Democrats also respectfully request the Department of Justice to investigate allegations of corporate fraud on the part of fossil fuel companies accused of misleading shareholders and the public on the scientific reality of climate change...

"...Democrats are unified in their strong belief that every student should be able to go to college debt-free, and working families should not have to pay any tuition to go to public colleges and universities...

"...Democrats believe that health care is a right, not a privilege, and our health care system should put people before profits...Democrats believe that all health care services should be culturally and linguistically appropriate, and that neither fear nor immigration status should be barriers that impede health care access..."[278]

From Congresswoman Ocasio-Cortez' Website

"...Representative Ocasio-Cortez believes that in a modern, moral, and wealthy society, no one should be too poor to live. For this reason, she is fighting every day to level the playing field... strongly supports a wealth tax, union rights, and pay equity...seeks to usher in a new era of shared prosperity and lift millions out of poverty...would forgive outstanding federal and private student loans of all previous and current students in our education system...would amend the Higher Education Act of 1965 to ensure college for all...is an unapologetic advocate of Medicare for All, which would create a universal, single payer healthcare system... announced the Climate Equity Act... ensuring that frontline communities are at the center of environmental and climate-related policies, rules, regulations, and investments...

"...Supports the federal legalization of marijuana, ending for-profit prisons, the release of individuals incarcerated for non-violent drug offenses, the end of cash bail, and independent investigations for any and every time an individual is killed by law enforcement...would prohibit Federal agencies and Federal contractors from requesting that an

---

[278]   Democratic Party Platform, 2016.

applicant… disclose criminal history record information before they have received a conditional offer…consistently called for a federal ban on assault weapons, high capacity magazines, and bump stocks… would establish new background check requirements for firearm transfers between private parties…

"…committed to transformative, empathetic, and just immigration reform…would provide a pathway to citizenship to undocumented immigrants who were brought to the U.S. as children (known as Dreamers) and many immigrants with temporary humanitarian protections… would lift the Hyde Amendment and make reproductive health accessible and affordable to all women, despite their income…believes that the people of Puerto Rico have the right to self-determination. For too long, Puerto Rico has suffered the political, social, and economic consequences of disenfranchisement…advocates for the cancellation of all of Puerto Rico's debt…

"…Committed to preventing the discrimination against any individual on any basis, including sexual orientation or gender-identity… dedicated to ensuring equal rights and protections for the LGBTQIA+ community across the nation…"[279]

Today's Democratic Party harbors revolutionaries linked by their shared desire to install a socialist government in the United States. They want a transformation of America into a communist utopia. The 2016 Democratic Party platform was heavily influenced by the ideology of communism, adopted from pages of writings of the CPUSA, DSA, WU, and BPP.

There are a large number of current and former Democratic Party elected officials who are true believers. For now, Alexandria Ocasio-Cortez, as a vocal, self-avowed member of the Democratic Socialists of America, has become the national spokesperson for them all.

---

[279] "Alexandria Ocasio-Cortez," website, https://ocasio-cortez.house.gov

CHAPTER ELEVEN

---

*"There is no country that poses a more severe
counterintelligence threat to this country right
now than China..."*
FBI Director Christopher Wray

M ost Americans are unaware of the range and scope of Chinese
intelligence collection efforts inside the United States. Arguably,
America's intelligence agencies are badly outnumbered and engaged in
overdrive to counter the scope and dimensions of the Chinese threat
here at home.

Bill Priestap, the FBI's head of counterintelligence in 2018 told the
Judiciary Committee of the U.S. Senate, "make no mistake... the Chinese government is proposing itself as an alternative model for the
world, one without a democratic system of government, and it is seeking to undermine the free and open rules-based order we helped establish following world war two." [280]

Senator Diane Feinstein, who sat on the Judiciary Committee

---

[280]　"China's Non-Traditional Espionage Against the United States: The
Threat and Potential Policy Responses," Bill Priestap Assistant Director,
Counterintelligence Division Federal Bureau of Investigation Statement Be-
fore the Senate Judiciary Committee Washington, D.C. December 12, 2018.

during the hearing with Priestap, along with officials from the Department of Justice and Homeland Security, reflected on her own past decisions.

Senator Diane Feinstein's Sister City Relationship with China-a Tsunami of Intellectual Property Theft

When she was mayor of San Francisco in 1979, Feinstein traveled to Shanghai, China to establish a sister city relationship, saying she had been, "very proud of China's economic and technological development." She has since understood the damage that China has been doing, with cyberattacks on American computer networks and aggressive intelligence operations targeting United States citizens, companies and technologies. [281]

Feinstein acknowledged these operations are causing "enormous damage between a relationship that I had hoped way back in the 1970's was really going to change that big Pacific Ocean into a small river of friendship, goods, services and interchanges."[282].

Fifty years of watching the Chinese evolve in their sophistication at stealing America's intellectual property, has transformed Senator Feinstein's naivete of the 1970's. Instead of her "big Pacific Ocean" turning into a "small river of friendship," it has become a tsunami of intellectual property theft. Feinstein herself described the dimensions:

"The Communist Party of China's use of illegal tools like cyber theft to acquire American intellectual property is now well documented...the Chinese government's cyber theft activities cost the United States annually $300 billion in intellectual property, $100 billion in lost sales, and 2. 1 million lost jobs...other more non-traditional forms of

---

[281]   Statement of Senator Diane Feinstein, China Non-Traditional Espionage Hearing, Senate Judiciary Committee, Washington, D.C., 12/12/2018.

[282]   Ibid

espionage...are equally troubling in the context of china's overall economic and military objectives. "[283]

In July 2019 FBI Director Christopher Wray testified that, "There is no country that poses a more severe counterintelligence threat to this country right now than China... It is a threat that's deep and diverse and wide and vexing...It affects basically every industry in this country." [284]

China uses its intelligence services to:

- Identify, target and recruit agents of influence inside the American Government.

- Identify, target and recruit individuals who have access to classified military information.

- Identify employees inside businesses with access to proprietary business information

- Target and recruit Chinese emigres with relatives still living in China.

One indicator of the threat posed by Chinese intelligence services inside the United States is the FBI's arrest of nineteen individuals as a result of their involvement in Chinese espionage during the 33 years between 1985 and 2017. Fifteen individuals have been arrested for espionage and theft of trade secrets in connection with Chinese spying during just the past two years (2017-2019) alone. These figures reflect a steep rise in Chinese intelligence operations directed at America. [285]

The numbers fail to reflect how successful the Chinese intelligence services have become at penetrating U.S. government agencies respon-

---

[283]   Ibid.

[284]   "FBI Chief Says China is Trying to Steal Their Way to Dominance," by Steven T. Dennis, 7/23/2019, *Bloomberg*.

[285]   "List of Chinese Spy Cases in the United States," *Wikipedia*.

sible for defending America against hostile intelligence threats.

In 2017, Kun Shan Chun was sentenced in a New York courtroom following his conviction for acting as an agent of the Chinese government. Chun was a native Chinese and naturalized United States citizen. Chun possessed a Top- Secret clearance, having worked for the FBI as a technician since 1997.

In April 2019 Candace Claiborne pleaded guilty to lying to FBI agents. She concealed numerous contacts with Chinese intelligence agents. She received gifts from Chinese intelligence in exchange for documents she accessed due to her employment with the U.S. State Department.

Kevin Mallory, a graduate of Brigham Young University, was convicted in June 2018 and sentenced in May 2019, for providing Top- Secret documents to Chinese intelligence officers. Mallory had served in the U.S. Army and had worked for the CIA, State Department Diplomatic Security Service, Defense Intelligence Agency and American Institute in Taiwan. Mallory's Chinese handlers provided him with communications technology in furtherance of his espionage efforts on their behalf. Mallory's Chinese contacts had posed as members of the Shanghai Academy of Social Sciences.

Between 2010 and 2013, close to 20 Chinese informants providing information on China to the CIA were murdered. An FBI investigation identified a former CIA officer, Jerry Chun Lee, who had worked for the Agency between 1994 and 2007. Lee had a Top -Secret security clearance. He gave his Chinese contacts the identities of human sources working for the CIA. Lee received hundreds of thousands of dollars from China in return. Lee's relationship with Chinese intelligence began after he met two Chinese officers from China's Ministry of State Security in Shenzhen province in 2010.

John Rockwell Hansen was sentenced in September 2019 on espionage charges resulting from charges of spying on behalf of China. Hansen was a former officer in the U.S. Army and was working with the Defense Intelligence Agency when he was arrested by the FBI. At the time of his arrest, Hansen was in route to the Seattle Tacoma airport to board a connecting flight to China. He was in possession of national security defense information.

Despite China's growing economic power, advancing technology, and expanding military, the Chinese intelligence services consider its own citizens as the number one weapon of choice to target America and Americans. Constantly on the prowl to penetrate our military, government, academic, and scientific institutions, the Chinese government engages in thousands of cultural and business exchanges every year.

From banking to agriculture, health care to entertainment, the Chinese government is investing hundreds of billions of dollars to sell Americans on China's peaceful intentions in the world. It relies on its intelligence services to make sure its money is well spent. And it relies on ethnic Chinese citizens, regardless of where they live, to secure its interests.

The FBI arrested Edward Peng in the San Francisco Bay area in September 2019 for delivering classified national security information to the Chinese and for working as a foreign agent. Peng operated tours for Chinese students and visitors. Peng is alleged to have worked on behalf of the Chinese Ministry of State Security.

He became a naturalized citizen in the United States in 2012, having come to the country on a temporary business visitor visa years earlier. Peng served as a conduit between double agents and his Chinese handlers, paying cash for services and then carrying the classified information back to China. He used secure hotel rooms to make the exchanges of cash and information with the double agents. They never saw him or were in the room with him at the same time.

The Chinese intelligence services have a huge appetite for theft. Over the decades, they have saved the Chinese government many billions of dollars in research and development by simply stealing America's technological secrets. Then, they create their own manufacturing base in a specific product, mass produce it for much less than the United States and sell it on the open market, effectively competing with America on the world stage.

"Yi-Chi Shih, an electrical engineer and a University of California,

Los Angeles professor, was found guilty in June 2019 by a Los Angeles jury on 18 counts related to smuggling computer chips containing military secrets to China." [286]

In another investigation, a Chinese citizen, Yanjun Xu, working for China's Ministry of State Security, was arrested in Belgium in 2018. A criminal complaint had been filed in Cincinnati charging him with theft of trade secrets and economic espionage. Xu had multiple targets of interest, including aerospace companies and GE Aviation. Xu had important contacts at Nanjing University of Aeronautics and Astronautics.

The Chinese make extensive use of human intelligence, cyber targeting, cyber penetration, intelligence collection, military and economic information.

Retired FBI Special Agent Al Heiman worked the Chinese target during his career in the FBI. He spent another twenty years keeping Lawrence Livermore National Lab safe from hostile intelligence recruitment of America's premier nuclear scientists. Heiman said the Chinese are increasingly turning to the use of computers in their operations.

"China and its intelligence services have lots of resources they can throw at people these days. There's pretty clear evidence they have access to information with the identities of government employees who have security clearances. There've been many instances of successful hacking and penetration operations where Chinese intelligence has stolen that kind of information from U.S. government computers...

"Chinese agents used to do everything face to face in the old days. Now they have just about completely transitioned to computers. They can reach out to people from the safety of the Chinese mainland. They don't even have to leave their office to target Americans. Security and comfort are multiplied when the talking is done machine to machine. It's more amorphous. They put things out on Linked in. They throw out the possibility of a job and then offer a position that is way too good to

---

[286] Chinese American Engineer Guilty of Exporting Military-Grade Semiconductors," *South China Morning Post*. July 3, 2019.

be true. But people bite-and then they're stuck. All of these things are taking place in the changing nature of Chinese intelligence work these days." [287]

The types of attacks Heiman described are not new. In 2007 the Chinese directed cyberattacks against the computer networks of several U.S. Government agencies, including the nation's leading national weapons laboratories. The FBI opened an investigation code-named, *Titan Rain*, subsequently connecting massive penetration efforts attributed to the intelligence services of the People's Republic of China. [288]

Vice-President Al Gore's Fundraising with Chinese Spies

The involvement of key leaders of the Democratic Party in a variety of conflicting situations involving the People's Republic of China isn't new.

Al Gore, Bill Clinton's Vice-President, became involved in fund raising efforts with the Chinese on behalf of the Clinton re-election campaign. The result was a campaign financing investigation by the FBI, which became known as CAMPCON. The investigation became the third largest FBI investigation in terms of resources, money and manpower, during the time frame between 1995-2002.

CAMPCON created severe conflict between the FBI and the Department of Justice. FBI Director Louis Freeh wanted a special prosecutor appointed. Attorney General Janet Reno refused the request.

There were multiple aspects to the CAMPCON investigation, but the most significant involved a shadowy figure from the Democratic

---

[287] Interview of retired FBI Special Agent Al Heiman, FBI China expert, by Terry D. Turchie, 10/8/2019

[288] "The Invasion of the Chinese Cyber-spies (And the Man Who Tried to Stop Them)," by Nathan Thornburgh, 9/5/2005, *Time*.

National Committee fundraising crowd named Johnny Huang. In 1993 President Clinton appointed Huang a deputy assistant secretary for international economic affairs at the Department of Commerce. Huang specialized in Asia.

The relationship between Huang and Bill Clinton dated back to 1980, when Clinton gave a speech at a financial seminar of the Lippo Group. The Lippo Group was owned by Mochtar and James Riady, a father and son. The two had a history of raising funds, then concealing the true sources of the donations through banking transactions. In 1998 the U.S. Senate Committee on Governmental Affairs concluded that James Riady and his father, Mochtar, "had a long -term relationship with a Chinese intelligence agency."

Maria Hsia, affiliated with the *His Lai Buddhist Temple* in Los Angeles, was friends with Johnny Huang and James Riady. Hsia had sent a letter to Al Gore in 1988, inviting him to visit Taiwan. Gore accepted, and Hsia successfully began a friendship with the man who would become Bill Clinton's Vice-President.

Gore attended one of the DNC/Johnny Huang fundraising drives at the Buddhist Temple in Los Angeles. Huang had raised $3.4 million for the Democrats, with $140,000 coming from fundraising at the Temple.

When FBI agents sought records and documents from the Buddhist Temple and a video allegedly showing Vice-President Gore at the fundraiser where Chinese intelligence operatives were in attendance, the evidence disappeared. But the FBI found two witnesses who admitted destroying evidence of Gore's attendance.

Vice-President Gore told the media, "I did not know that it was a fund raiser…I knew it was a political event…I knew there were finance people that were going to be present."

In a June 22, 2000 letter to President Clinton, then U.S. Senator Jeff Sessions was critical of the decision by Attorney General Janet Reno not to appoint a special prosecutor in the investigation. Sessions released information describing Gore's treatment of the FBI agents who interviewed him. "News accounts in the 'New York Post' recently reported that at the interview, the vice president 'blew his top…'because they asked about his illegal Buddhist temple fundraiser for the first time…the interview 'ended in a yelling match between Gore and federal investigators.'"

President Bill Clinton Grants Export Waivers for Sale of Satellite Technology to China-Raises $400,000

Another avenue in the CAMPCON investigation concerned the DNC fundraising efforts of Johnny Chung. Chung raised $366,000 for the Democratic Party between 1994 and 1996, while visiting the Clinton White House 49 times. Chung was convicted on campaign financing charges, telling the FBI he received $300,000 from a Lieutenant Colonel in the Chinese army. The Chinese Lieutenant Colonel was the daughter of a Chinese military official and vice president of state-owned China Aerospace. He was photographed with President Clinton at a Democratic fundraiser in Los Angeles in 1996.

During Clinton's time in the White House, export waivers were granted to Loral Space and Communications, so that Loral could send satellite technology to China Aerospace. A report to Congress dated September 5, 2001, titled, "China: Possible Missile Technology Transfers from U.S. Satellite Export Policy- Actions and Chronology," states:

"Congress has been concerned about whether U.S. firms, in exporting satellites, provided expertise to China for use in its ballistic missile and space programs and whether the administration's policies might facilitate transfers of military-related technology to China." [289]

In 2007, the Chinese military tested laser weapons over the Taiwan Straits. The weapons have the potential to blind American military satellites supporting the U.S. Navy operating in the Straits. In a war, the

---

[289]   Congressional Research Service, "China: Possible Missile Technology Transfers from U.S. Satellite Export Policy – Actions and Chronology," by Shirley A. Kan, Congressional Research Service, *USC US China Institute*, September 5, 2001

Chinese could be victorious because of the possession of such technology. This is the 2019 consequence of Bill Clinton's decision in 2001 to grant export waivers to the Chinese, so they could acquire satellite technology from the United States.

In the Loral satellite case, for example, the Clinton re-election campaign received hundreds of thousands of dollars from a long time Democratic operative who told the FBI he got the money from a relative of the vice president of China Aerospace. State-owned China Aerospace then received Loral's satellite technology, which the Chinese have put to work building weapons directed against the U.S. Navy.

Twenty percent of U.S. Uranium Production and Bill Clinton Go to Russia-Clinton Raises $500,000

Shortly after Hillary Clinton, as Secretary of State, returned from official travel to Russia in 2010, former President Bill Clinton requested an opinion from the Department of State on plans to visit with fourteen high level officials during his own June 2010 travel to Russia. Bill Clinton ended up meeting with Vladimir Putin instead, receiving $500,000 in speaking fees for a ninety- minute speech he gave while in Russia.

During the same time frame Bill and Hillary were traveling to Russia, the Obama State Department was preparing for the transfer of American uranium to Russia through Canadian company Uranium One. Rosatom, Russia's state-owned energy company, was buying Uranium One, as Russia's Renaissance Capital was "talking up" the purchase. Renaissance Capital actually paid Bill Clinton's $500,000 speaking fee.

In October 2010 the Committee on Foreign Investment in the United States (CFIUS), approved the Uranium One deal, effectively transferring 20% of America's uranium production to Russia's Rosatom. According to The Hill, the FBI "uncovered evidence that Russian nuclear officials were engaged in a massive bribery scheme before CFIUS approved the deal." [290]

---

[290] "Bill Clinton Sought State's Permission to Meet with Russian Nuclear

How the PRC Targets America's Politicians

Perhaps most significant-Chinese intelligence agencies will aggressively use the tactics and techniques that have worked for them in the past. And they never forget the people and the relationships that make it all work. According to former FBI China expert, Al Heiman:

"Guanxi is a Chinese word that translates in English into connection. It's all about the art and practice of taking advantage of connections to build reciprocal relationships. Its significance in Chinese culture is immense. The Chinese can carry on hundreds of thousands of conversations at any one time, all for the purpose of relationships. And they don't forget. In fact, the Chinese developed lots of relationships with the husband of Senator Diane Feinstein back in the 1970s..." [291]

Former FBI Special Agent Heiman's comment about the Chinese intelligence services "guanxi" and Chinese business connections with Senator Diane Feinstein's husband in the 1970's, may help explain the predicament Senator Feinstein found herself in just a year ago.

"Imagine if it emerged that the Republican chairman of the House or Senate intelligence committee had a Russian spy working on their staff. Think it would cause a political firestorm? Well, this month we learned that Sen. Dianne Feinstein (D-Calif) had a Chinese spy on her staff who worked for her for about 20 years, was listed as an 'office director' on payroll records and served as her driver when she was in San Francisco, all while reporting to China's Ministry of State Security through China's San Francisco Consulate.

"'Feinstein acknowledged the infiltration but played down its significance. 'Five years ago, the FBI informed me it had concerns that an administrative member of my California staff was potentially being sought out by the Chinese government to provide information,' Feinstein said in a statement — which means the breach took place while

---

Official During Uranium Decision," by John Solomon and Alison Spann, *The Hill, 10/19/2017*

[291]   Ibid.

Feinstein was heading the Intelligence Committee. But, Feinstein insisted, "he never had access to classified or sensitive information or legislative matters" and was immediately fired. In other words: junior staffer, no policy role, no access to secrets, quickly fired — no big deal." [292]

Back then, during the rigors of the CAMPCON investigation, the FBI agents assigned to the case didn't trust the wisdom of the Democratic loyalists working in the Department of Justice. They had good reason: four of the FBI agents involved in CAMPCON testified before Congress in 1999. They criticized Department of Justice prosecutor Laura Ingersoll who directed them "not to pursue any matter related to solicitation of funds for access to the president." [293]

The Chinese are keenly interested in the American Government-the power structure within the United States, in who makes decisions and what they are thinking. They are not only interested in how Americans think about China, but in actively shaping impressions of China as a peace -loving nation with a growing economy and a billion very happy people who are intensely loyal to their country.

Consider the example of Democratic United States Congresswoman Judy Chu:

Judy Chu was first elected to the United States Congress in 2009, and today represents the 27th District of California. Chu earned undergraduate degrees in mathematics from UCLA and a PhD in psychology. She taught psychology in colleges in Los Angeles until running for Congress.

Chu considered herself an activist during the 1970's. By early May 1982, she was identified as a member of the steering committee of the newly founded Federation for Progress (FFP). The purpose of the FFP was to build a coalition to oppose President Ronald Reagan's agenda.

---

[292]   "Explain the Chinese Spy, Senator Feinstein," by Marc Thiessen, The Washington Post, 8/9/2018.

[293]   "The Obstruction of Justice Department," *The Wall Street Journal*, 9/30/1999.

Chu attended the first meeting of the FFP in Washington, D.C. Other elected officials who attended were, Nelson M. Johnson, chairman of the Maoist oriented Communist Workers Party; Congressman Ron Dellums; Congressman Parren Mitchell, a Democrat from Maryland; Georgia State Senator Julian Bond and Mayor Richard Hatcher.

Chu has a history of involvement with people and organizations espousing the ideology of communism. She has authored articles for communist publications, been a speaker at gatherings of communist leaning organizations and associated with known members of the Communist Party of the United States.

For example, Chu wrote an article for the Maoist publication, *Gidra*, in April 1974, titled "The prisons and the Asian American." While serving in the California Legislature, Chu's Legislative Assistant was Marilyn Calderon. Calderon was married to Jose Calderon, a leader of the Colorado Communist Worker's Party.

In 1983, the FFP organized an international solidarity conference in connection with the 1984 Olympics held in Los Angeles. An article in the Communist Workers Party, *Worker's Viewpoint,* on March 9, 1983, described the attendees and speakers at the solidarity conference.

They included the Committee in Solidarity with the People of El Salvador (CISPES); National Lawyers Guild; and National Resistance Coalition. Other individuals in attendance were Maxine Waters, Ramsey Clark, and Judy Chu. Chu attended and spoke at a follow-up meeting in July 1983.

The year 1984 was a busy one for Judy Chu. She served as the president of the Los Angeles chapter of the FFP. She signed a letter to the International Olympic Committee (IOC) asking for the resignations of two of its officials for comments they made in connection with efforts by the South African Olympic Committee to regain membership in the IOC. Signing the letter with Chu was Mike Young, representing the organization, "84 Mobilization for Peace and Justice" and the Communist Workers Party.

In January 2011 Chinese President Hu Jintao visited the United States and was met at the airport by Vice-President Joe Biden. President

Obama hosted a private dinner for Hu Jintao on one night of his visit and a state dinner the second. At the dinner was Chinese American Mayor Ed Lee of San Francisco; Mayor Jean Quan of Oakland, California; Energy Secretary Steven Chu; and Representative Judy Chu.

Four days later, Congresswoman Chu was invited to dinner by the Chinese Counsel General in Los Angeles, where there was a discussion of agriculture between China and California.

On July 17, 2011, Chu and the Committee of 100 held a dinner for a Chinese delegation at the Atherton, California home of Ta-lin Hsu, the chairman of H & Q Asia Pacific. The Chinese delegation, led by the Governor of Jiangsu Province, was accompanied by Chinese solar energy executives. Among the invited guests were Judy Chu, Mike Honda and former Governor of California, Gray Davis.

In August 2011 Chu led a delegation to China, after an invitation from the Chinese People's Institute of Foreign Affairs. While in Beijing, Chu encouraged the enhancement of U.S. China relations. After leaving Beijing, she traveled to Jiangsu Province, the financial hub of Shanghai.

Chu and her delegation met with the Secretary of the Chinese Communist Party for the Jiangsu Provincial Committee. Chu extended regrets over the "Chinese Exclusion Act of 1882, a Congressional bill suspending Chinese immigration" While in China, agreement was reached on establishing a sister city relationship Jiangsu and California.
294

Chu visited her Chinese ancestral home upon leaving the country, and had these comments upon her departure:

"Going to my home village and the Jiangmen museum of overseas Chinese it exemplified so greatly the hardships of the Chinese experience when they went abroad and had been treated so poorly by the immigration officials and experienced such hardships as they were trying to settle in America.

---

294 "Pro-Vice-Chancellor of Durham University visits Peking University," Peking University, 9/15/2011

"It just brought home for me what kind of difficulties that my own grandfather and parents must have experienced as they came over.

"There are some in Congress who are saying negative and angry things about China.

"I felt that we needed to have this trip in order to help balance the perspective that is out there. We have more to gain in our relationship between US and China than we have to lose.

"We need to explain what great progress China has made, with some great advances that we can learn from. For instance, on high-speed rail. We actually rode the high-speed rail from Nanjing to Shanghai and we were incredibly impressed at how China could make these advances when we in the US actually have not been able to get our first high-speed train going.

"I am a daughter of China, now I am coming home. This most incredible eight days visit has made me better understand what China is about. I had a memorable visit to my home village of Jiangmen. I am truly coming home.

"China has really made great progress…21 years ago when I was last in Jiangmen, single lane roads, no bridges cross the river. But this time I see 3-lane highways, magnificent highways, and all kinds of industry." Judy Chu Exposed, Part 5: Judy Chu – [295]

Judy Chu was at the opening ceremony of the Global Chinese Broadcasting Corporation Annual Meeting in Los Angeles on May 23, 2012, attended by the Chinese Council General.

In her talk, Chu raised one of her key issues- the Chinese Exclusion Act of 1882, stating that Chinese immigrants were made "scapegoats for the Americans here." Chu continued, "It was the relationship between the U.S. and China that actually got that act repealed in the first place. So, we must know that we have to value that relationship." [296]

---

[295] "I Am a Daughter of China, Now I Am Coming Home" by Trevor Loudon March 18, 2013.

[296] "New Age of U.S.-China Relations," 2012 Western Regional Conference of US-China Peoples Friendship Association, October 2012

Key Wiki provided this assessment of a November 3, 2012 article in the Chinese newspaper *People's Daily* on "overseas Chinese" in politics:

"China laid a claim to human resources around the world that no other country can match: 50 million ethnic Chinese, mostly citizens of other countries whom Beijing sees as 'sons and daughters of the Chinese nation.'

"It cited U.S. congresswoman Judy Chu of California, the only Asian among 35 national campaign co-chairpersons for Barack Obama's campaign committee.

"Even though the article appeared in English in the paper's online edition, it did not refer to her as "Judy Chu" but as Zhao Meixin, using her Chinese name.

"It called her an example of a successful overseas Chinese 'participating in politics in foreign countries.' The article referred to the congresswoman and others as 'ethnic foreigners,' as though she will be forever a foreigner in the land of her birth and will always be Chinese.

"In fact, China is claiming credit for the achievements of people such as Judy Chu. The People's Daily said: 'As China's national strength is constantly enhancing, the status of overseas Chinese is also upgraded in the countries they live in.' It said that participation in politics had become an "irresistible trend" for overseas Chinese." [297]

In April 2016 the Committee of 100 held a conference in Los Angeles attended by its official supporters, which included Judy Chu and a number of other high -profile Democratic politicians and businesspeople.

Edmund G. Brown Jr., Governor of California; Eric Garcetti, Mayor of Los Angeles; Cui Tiankai, Ambassador of the People's Republic of China to the United States; Penny Pritzker, U.S. Secretary of Commerce; Cory Gardner, United States Senator; Mark Kirk, United States Senator; Ed Royce, Congressman, Chairman, House Foreign Affairs

---

[297] "The 'Sons & Daughters of China' by Frank Ching, *The China Post,* November 7, 2012.

Committee; Congressman Charles Boustany; Congressman Xavier Becerra; Congressman Mike Honda; Congressman Ted Lieu; Liu Jian, Council General of the People's Republic of China in Los Angeles; Anthony Rendon, speaker of the California State Assembly; Ed Chau, member of California State Assembly; Betty Yee, California State Controller; and -*Congressman Adam Schiff, now heading the Intelligence Committee of the House of Representatives, and a leading Congressional advocate of impeaching President Trump.*

Congresswoman Judy Chu has been involved in a number of *Committee of 100* meetings over the years. The Committee describes its mission as:

"...a non-partisan leadership organization of prominent Chinese Americans in business, government, academia, and the arts. The concept of founding the Committee came from architect, the late I.M. Pei and Dr. Henry Kissinger, 56th U.S. Secretary of State in 1988. Membership is open to American citizens of Chinese heritage. The Committee of 100 aims to harness 'its distinguished membership to address significant and complex issues pertaining to Americans of Chinese descent and U.S.-China relations.'" [298]

The PRC has brilliantly manipulated Judy Chu as an advocate for China's "benign" intentions. Whether witting or unwitting, Chu is a valuable agent of influence for the Chinese government.

Of course, Judy Chu isn't alone. When Obama's Vice-President Joe Biden stepped off of Air Force Two in China, with his son Hunter behind him, Chinese intelligence agents must have gone into warp speed with operations designed to gain access to the Obama White House. After all, look how close they became to another Democratic Party Vice-President twenty-four years ago.

---

[298]   committee100.org

PART TWO

CHAPTER TWELVE

Weather Underground, Black Panther Party and the Weapon of Racism

---

"This country... was founded on racism, has existed through racism and is racist today..."
Beto O'Rourke

The leaders of the Weather Underground (WU) recognized the significance of the Black Power Movement. They were effusive in their praise of Black Power as a vanguard of the revolution in the 1970's to topple the United States Government and usher in an era of socialism, followed by communism. WU members viewed black citizens inside America as the second largest *"Black Nation"* on the earth. They represented millions of people who could contribute to the mass movement that was necessary for the revolution to succeed.

Racism- the Weapon of Choice of the Communist -Minded Men and Women of the Weather Underground

Combined with other *"oppressed peoples"*-women, Native Americans, Chicanos, youth, and those from the Third World, the Weather Underground believed it had found, and was developing, the ideal political and potentially violent force it needed to carry through with its ambitious plans:

"US imperialism is the greatest destroyer of human life on earth... In the people's culture lie the seeds of resistance and rebellion... Oppressed peoples, women and youth and other anti-imperialist forces can and should deliver telling blows against the empire now; the actual building of socialism cannot succeed without the active support of the industrial proletariat...In the face of imperial decline, the rulers make fascistic appeals to whites to try to recoup economic stability and privilege by going along with and enforcing even more intensified oppression of Third World people..."[299]

An ongoing challenge for the revolutionaries in pushing the movement forward was consistently motivating the masses to action. The weapons of choice, then and now, are racism, white supremacy and white privilege. Aimed at building a racial divide in America, the Weather Underground's 181- page *Prairie Fire* manifesto, references racism, white supremacy and white privilege throughout.

- "Creation of an anti-racist white movement is the necessary foundation for the functional unity of Third World and white enemies of the empire. Anti-racist organizing and action can create this unity."

---

[299] *Prairie Fire*

- "…Organizing a Base for Fascism. In the US this means racism: building explicitly or thinly -disguised anti-Black and Third World campaigns…"

- "If we do not create an anti-racist left, the masses of white people being bombarded with these measures have little alternative but to resolve these fears and these conflicts the traditional way —in complicity with racism."

- "Anti-crime legislation mobilizes racist fears in the white population."

- "…Distinctions of color and origin were promoted into an entire system of racism."

- "Racism is not only directed at Black people-it is also aimed at controlling whites…"

- "Racism as a prime social and cultural dividing line was born in North America, out of slavery —it was born out of greed for profit, perpetrated by deception and a monopoly of firearms…"

- "Racial and cultural inferiority of African and other Third World peoples has been deeply embedded into every US institution as the chief means of brainwashing and using the white population."

- "Imperialism has intensified and spread worldwide the most virulent racist practices and ideology. Racism is built into US imperialism and imperial culture feeds on and creates racism. Racism is institutionalized as a system of control and containment, necessary to enforce the exploitation and oppression of colonized people. In the Third World, racism takes the form of cultural warfare, the displacement of populations and genocide."

- "The Communist Party (CP) stressed the special importance of Black liberation. Black people were recognized as an oppressed nation in the South (then called a Negro nation) with the right of self-determination, which white revolutionaries were bound to support. This was a great breakthrough. Communists engaged in persistent battles against white chauvinism and white supremacy both within and outside the Party. CP organizers challenged racism in the labor movement..."

- "Racism bloats and disfigures the face of the culture that practices it." The imperialists create racial identification with one's oppressors among the domestic white population in support of wars of conquest. They also draw on xenophobia and national chauvinism..."

- "Institutionalized racism is mainlined and perpetuated over the generations by the schools, the unemployment... the drug trade, immigration laws, birth control, the army, the prisons."

- "All forms of racism, class prejudice, and male chauvinism must be torn out by the roots."

- "...Their main weapon is white supremacy...Socialism is the rejection of empire and white supremacy."

- "History is a weapon only if used honestly, only if reverses as well as highlights accommodation with empire and white supremacy as well as resistance to it...U.S. history is a product of the...white masters and black slaves...distinctions of color and origin were promoted into an entire system of racism...Coupled with the economic bribe of white privilege, it is the cornerstone of U.S. history."

- "Crushing Reconstruction involved the conscious reinstatement of white supremacy patterns in order to destroy a kind of people's unity... Jim Crow laws and wholesale disenfranchisement, and white skin became the cultural definition of power once again. While there were scattered attempts at Black-white unity in these days, they fell apart as many poor whites destroyed the basis for genuine alliance by defending white supremacy."

- "This has created a new level of militant leadership from below, challenging white supremacy in the unions, confronting and radicalizing white co-workers."[300]

Before he was elected as President of the United States, Donald Trump was targeted by name in the 2016 Democratic Party platform. Although Trump had previously been a registered Democrat who provided contributions to the political campaigns of influential Democrats, he found himself characterized as a man who uses "divisive and derogatory language" and whose "offensive comments about immigrants and other communities have no place in our society."[301]

In its 2016 platform, the Democratic Party adopted "ending systemic racism," as a weapon of its societal transformation:

- "we know that our nation's long struggle with race is far from over."

- "from the enduring scourge of systemic racism..."

- "Democrats will fight to end institutional and systemic racism in our society. We will challenge and dismantle the structures that define lasting racial, economic, political, and social inequity."

- "Democrats will promote racial justice through fair, just, and equitable governing of all public-serving institutions and in the

---

[300] Ibid. *Prairie Fire.*

[301] Democratic Party 2016 platform.

formation of public policy."

- "Democrats support removing the Confederate battle flag from public properties, recognizing that it is a symbol of our nation's racist past that has no place in our present or our future."

- "We will push for a societal transformation to make it clear that black lives matter and that there is no place for racism in our country."

- "this is environmental racism; energy poverty…During the clean energy transition, we will ensure landowners, communities of color, and tribal nations are at the table."

- "low income communities and communities of color are disproportionately home to environmental justice 'hot spots,' impacts of climate change will also… affect low-income and minority communities, tribal nations, and Alaska Native villages—all of which suffer the worst losses during extreme weather and have the fewest resources to prepare."**4** [302]

The above excerpts from the Democratic Party 2016 platform are extraordinary, especially considering that the 2020 platform will be far more progressive. In just a few short statements from a 43- page platform, the Democrats have condemned American history, propose erasing elements of America's history and call for a "societal transformation."

The "societal transformation," sounds a lot like the "fundamental transformation," promised by Barack Obama in 2008; the "total transformation" mentioned by Huey Newton at Boston College in 1970; and the "revolutionary transformation," favored by the Communist party of the United States. These transformations share the same vision- moving America to socialism.

An evaluation of the Weather Underground's (WU) *"Prairie*

---

[302]   Democratic Party 2016 platform.

Fire," and the Black Panther Party's *Ten Point Program* makes it clear that democratic socialism is an important step in the incremental installation of a communist utopia that now fuels the appetite of Democratic Party politicians and their lust for power.

The Democratic Party Adopts the Weather Underground's Racism as a Political Weapon

Towards this end, Democratic Party candidates have evoked racism at every turn, as they fight for their Party's Presidential nomination in 2020.

Elizabeth Warren

In May 2019, Elizabeth Warren, using information from a George Soros think tank study on maternal health care in the United States, said that black women are treated differently than white women due to the prejudice of doctors and nurses. She wrote, "black women are three to four times more likely than white women to die from pregnancy or childbirth-related causes. This trend persists even after adjusting for income and education. One major reason? Racism…"[303]

In July 2019, after the President tweeted that Baltimore is "a very dangerous and filthy place," and called the late Democratic Congressman Elijah Cummings a "brutal bully," Warren reacted, saying, "Donald Trump, once again, is a racist who makes evermore outrageous, racist remarks."[304]

Over a year ago, Warren called America's criminal justice system

---

[303]   "Sen. Elizabeth Warren on Black Women Maternal Mortality: 'Hold Health Systems Accountable for Protecting Black Moms'" by Senator Elizabeth Warren, *Essence*, 4/30/2019.

[304]   "Donald Trump Insults Baltimore Again: "It's Worse Than Honduras," by Angela Wilson, *BET*, 7/31/2019

racist while giving a speech at a college in New Orleans. Warren declared that "the hard truth about our criminal justice system: It's racist . . . I mean front to back."[305]

Cory Booker

When President Trump challenged four Democratic Congresswomen after they made negative comments about America, Cory Booker told CNN "the reality is this is a guy who is worse than a racist. He is actually using racist tropes and racial language for political gain. He *is* trying to use this as a weapon to divide our nation against itself." "And this is somebody who is very similar to George Wallace, who -- a racist -- he's using the exact same language."[306]

In a forum of presidential candidates, Booker made the point that anyone who is not actively against, and fighting racism, is complicit in racism. If this sounds like a familiar refrain, it is. The Eric Holder Department of Justice, along with the Democratic Party, as a matter of policy, turned up the heat on America's police departments using consent decrees and a variety of other means available, to begin educating every American police officer in the area of "implicit bias."

Developed in liberal academia think tanks, *"implicit bias"* means that every police officer has a subconscious racial bias, of which he or she is completely unaware. Proper training is the proposed remedy for "implicit bias."

If Booker has his way, every American will have their opportunity to share in a re-education of their thought process to treat their "complicit bias." "It's not enough to say you're not racist, you need to attack racism." "If you just sit by and content yourself with just not being what

---

[305] "Police, Opponents Criticize Warren's Remarks on 'Racist' Justice System," by Eric Garcia, *Roll Call*, 8/13/2018.

[306] **8** "Cory Booker: Donald Trump is 'Worse Than a Racist'" by Devan Cole, *CNN*, 7/21/2019.

Donald Trump is…this is a letter to white moderates."[307]

In 2018, during the hearings for Supreme Court Justice Brett Kavanaugh, Booker announced that America's founding fathers were racist. In a Senate exchange, he said:

"I love that my colleagues keep going back to the Constitution but understand this: I laud our Founders. I think they were geniuses. But I understand that millions of Americans understand that they were also flawed people…"

"We know our Founders and their values and their ideals, but we also know that they were flawed and you can see that in the documents. Native Americans were referred to as savages, women weren't referred to at all, African Americans were referred to as fractions of human beings…As one civil rights activist -- I think it was Stokely Carmichael -- used to always say: 'Constitu, constitu. I can only say three-fifths of the word.'"[308]

Kamala Harris

Campaigning in Iowa, Kamala Harris was asked outright about whether President Trump is a white supremacist.

"I as a prosecutor handled hate crimes. As the attorney general running the California Department of Justice - the second largest Department of Justice in the United States - I would publish hate crime reports every year. This is not new in America. Hate is not new. Hate that takes the form of racism, antisemitism, homophobia, transphobia, Islamophobia is not new in our country."

"I will not participate in a conversation that simplifies this issue without recognizing one - the history, speaking the truth about it and recognizing it happened before [Trump] was in the White House and it

---

[307] "Cory Booker Says to White Moderates, "It's Not Enough to Say You're Not Racist," by Chrissy Clark, *The Federalist Papers*, 7/18/2019.

[308] Transcripts, *CNN*, 9/4/2018

will continue after this guy in the White House."[309]

Beto O'Rourke

In an appearance in Texas following the El Paso shooting, O'Rourke offered his opinion on racism in America, "this country, though we would like to think otherwise, was founded on racism, has existed through racism and is racist today…"[310]

Kirsten Gillibrand

Senator Gillibrand was in Ohio when a white woman expecting a baby asked her about the Democratic Party focus on white supremacy.

"…What that conversation is about is when a community has been left behind for generations because of the color of their skin. When you've been denied job after job after job because you're black or because you're brown. Or when you go to the emergency room to have your baby — the fact that we have the highest maternal mortality rate, and if you are a black woman you are more likely to die in childbirth because that health care provider doesn't believe you when you say, 'I don't feel right.'"

"So institutional racism is real… It doesn't take away your pain or suffering. It's just a different issue. Your suffering is just as important as a black or brown person's suffering. But to fix the problems that are happening in the black community, you need far more transformational efforts that are targeted for real racism that exists every day."[311]

---

[309]   "Kamala Harris Says She 'Will Not Participate' in Conversation that Reduces Racism to Just Donald Trump," by Donica Phifer, *Newsweek*, 8/10/19.

[310]   "Attacks on Racism and Trump Resonate for Texans Beto O'Rourke and Julián Castro," by Bill Lambrecht, Washington Bureau, *San Antonio Express News* Aug. 20, 2019

[311]   "Kirsten Gillibrand Delivers Powerful Explanation of White Privilege,"

Bernie Sanders

Sanders is well versed at integrating racism into the argument for a socialist America:

"One of the ongoing crises in America is institutional racism. We have a very broken criminal justice system. We live in a country where there are more people in jail than any other country on Earth. There are some 2.2 million people currently incarcerated and they are disproportionally African American and Hispanic. Unarmed African Americans have been abused and sometimes killed while in police custody. Clearly these are issues that must be dealt with and changed."

"We've got to stand with those people who are being attacked today, but at the same time, it`s not good enough to say that racism and xenophobia is bad. We've got to reach those people today who are so angry, who are so hateful and say, yes, you have a right to be angry, don`t take it out on the Muslims. Work with us to create an agenda and political movement that will make your life better, not just other people`s life worse."

"In America, we have struggled too much, too long as a country trying to overcome racism and sexism and homophobia. We cannot go back to a more discriminatory society."

"What we have got to do immediately is to say that racism and xenophobia is totally unacceptable, and we will stand with the 1 percent of our population who are Muslims, for undocumented people in this country. Absolutely, we will stand."[312]

While this book was being written, 21- year old Patrick Crusius walked into a Walmart in El Paso, Texas carrying a semi-automatic rifle. He opened fire killing twenty-two people and injuring dozens more. As the FBI and police investigation of background and motive developed, an anti-immigrant manifesto attributed to the shooter was found.

Headlines in newspapers and magazines across the country used

by Sanjana Karanth, *Huff Post,* 7/11/2019.

[312]   "All Bernie Sanders Quotes About Racism," *Inspiring Quotes.*

words like "white supremacy," "white nationalism," and "racism," to call attention to the El Paso and other similar shootings, concluding that a rise in white nationalism since the election of President Trump is the reason for these attacks.

Democratic candidates for President traveled the country, hit the air waves, interviewed with a variety of media organizations and spoke at countless forums, all accusing President Trump of bearing some measure, to all of the responsibility, for the El Paso mass shooting. Democrats accused President Trump of being a "white supremacist and a "racist," who is tearing the county apart.

At least one United States Congresswoman told the President to stay away from El Paso while people mourned. Democratic Party strategists appeared on network news and talk shows calling for stricter regulations on firearms possession. Some claimed that tougher regulations, combined with getting President Trump removed from office, was the only way to stop the mass shootings. Others argued that only Trump's removal from office can stop the rise in white nationalism, white supremacy, and racist hate crimes Several weeks prior to the El Paso shooting, FBI Director Christopher Wray told Congress most domestic acts of terror are related to white supremacists. The FBI authored a report that was intended for law enforcement eyes only. The report leaked to the public. It expressed concern over the rise in white nationalism reflected in the FBI's terrorism case load.

And yet two years ago, the FBI published a report expressing alarm over the rise in Black Extremism in the United States. In the final years of the Obama Presidency attacks on police officers in locations such as Louisiana and Texas were being committed by black males, who tied their murder sprees to police brutality against blacks.

The Congressional Black Caucus immediately assaulted the FBI's findings and conclusions. Hakeem Jeffries, a Democratic Congressman from New York state, questioned Wray over the report on Black Extremists. "He (Wray) was asked to publicly clarify that there is no scintilla of evidence, as far as we can tell, to provide an example of the black identity extremist movement or any groups that fall in that category. That clarification should be made publicly, it seems to many of us, and not privately behind closed doors."[313]

The Democratic Party has resurrected the Weather Underground's communist ideology to breathe life into their new political revolution. The Weather Underground worked in the 1960's and 1970's to create massive division and civil unrest in America to further the revolution. The use of words like white nationalism, white privilege, white supremacy, and racism, are indicative of today's Democratic Party ties to the revolutionary language of the Weather Underground and Black Panther Party.

President Obama says words matter. Cory Booker speaks of President Trump's racist language. The Democratic Party platform proposes removing all Confederate flags as they are a symbol of America's racist past. Every Democratic Party candidate for President uses the battle cry of "systemic racism" in America.

It's good that leaders in the Democratic Party accept the premise that words and past history matter. Their own party now lives by the words and past history of the Weather Underground and Black Panther Party-the violent revolutionaries of the *Days of Rage*, whose shared desire was the transformation of America into a socialist society-followed by communism.

---

[313] "Lawmakers Confront F.B.I. Director Over Report on Black Extremists," by Adam Goldman and Nicholas Fandos, *The New York Times*, 11/29/2017.

CHAPTER THIRTEEN

Organizing the Masses- a Weapon of Socialist Revolutions

---

*"Organize the masses of people and build the
fight...to seize power and build the new
society."*
The Weather Underground

A merican politicians pushing Democratic Socialism have become experts at subterfuge and subversion. They call themselves activists, progressives, and social justice warriors. While too many of the rest of us have sat on the sidelines, they have turned government away from moderation and fairness, into a tool to enhance socialist agendas, personal power and the authority of government over the individual.

All of this has happened in a relatively short period of time, despite Thomas Jefferson making clear in the Declaration of Independence that government should be a secondary influence in our lives-guided by "inherent and inalienable rights" bestowed by our Creator.

243

"We hold these truths to be self-evident, that all men are created equal; that they are endowed by their Creator with inherent and inalienable rights; that among these, are life, liberty, and the pursuit of happiness; that to secure these rights, governments are instituted among men, deriving their just powers from the consent of the governed; that whenever any form of government becomes destructive of these ends, it is the right of the people to alter or abolish it, and to institute new government, laying its foundation on such principles, and organizing its powers in such form, as to them shall seem most likely to affect their safety and happiness."

Authoritarian governments, tyrants and the "dictator" class have never accepted a Creator or "life, liberty and the pursuit of happiness" as the foundation for our earthly existence. America's governmental structure has continuously evolved to add substance to the idea that "all men are created equal." Each successive generation of citizens and leaders have worked to create more opportunity for every individual. Until recently, both mainstream American political parties have united around this key principle that is the essence of our constitutional Republic. Not any longer.

The writing of the Declaration of Independence and the nation it helped to create, was one of the most significant events in the history of mankind. Yet today Democratic Party politicians are working their own brand of subversion from inside the United States Government to impair and eventually replace the "inalienable rights" enjoyed by Americans since the nation's founding.

Democratic Party politicians are now actively building a "victim class," and promising them equality- not equal opportunity. Equality for some will come at the expense of "life, liberty and the pursuit of happiness for many. Equality will replace freedom, liberty and our Creator, with an all- powerful Government, transformed from a moderator of fairness into an enforcer of unworkable socialism. By the time Americans wake up to the mistake they have made in allowing socialists to install incremental communism in place of our constitutional Republic, we will have already entered that period of instability foreshadowed by the Weather Underground's *Prairie Fire*. It will be too late.

The Democratic Party is using the subterfuge of "equality." They are deploying the weapons of racism and white nationalism to create divisions among the American people. The government now wants to harness the power and wealth generated by capitalism as its own, to distribute as the activists among us see fit.

They will use that wealth and power to solidify the growth of an elite ruling class, while redistributing a share of it to every citizen. They will realize their vision of a communist utopia where every citizen is equal and cared for by the grace of whoever is in power at the time and through inalienable political correctness.

Strategy for Revolution- the Democratic Socialists of America

The Democratic Party's vision will change the country and the lives of Americans forever. There will be no turning back. The Democratic Socialists of America (DSA) website offer a forecast of the future:

"...Our strategy...consists of fighting on a number of interconnected fronts in the short-term, leveraging gains made in these struggles into more structural, offensively-oriented changes in the medium-term and ultimately employing the strength of a mass socialist party or coalition of leftist and progressive parties to win political power and begin the process of socialist transformation..."[314]

Strategy for Revolution- the Communist-Minded Men and Women of the Weather Underground

This is the way the self-described "communist-minded" Weather Underground (WU) viewed the strategy for revolution in America almost fifty years ago:

---

[314]   Democratic Socialists of America (DSA) website. 1

"...Here is PRAIRIE FIRE, our political ideology —a strategy for anti-imperialism and revolution inside the imperial US...The politics cannot be realized unless and until the content of the program is activated in thousands of situations, among thousands of people in the coming period, PRAIRIE FIRE will be a growing thing...

"We hope the paper opens a dialectic among those in the mass and clandestine movements...We need to battle for a correct ideology and win people over. In this way we create the conditions for the development of a successful revolutionary movement and party. We need a revolutionary communist party in order to lead the struggle, give coherence and direction to the fight, seize power and build the new society...

"Getting from here to there is a process of coming together in a disciplined way around ideology and strategy, developing an analysis of our real conditions, mobilizing a base among the US people, building principled relationships to Third World struggle, and accumulating practice in struggle against US imperialism...

"...PRAIRIE FIRE is written to communist-minded people, independent organizers and anti-imperialists...It is written to prisoners, women's groups, collectives, study groups, workers' organizing committees, communes, GI organizers, consciousness-raising groups, veterans, community groups and revolutionaries of all kinds...It is written as an argument against those who oppose action and hold back the struggle...

"Revolutionaries must...organize the masses of people and build the fight."[315]

The Democratic Socialists of America, speak of the need to engage in "fighting" over the short, mid and long term, to leverage gains made in "these struggles," employing a "mass socialist party or coalition of leftist and progressive parties," to "win power and begin the socialist transformation."

The Weather Underground wrote *Prairie Fire* to "give direction to the fight," "against those who oppose action and hold back the strug-

---

[315] *Prairie Fire 2*

gle," "to organize the masses of people and build the fight," "to seize power and build the new society."

Strategy for Revolution- the Communist Party of the United States of America (CPUSA)

The Communist Party of the United States (CPUSA) presents the same vision using different words:

"Organization is the characteristic weapon of the working class and popular movements...The Communist Party seeks to build broad unity to achieve the strategic and tactical goals of the working class. The major obstacle to working class unity is capitalist class-promoted racism, which must be fought by all. Full unity will only be built when substantial numbers of white workers participate in the fight for full equality and against racism, based on an understanding of their self-interest in class unity. This principle is not just true in struggles in the workplace, on the campus, or in the neighborhood, but is equally true at the ballot box..."[316]

During the past two decades, various researchers have identified by name dozens of Democratic Party politicians who have been directly or indirectly affiliated with the Democratic Socialists of America. Although these politicians have taken an oath of office to "preserve, protect and defend the Constitution of the United States against all enemies, foreign and domestic," they are part of a growing movement that seeks to join with other leftist, progressive and communist organizations who have made it clear their new strategy is to win power at the ballot box and begin the "societal transformation."

Congressman Dick Durbin's Rally with the Communist Party at Haymarket Square

The underlayment of international solidarity that binds together

---

[316] CPUSA website.

powerful Democrats, communists, anarchists, and the Weather Underground's "communist minded men and women" was on full public display in Chicago on May 1, 2013. Several thousand people with clenched
fists began a major protest at the site of Chicago's Union Square Haymarket Monument, subsequently marching to Federal Plaza.

The Haymarket location has become an important symbol to those
who believe in the ideology of communism. Rallies and speeches involving labor and anarchists at Haymarket Square on May 4, 1886
turned deadly when Chicago police tried to break up demonstrations
that were becoming more volatile as midnight approached.

In the ensuing confrontation, a homemade bomb was thrown at the
police, setting off gunfire. Seven police officers and four civilians were
killed. Sixty officers were wounded. Several years later, the first day in
May was set aside by the Communists and Socialists of the Second International to remember the Haymarket affair and pay tribute to the International Workers Movement.

Underscoring the importance of what happened at Haymarket in
1886 to the worldwide communist movement, the Weather Underground struck twice at the location during the *Days of Rage*. In October
1969, a Weather Underground bombing attack severely damaged the
Haymarket Memorial Statue as a symbolic protest against police brutality. The statue was rebuilt only to be attacked by the Weather Underground again a year later in October 1970.

Against this history, Illinois Senator Dick Durbin, the Democratic
Party Whip, and second highest ranking person in the Senate, was
standing near the statute waiting to speak to the crowd. He was challenged by an aggressive reporter from *Rebel Pundit*. The following exchange occurred:

Rebel Pundit: "There is a large contingent of Communist Party
USA, anarchists, international socialist groups here today that you just
spoke to…"

Durbin: "How do you know that?"

Rebel pundit: "Because I've filmed them all day and you just spoke
to them, so I'd like to ask about your participation, why you decided to

come out today?"

Durbin: "Well let me just say something, because [pause] I believe in the Constitution. Do you believe in it?"

Rebel Pundit: "Because you believe in the Constitution you decided to come out to a rally full of communists and socialists?"

Durbin: "And you know why?"

Rebel Pundit: "Why?"

Durbin: "Because we have freedom of speech in America, and that's why you can record this and not be arrested."

Rebel Pundit: "You think I should be arrested?"

Durbin: "No, not at all, you have a right to your constitutional rights, and I do, too."[317]

The words of the Communist Party of the United States of America make it clear that advancing a narrative of racism and equality are vital to the building of a mass movement to collapse the United States Government from the inside. Illinois Senator Durbin confirmed in his answer to the reporter that he knew he was speaking to a rally of communists and anarchists.

Senator Durbin was doing his part to build the mass movement. He was right to say that the reporter had every right to freedom of speech. But the reporter wasn't an elected official who took an oath of office to preserve the Constitution and to protect and defend America. Senator Durbin did take such an oath. Yet he chose to spend his time as an elected official addressing a rally of people who believe in an ideology that wants to see America destroyed.

Building a Mass Movement to "Restructure" America- The DSA and Democratic Party Have the Same Plan

If racism is the weapon of choice wielded by the revolutionaries

---

[317]   "Senator Durbin Defends Rallying with Communists and Anarchists at May Day Chicago" Rebel Pundit 5/2/2013

who want to see America fundamentally transformed, equality is the revolutionary battle cry to appeal to the masses. Without the masses-who perceive themselves as the disenfranchised victims of the United States Government and capitalism, there can be no successful uprising and revolution.

The Democratic Socialists of America have identified the groups of Americans who will constitute the masses. They've gone into great detail as to how they will organize and use them as a pathway to unlimited government power, and to permanently terminate the liberties Americans now enjoy as their inalienable right. Equal opportunity, life, liberty and the pursuit of happiness will be replaced by equality- as determined by government officials at the local, state and federal level.

Developing the Masses: The Democratic Socialists of America

Labor

"...The best recruits for socialism are experienced and radicalized workers, and the best workplace organizers are socialists....For these reasons we must place the trade union movement... front and center in our priorities...We can... encourage and support our members who become rank-and file activists, as well as shop stewards and local union officers...in sectors where many DSA members work, such as health care, social services and teaching."

Community Organizing

"...Community organizing is a crucial complement to labor organizing...DSA members...should talk to their neighbors, determine which issues most urgently face the community (for example, tenants' rights, police brutality or shoddy, under-funded public services) and organize strategically around those issues."

Organizing in Higher Education

"...Free public higher education is a key example of what we might call a "transformative" reform that helps to popularize the idea of socialism and to make further, more dramatic reforms possible in the future. Free public higher education would mean taking what should be a universal public good out of the marketplace, putting it under democratic control and guaranteeing it as a right to all citizens — and funding it by a truly progressive tax system that makes the wealthy and corporations pay their fair share of government revenue.

Beyond its inherent benefits, such a campaign would also show people that socialist policies are both desirable and achievable..."

Electoral Organizing

"Achieving our goals... will require a critical mass of political office holders to implement them. Although elections in and of themselves will not bring about major political, economic or social reforms — let alone establish a pathway to socialism — it is difficult to imagine how we could achieve any of our objectives in the United States without taking part in the electoral process...

"The nature of our electoral activism... will include supporting progressive and socialist candidates running for office, usually in Democratic primaries or as Democrats in general elections but also in support of independent socialist and other third-party campaigns outside the Democratic Party...."

Environmental Organizing

"...We will participate in the climate justice movement against the devastation wreaked by global capitalism on the most vulnerable people, cultures and ecosystems. Our commitment to this movement aligns us with the struggles of indigenous peoples against the plunder of their fossil fuel and forest resources and the life-destroying pollution of our air and water...

"Organizing as open socialists gives DSA members the opportunity to organize around widely supported "green" causes under the banner of the anti- capitalist "red" movement. Participation in the climate justice movement also enables DSA to stress its internationalist politics, as this movement is part of a broader fight against corporate domination of social and economic life, and in favor of a democratic international order that enhances global labor, human rights and environmental standards...."

International Organizing

"...In a globalized economy, the commitment of socialists to international solidarity is not just a moral imperative, but a pragmatic necessity. DSA will stand in solidarity with movements around the world fighting to raise global labor, environmental, and human rights standards in opposition to corporate "race to the bottom" policies.

"Such solidarity often will take the form of opposing our government's own foreign policy, which supports undemocratic international institutions (including pro-corporate "free trade agreements"), and which backs, often through military intervention, authoritarian regimes that support U.S. government and economic interests..."

The Democratic Socialists of America have an ultimate destination in mind that will come from their organizing of the masses:

"Success across this spectrum of struggles should lead to a period when we can talk seriously about the transition to democratic socialism through reforms that fundamentally undermine the power of the capitalist system, such as the nationalization of strategic industries (banking, auto, etc.) and the creation of worker controlled investment funds (created by taxing corporate profits) that will buy out capitalist stakes in firms and set up worker-owned and -operated firms on a large scale... "[318]

---

[318]   Ibid. DSA

Developing the Masses: 2016 Democratic Platform:

The 2016 Democratic Platform (the most progressive in the party's history) appears to have adopted many of the visions of the Democratic Socialists of America. Consider the language from the 2016 Democratic Party platform:

Labor

"Democrats will make it easier for workers, public and private, to exercise their right to organize and join unions. We will fight to pass laws that direct the National Labor Relations Board to certify a union if a simple majority of eligible workers sign valid authorization cards, as well as laws that bring companies to the negotiating table…Democrats believe so-called "right to work" laws are wrong for workers—such as teachers and other public employees who serve our communities every day—and wrong for America…"

Community Organizing

In a prime example drawn directly from the pages of the Democratic Socialists of America and their desire to focus on local issues of interest (or in this case issues in the national spotlight), the Democratic Party platform calls for promoting, "racial justice through fair, just, and equitable governing of all public-serving institutions and in the formation of public policy. Democrats support removing the Confederate battle flag from public properties, recognizing that it is a symbol of our nation's racist past that has no place in our present or our future…"

Organizing in Higher Education

"…Democrats are committed to making good public schools available to every child, no matter what zip code they live in, and at last making debt-free college a reality for all American…Democrats believe that in America, if you want a higher education, you should always be able to get one: money should never stand in the way. Cost should not be a barrier to getting a degree or credential, and debt should not hold you back after you graduate...

"...We will also make community college free, while ensuring the strength of our historically Black colleges and universities, and minority-serving institutions. The federal government will push more colleges and universities to take quantifiable, affirmative steps in increasing the percentages of racial and ethnic minority, low income, and first -generation students they enroll and graduate. Achieving these goals depends on state and federal investment in both students and their teachers. Whether full-time or adjunct, faculty must be supported to make transformative educational experiences possible...

"...To make progress toward these goals, the government should offer a moratorium on student loan payments to all federal loan borrowers so they have the time and get the resources they need to consolidate their loans, enroll in income-based repayment programs, and take advantage of opportunities to reduce monthly payments and fees..."

Electoral Organizing

"...We believe that we must protect Americans' right to vote, while stopping corporations outsized influence in elections...We must restore the full protections of the Voting Rights Act. We will bring our democracy into the 21st century by expanding early voting and vote-by-mail, implementing universal automatic voter registration and same day voter registration, ending partisan and racial gerrymandering, and making Election Day a national holiday. We will restore voting rights for those who have served their sentences. And we will continue to fight against discriminatory voter identification laws, which disproportionately burden young voters, diverse communities, people of color, low-income families, people with disabilities, the elderly, and women."

Environmental Organizing

"...we must ensure federal actions do not "significantly exacerbate" global warming. We support a comprehensive approach that ensures all federal decisions going forward contribute to solving, not significantly exacerbating, climate change...During the clean energy transition, we will ensure landowners, communities of color, and tribal nations are at the table...

"...All corporations owe it to their shareholders to fully analyze and disclose the risks they face, including climate risk. Those who fail to do so should be held accountable. Democrats also respectfully request the Department of Justice to investigate allegations of corporate fraud on the part of fossil fuel companies accused of misleading shareholders and the public on the scientific reality of climate change..."

"...The impacts of climate change will also disproportionately affect low-income and minority communities, tribal nations, and Alaska Native villages—all of which suffer the worst losses during extreme weather and have the fewest resources to prepare. Simply put, this is environmental racism..."

International Organizing

"...We believe the United States must lead in forging a robust global solution to the climate crisis. We are committed to a national mobilization, and to leading a global effort to mobilize nations to address this threat on a scale not seen since World War II. In the first 100 days of the next administration, the President will convene a summit of the world's best engineers, climate scientists, policy experts, activists, and indigenous communities to chart a course to solve the climate crisis...

"...Democrats support progress toward more accountable governance and universal rights. As autocrats and strongmen around the world crack down on civil society and imprison those who speak out to demand greater freedom, we will continue to bolster groups and individuals who fight for fundamental human rights, democracy, and rule of law. We will support strong legislatures, independent judiciaries, free press, vibrant civil society, honest police forces, religious freedom, and equality for women and minorities. We will bolster the development of civil society and representative institutions that can protect fundamental human rights and improve the quality of life for all citizens, including independent and democratic unions…

"In non-democratic countries, we will work with international partners to assist the efforts of those struggling to promote peaceful political reforms. Democrats will protect American citizens abroad. We condemn the practice of unlawful detentions or imprisonment, especially of journalists and civil rights activists…"[319]

Many of the leading Democratic Party presidential candidates for 2020 are already doubling down on the issues driven by the Democratic Socialists of America and injected into the 2016 Democratic Party platform.

Indiana Mayor Pete Buttigieg has implied that only the Democratic Party position is reflective of the American people, therefore everyone is a crazy socialist.

"If we are crazy socialists, then they're saying the American people are a bunch of crazy socialists…" "Most of what we stand for, the American people stand with us, whether it's the idea that we ought to have universal healthcare or the fact that the minimum wage ought to be higher or what we think ought to happen around gun control."[320]

The Democratic Party platform of 2016 reflects the major goals and objectives of the Students for a Democratic Society (SDS), Weather Underground (WU), the Black Panther Party (BPP), the Communist Party of the United States (CPUSA), and the Democratic Socialists of America (DSA). Organizing the masses and international solidarity are a key part of accomplishing their goals.

Despite Nancy Pelosi's proclamation that the Democratic Party *is*

---

[319] Ibid. Democratic Party 2016 Platform

[320] "Buttigieg: If We're Crazy Socialists, Americans Are Too," by Sandy Fitzgerald, *Newsmax*, 7/31/2019

not under the spell of the progressives and socialists inside its corridors of power, the evidence suggests that *it is*.

The key to success for the communists and democratic socialists to gain the political power they need to fundamentally transform our constitutional republic, rests with their success at organizing the "mass movement" by building the victim classes highlighted in their manifestos and platforms. At the same time, those who refuse to yield to their ideology will be attacked and branded as racists and white supremacists.

CHAPTER FOURTEEN

International Solidarity and the Socialist Revolution

"...As democratic socialists, we believe we must also be internationalists. We believe that working people around the world have more in common with each other than they do with the bosses in their own countries." Website, Democratic Socialists of America

---

There isn't any tie that more clearly links the agenda of the Democratic Party and the ideology of the Communist Party of the United States; the Democratic Socialists of America; the Weather Underground; and Black Panther Party of the 1960's and 1970's than international solidarity.

In the flooring business, the supporting layer of sub- flooring to a main floor of a structure is called the underlayment. Regardless of how shiny and sturdy the main flooring might look, if the underlayment is faulty, the main floor will collapse. International solidarity is the underlayment that ties international progressive organizations and their "democratic socialist" ideology to America's Democratic Party.

Democratic Party politicians and organizations within Congress, such as the Congressional Black Caucus and the Congressional Progressive Caucus, operate under the banner of global climate change, international labor, and a range of other initiatives. These are arguably viewed as part of the globalist movement. In five decades, the communist-minded ideology, under the cloak of international solidarity and democratic socialism, has attached itself to the Democratic Party.

When Democratic Party presidential candidates scream racism and white supremacy, police brutality and oppression, it's the sound of the underlayment giving way, and the main floor collapsing. The communist-minded revolutionaries are now the underlayment of the Democratic Party. Whether they collapse the Democratic Party or America first, is in the hands of the voters in 2020.

Communist- minded governments have long deployed the clenched fist radical as a symbol of the solidarity between government, the workers, and their unions. In today's world, communist governments and their intelligence services have once again raised the clenched fists and reissued the battle cries and slogans of past decades to influence a new generation of American youth and minorities who view themselves as oppressed masses.

With help from some of America's own political leaders, Cuba, China, Russia and Iran, target technology, military secrets, government employees, and emigre communities inside the United States. They target politicians and their staffs as well. The battle over ideology to influence public policy is every bit as important as the battle for unlocking the most sensitive secrets of the Pentagon.

Efforts to influence public perception inside America can grow deep roots and take a human lifetime to fully develop. There is no intelligence service in the world with the patience of China's Ministry of State Security. Operations to recruit an American politician as an "agent of influence" can easily begin in one decade and continue into the next. China's quest to subvert America's political system, steal our technology, compromise our military advantage, and paint a benign picture of its own intentions is never ending.

The Black Panther Party (BPP) Gains Credibility as China and Cuba Recognize Black Power in the U.S.

China's early recognition of Huey Newton and his Black Panther Party, and Mao Zedong's invitation to Newton to visit China in 1971, continues to help China exert influence inside America's Black Power movement today.

One former Black Panther Party member described the importance of the Chinese relationship at the height of the Black Power movement in America, "the Black Panther Party (BPP) has always had an international outlook and believed in worldwide revolution. It was a monumental event for The People's Republic of China to recognize the Black Panther Party in solidarity and to invite Huey P. Newton to visit."[321]

In *Panther on the Prowl,* Elbert, "Big Man" Howard, a Black Panther Party member for twelve years, wrote that solidarity with other revolutionary and progressive groups worldwide, contributed to the Party's influence at home:

"As the Black Panther Party (BPP) developed in the Black Community of Oakland, it also became known across America and the world. As our impact became effective, we started to receive correspondence from countries around the world. Many groups such as student, labor, and political organizations sent letters of support and invitations to come and speak in their countries. One of our first invitations outside of the U.S. came from an international labor party in Montreal, Canada,

---

[321] "Huey P. Newton Returns from China - 1971," by Billy X, Black Panther Party Legacy and Alumni

as a Solidarity Group... many... groups who were in protest; students, women, labor organizations, all who showed solidarity with the BPP... Working in solidarity made some of it happen."[322]

When he returned from his China travels, Huey Newton wrote observations on the ten days he spent as a personal guest of the People's Republic. His words became the topic of a video, *"China, Huey P. Newton's Account,"* by Dr. Huey P. Newton. In telling his story, Newton heaped praise on the Chinese people and their government, while condemning the oppression of black Americans by an imperialist United States. Newton's words reflect a heavy reliance on international solidarity as integral to the coming revolution in America.

"...What is important is the effect that China and its society had on me- and that impression is unforgettable. While there, I achieved a psychological liberation I had never experienced before. It was not simply that I felt at home in China. The reaction was deeper than that. What I experienced was a sensation of freedom, as if a great weight had been lifted from my soul, and I was able to be myself without defense or pretense or the need for explanation...

"I feel absolutely free for the first time in my life. Completely free among my fellow man, this experience of freedom had a profound effect on me, because it confirmed my belief that an oppressed people can be liberated if their leaders persevere in raising their consciousness and in struggling relentlessly against the oppressor."

"The behavior of the police in China was a revelation to me. They are there to protect and help the people, not to oppress them. Their courtesy was genuine. No division or suspicion exists between them and the citizens. This impressed me so much, that when I returned to the United States and was met by the tactical squad at the San Francisco airport, they had been called out because nearly a thousand people came to the airport to welcome us back, it was brought home to me all over again that the police in our country are an occupying and oppressive force...

---

[322] "Panther on the Prowl," by Elbert "Big Man" Howard, Black Panther Party Legacy and Alumni

"…As we crossed into China, the border guards held their automatic rifles in the air as a signal of welcome and well wishing… the Chinese truly live by the slogan political power grows out of the barrel of a gun and their behavior truly reminds you of that… for the first time I did not feel threatened by a uniformed person with a weapon… the soldiers were there to protect the citizenry…

"… Everywhere we went large groups of people greeted us with applause…at every airport thousands of people welcomed us applauding, waving their little red books and carrying signs that read, 'we support the Black Panther Party, down with imperialism, we support the American people…but the Nixon imperialist regime must be overthrown…'

"…The press was constantly after us to find out why we had come… A Canadian reporter would not leave my table…I ordered him to leave… Second later, the Chinese comrades arrived with the police and asked if I wanted him arrested. I said no, I only wanted them to leave my table. After that we stayed in a protective villa with the Red Army honor guide outside… this was another strange sensation… to have the police on our side. We did have two meetings with premier Chou-En Lai… we discussed world affairs, oppressed people in general and black people in particular…

"…Everything I saw in China demonstrated that the People's Republic is a free and liberated territory with a socialist government…the way is open for people to gain their freedom and determine their own destiny… It was an amazing experience to see and practice a revolution that is going forward at such a rapid rate… to see a classless society in operation is unforgettable… here Marxist dictum, 'from each according to his abilities to each according to his needs is in operation…'"[323]

China wasn't alone in extending the clenched fist of solidarity and encouragement to the Black Panther Party. The Panthers found enduring soul mates in Fidel Castro and his Cuban revolution. Castro's over-

---

[323] "China, Huey P. Newton's Account of his Visit to China During the GPCR, "You Tube, 7/2/2019

throw of the government of Fulgencio Batista in 1958 was an inspiration for the Black Panther's own struggle inside the United States. Castro and the Panthers found a common ideology in their love of Marx and Lenin, as well as their belief that America was an imperialist and oppressive country.

As law enforcement authorities in the United States tightened dragnets on Newton, Eldridge Cleaver, the Black Panther Party Information Minister, and Angela Davis, for their involvement in violent crimes committed in America, Castro gave them sanctuary inside Cuba. Even with Fidel Castro's death, Cuba continues to provide sanctuary to cop-killing fugitive Joanne Chesimard, a former member of the Black Liberation Army, who has changed her name to Assata Olugbala Shakur.

When Barack Obama declared a normalizing of relations with Cuba in 2014, Shakur stayed put, depriving the family of New Jersey State Trooper Werner Foerster of justice for a father and husband who died in the line of duty at the hands of a Black Power revolutionary and terrorist.

China and Cuba cultivated the Black Power movement early on, knowing there would be dividends down the road.

- Having a relationship with Newton and people inside the movement, gave both China and Cuba important visibility worldwide when they needed it most in their struggle with the United States.

- The recognized international solidarity with China and Cuba gave stature to the Black Panther Party and leverage to the Chinese and Cubans inside America and with other progressive, leftist, communist and socialist movements in the world.

- China and Cuba sent a clear message to the United States that the Marxist communist revolution was alive and well, and its tentacles extended into the "empire."

- The Black population, at least those influenced by and reached through the Black Panther Party, were a perfect audience for the Chinese and Cuban propaganda about the wonder of communism and how it could end the racism and oppression faced by Black citizens inside America.

- On the backs of the Black Power movement, China and Cuba could build a capable, effective and far reaching intelligence network inside America for generations to come.

To the latter point, this has happened. Neither Cuba nor China gave up on the idea that a key foundation for their unique blend of intelligence and subversion would be the Black Power movement. The investments they made in the early 1970's are paying off today. *"Struggles," "white nationalism," "oppression," "racism," "equality," "police brutality," "imperialism," "white supremacy," "socialism," "democratic socialism," "empire," "racist government," "white racist government," "sexism," "anti-imperialist," anti-capitalist,"* are all words of the revolution designed to reach not only black Americans, but white, Hispanic, Asian, gay, straight, the young, the old, and every other individual living in America who feels disadvantaged and oppressed by capitalism.

International Women's Day as a Symbol of International Solidarity and the "Movement"

The Communist Party of the United States embraces international solidarity in all its forms and claims credit for, "organizing workers to fight for their interests and struggling to win socialism in the United States."[324]

Celebrating one hundred years of existence in the United States, the Communist Party has highlighted its support for international solidarity across the world and inside the country:

"Communists helped lead the student free speech movement and

---

[324] Communist Party USA: by People's World Editorial Board, 100 years in struggle for peace, democracy, socialism August 30, 2019

the anti-Vietnam War movement in the 1960s and early '70s. They also spearheaded the campaign to free Angela Davis, Rev. Benjamin Chavis Jr., and all political prisoners, working as part of the National Alliance Against Racist and Political Repression (NAARPR) during that period."[325]

Even International Women's Day is a favorite worker's holiday and day of celebration for socialists and communists across the world, specifically symbolizing international solidarity and women's suffrage.

"International Women's Day...calls us to celebrate—and to advance—the leadership of women in the fight for a better world. Today, women are leading major struggles for democracy and equality–from the movement for Black lives, to the teachers' and fast food workers' strikes that are redefining the labor movement; from the Water Protectors of Standing Rock, to the Women's Marches against the Trump regime; from protecting the rights of immigrants, to joining the ranks of progressive candidates, to breaking the silence on rape culture and violence against women.

"When the men kill," wrote German revolutionary Clara Zetkin, "it is up to us women to fight for the preservation of life." She wrote those words in 1914, when the leaders of the Socialist International had betrayed the working-class cause by joining in the war effort alongside the capitalists of their nations.

"Today her words resonate in a larger sense. Amidst a deepening capitalist crisis, escalating imperialist aggression, and the rise of the fascist right, women are leading the struggle for an equitable, sustainable, socialist future for the human race."[326]

International Women's Day is celebrated as an official holiday in Afghanistan, Armenia, Azerbaijan, Belarus, Burkina Faso, Cambodia, China (for women only), Cuba, Georgia, Guinea-Bissau, Eritrea, Ka-

---

[325]   "Communist Party USA: 100 years in struggle for peace, democracy, socialism," People's World, August 30, 2019

[326]   "Statement of the Communist Party, USA on International Women's Day," by Communist Party USA, cups.org 3/8/2018

zakhstan, Kyrgyzstan, Laos, Madagascar (for women only), Moldova, Mongolia, Montenegro, Nepal (for women only), Russia, Tajikistan, Turkmenistan, Uganda, Ukraine, Uzbekistan, Vietnam and Zambia. [327]

Today's Democratic Party now regards International Women's Day as a key moment in America's war against sexism. Just as the Weather Underground did when it called out International Women's Day as one of its weapons of resistance to topple the United States government in the 1970s.

Linda Sarsour, in a speech at the Women's Day March on Washington, January 21, 2017, pointed to the Resistance as a strategy directed at the election and inauguration of President Donald Trump:

"...My name is Linda Sarsour, and I am one of the national co-chairs for the Women's March on Washington. I stand here before you, unapologetically Muslim American, unapologetically Palestinian American; unapologetically from Brooklyn New York.

"Sisters and brothers, you are what democracy looks like. Sisters and brothers, you are my hope for my community.

"I will respect the presidency, but I will not respect this president of the United States of America. I will not respect an administration that won an election on the backs of Muslims and black people and undocumented people and Mexicans and people with disabilities and on the backs of women..."[328]

The Women's March, International Women's Day celebrations and *"systemic change"* are bound by the ideology of communism. But now mainstream, and so-called moderate Democrats, are linked to the same ideology.

In 2017 Senator Diane Feinstein delayed a vote on Jeff Sessions' nomination as Attorney General because of the Women's March. The nomination of Sessions by President Trump is, "a very big deal," Fein-

---

stein announced to the country. She continued by saying that Sessions, "must be a zealous advocate for the American people. All the American people...the least we can do is tell marchers we'll be as careful as possible about who we put in place to make these decisions..." [329]

Senator Feinstein made it sound as if Linda Sarsour and Angela Davis were representative of all the American people. That's highly unlikely.

During an interview in 2019, Sarsour provided her thinking regarding United States policy towards Israel, "This sentiment of ending occupation in Palestine, of supporting Boycott, Divestment, Sanctions (BDS), or at least at the minimum, the right for people to engage in Boycott, Divestment, Sanctions, the idea that being a staunch critic of the state of Israel does not equal being anti-Semitic. This is just mainstream now."[330]

A research study by Israel's Strategic Affairs Ministry concluded that:

"There are more than 100 links between the internationally-designated terrorist organizations Hamas and the Popular Front for the Liberation of Palestine (PFLP) with NGOs promoting the anti-Israel Boycott, Divestment and Sanctions (BDS) movement, some of which receive funding from European states and philanthropic funds..."

"Public Security Minister Gilad Erdan said the research 'reveals the true nature and goals of the BDS movement and its connection to terrorism and antisemitism.'

"'When people talk about the goals of the BDS movement, they don't bother to read official statements from its leaders,'" 'If you do, it becomes clear that the goals of its leaders are the same as those of the leaders of Palestinian terror organizations. BDS rejects Israel's right to exist as a Jewish state within any borders. They want to see Israel wiped

---

[329] "Feinstein delays Sessions' vote in name of Women's March on Washington," by Kelly Cohen, Washington Examiner, January 24, 2017

[330] "The Orwellian Universe of Linda Sarsour," by Steven Emerson, The Investigative Project on Terrorism News, 9/20/2019

off the map.'

"'Promoting boycotts is [just] a different means to achieve this goal.'" [331]

In a 2015 roundtable with other activists, Sarsour had this to say about solidarity and the movement:

"Organizing as a Palestinian American Muslim in the Black Lives Matter movement has been a blessing but has also brought some challenges. Building solidarity with Black communities when we as Palestinian Americans/Arab Americans have not holistically addressed anti-Black racism within our own ranks calls to question in some cases our solidarity…Solidarity is not a noun; it's a verb, its action…

"These experiences and the conversations about the clear connection between oppressed communities in the United States and Palestine are being derived through story-telling and relationship building. This struggle knows no borders and we know that all oppression is intertwined. We must continue to organize together… My investment in the Black Lives Matter movement is based on the belief that Black Liberation will lead to the liberation of all people, including Palestinians."[332]

On August 7, 1970, in a brazen and deadly daylight assault on the rule of law in America, several individuals associated with the cause of the Black Panther Party, kidnapped and murdered Superior Court Judge Harold Haley after gaining access to his courtroom at the Marin County Civic Center in Marin, California.

Jonathan Jackson entered Judge Haley's courtroom with a pistol, M1 carbine and sawed -off shotgun concealed underneath a long buttoned up raincoat. Jackson planned to force the release of his brother George from the criminal justice system. Angela Davis had purchased the shotgun at a San Francisco pawn shop and was the registered owner of all three weapons used in the subsequent attack inside the courthouse.

---

[331] "Watch: Dozens of Hamas members hold senior positions in BDS NGOs," By Lahav Harkov, The Jerusalem Post, 2/3/2019

[332] .) Roundtable on Anti-Blackness and Black-Palestinian Solidarity, by Anti-Blackness Roundtable, June 3, 2015

In the aftermath of the attack, Davis became a fugitive and had significant help as she tried to allude the FBI. "She was secreted to Chicago to meet up with fellow Communist leader David Poindexter Jr., who took her to Miami, Florida. In an effort to hide from authorities, Davis used false identification, cut off her afro, wore a wig, plucked her eyebrows, wore makeup, and donned business eyeglasses. On October 13, 1970, FBI agents found her at the Howard Johnson Motor Lodge in New York City."[333]

Two months after the attack, the same Marin County Courthouse building was bombed by the Weather Underground in retaliation for the death of Jonathan Jackson and two of his comrades.

Forty-seven years later, Angela Davis would be giving a speech at the Women's Day March:

"This is a country anchored in slavery and colonialism, which means for better or for worse the very history of the United States is a history of immigration and enslavement. Spreading xenophobia, hurling accusations of murder and rape and building walls will not erase history.

"No human being is illegal.

"The struggle to save the planet, to stop climate change, to guarantee the accessibility of water from the lands of the Standing Rock Sioux, to Flint, Michigan, to the West Bank and Gaza. The struggle to save our flora and fauna, to save the air—this is ground zero of the struggles for social justice.

"This is a women's march and this women's march represents the promise of feminism as against the pernicious powers of state violence. And inclusive and intersectional feminism that calls upon all of us to join the resistance to racism, to Islamophobia, to anti-Semitism, to misogyny, to capitalist exploitation.

"Yes, we salute the fight for 15. We dedicate ourselves to collective resistance. Resistance to the billionaire mortgage profiteers and gentrifiers. Resistance to the health care privateers. Resistance to the

---

[333]   Marin County Civic Center Attacks, Wikipedia

attacks on Muslims and on immigrants. Resistance to attacks on disabled people. Resistance to state violence perpetrated by the police and through the prison industrial complex. Resistance to institutional and intimate gender violence, especially against trans women of color.

"Women's rights are human rights all over the planet and that is why we say freedom and justice for Palestine. We celebrate the impending release of Chelsea Manning. And Oscar López Rivera. But we also say free Leonard Peltier. Free Mumia Abu-Jamal. Free Assata Shakur.

"Over the next months and years, we will be called upon to intensify our demands for social justice to become more militant in our defense of vulnerable populations. Those who still defend the supremacy of white male heteropatriarchy had better watch out."[334]

Like Senator Dick Durbin at the Haymarket rally of communists and anarchists, Senator Feinstein's treatment of Sarsour and Davis as representative of American women, is an outrage to justice and the rule of law. But international solidarity and equality will always prevail over the rule of law in a Democratic Party increasingly controlled by those who believe in the ideology of communism.

The International Committee of the Democratic Socialists of America

The Democratic Socialists of America has established an International Committee with the sole mission of developing international solidarity.

- "to connect in solidarity with like-minded activists, workers, movements and parties worldwide...we hope to contribute to international political education and to support the growth of international solidarity work in local chapters across the country. We additionally aim to support national campaigns for in-

---

[334]   "Here's the Full Transcript Of Angela Davis's Women's March Speech," by Lyndsey Matthews, Elle, 1/21/2017

ternational justice…we seek to serve as a conduit allowing comrades and interested parties from abroad to connect with DSA, either at the national or at the local level. We also hope to assist DSA leaders and membership to connect to movements and parties struggling abroad for racial, social, economic, and climate justice… we aspire to present DSA to international comrades, both in the U.S. and abroad, as the pluralistic, multi-tendency, democratic socialist organization that it is…

- "…The next step in our growth as a committee…supporting DSA as a truly internationalist democratic socialist organization…We look forward to you joining us in a solidarity that knows no borders.

- "…As democratic socialists, we believe we must also be internationalists. We believe that working people around the world have more in common with each other than they do with the bosses in their own countries. We believe that struggles ranging from peace to climate justice, from anti-racism to women's liberation, can only be won if we work together.

- "We believe that we are engaged in a common international struggle and are therefore concerned about what is happening to the working classes in other countries, about their human rights and worker's rights, about their struggles for democracy, for justice, and for socialism.

- "We often face the same enemies: multinational banks and corporations, as well as other financial, political, and military organizations. These enemies work together across borders, and to defeat them it will be necessary for us to unite in our struggle against the multifold oppressions they commit against poorer countries and the vast majority of people and our shared planet. This is why we do international work, and this is why we believe that DSA is and must always be an internationalist organization…"[335]

In its *Prairie Fire* manifesto, the Weather Underground recognized the importance of international solidarity with like-minded communist revolutionary movements. The Weather Underground's leaders were in awe of the progress of the Black Power movement in building international unity for their cause, especially with countries like Cuba and China. They understood the importance of international solidarity in bringing violence and political revolution to the United States.

In *Prairie Fire,* they analyzed the war in Vietnam through the lens of international solidarity:

"The Vietnamese built international solidarity around their struggle. They organized a broad united front against imperialism throughout the world. This international front —of which the movement in the United States is an important part- consisted of many Third World nations, the socialist countries and opposition movements within the imperialist countries. Mass anti-war movements grew, not only in the US. but in Japan. France. Great Britain, West Germany, Italy and Sweden…

"The Vietnamese say: 'if the resistance is strong, even a Hawk may be forced to withdraw. If the resistance is weak, even a Dove may be tempted to invade…

"But victory in revolution is not like the seventh game of the world series. Victory is built for over time, thru a series of successes and failures…"[336]

International Solidarity and the Democratic Party 2016 Platform

Remarkably, the Democratic Party platform for 2016 shares a number of common bonds with the *Prairie Fire* manifesto, the Commu-

---

[335] DSA International Committee, National Call to Action! DSA International, https://international.dsausa.org.

[336] Prairie Fire

nist Party of the United States and the Democratic Socialists of America, when it comes to viewing the world through the prism of international solidarity:

"Democrats believe we are stronger and safer when America brings the world together and leads with principle and purpose. We believe we should strengthen our alliances, not weaken them. We believe in the power of development and diplomacy... we know that only the United States can mobilize common action on a truly global scale, to take on the challenges that transcend borders, from international terrorism to climate change to health pandemics...

"... the Republicans... have nominated as the standard-bearer for their party and their candidate for President a man who seeks to appeal to Americans' basest differences... in 2016, the stakes can be measured in human lives—in the number of immigrants who would be torn from their homes; in the number of faithful and peaceful Muslims who would be barred from even visiting our shores...

"In Cuba, we will build on President Obama's historic opening and end the travel ban and embargo. We will also stand by the Cuban people and support their ability to decide their own future and to enjoy the same human rights and freedoms that people everywhere deserve. In Venezuela, we will push the government to respect human rights and respond to the will of its people. And in Haiti, we will support local and international efforts to bolster the country's democratic institutions and economic development...

"Africa is home to many of the fastest growing economies in the world. Democrats will strengthen our partnership and collaboration with the African Union, emphasizing trade while increasing development assistance to bolster the continent's domestic economies. We will engage our African partners on the full range of global challenges and opportunities, and we will continue to strengthen democratic institutions and human rights, fair trade and investment, development, and global health..."[337]

---

[337]   Democratic Party 2016 Platform

The Democratic Party addresses climate change in terms of global climate change and the need for international leadership to combat it:

"Climate change poses an urgent and severe threat to our national security, and Democrats believe it would be a grave mistake for the United States to wait for another nation to take the lead in combating the global climate emergency…"and even confronts head on the feeling of many Americans, including President Trump, that, "climate change is a hoax created by and for the Chinese."[338]

In the section of the platform titled, "International Labor, "the Democratic Party platform says, "we believe that we need to coordinate our economic actions with other countries to address economic insecurity, specifically youth un- and underemployment, gender inequality, the digital transformation, and the transition towards green jobs." [339]

International Solidarity and the Black Power Movement

Fred Hampton headed the Illinois chapter of the Black Panther Party. He was also the Deputy Chairman of the national Party in the late 1960's. Hampton's skills in organizing and his charismatic personality enabled him to forge an alliance between the Black Panther Party and several large Chicago street gangs, including the Young Patriots Organization and Young Lords.

Eventually, Hampton's coalition was joined by the Students for a Democratic Society, the Brown Berets, the American Indian Movement, and the Red Guard Party. Hampton called his alliance the Rainbow Coalition-a name subsequently picked up by the Reverend Jesse Jackson. when he named his own creation, Rainbow/PUSH.

In November 1969, while Hampton was in California, members of

---

[338]   Ibid

[339]   Ibid

the Illinois Black Panthers engaged in a shoot -out with the Chicago police. Two officers were killed and nine were wounded during the gun battle. Less than a month later, Chicago police raided Hampton's apartment. Hampton and another Party member were killed during the raid, and seven others were arrested. A Coroner's Jury inquest concluded the shooting deaths were justifiable homicide.

Hampton made no excuses for being a revolutionary and an activist, "we don't think you fight fire with fire best; we think you fight fire with water best. We're going to fight racism not with racism, but we're going to fight with solidarity. We say we're not going to fight capitalism with black capitalism, but we're going to fight it with socialism. We're going to fight their reactions with all of us people getting together and having an international proletarian revolution."[340]

The Reverend Jesse Jackson and Ralph Abernathy, who replaced Dr. Martin Luther King as the head of the Southern Christian Leadership Conference, gave eulogies at Hampton's funeral. Bobby Rush, the founder of the Illinois chapter of the party, and its deputy minister of defense at the time of the shooting, said the police raid was an "execution squad." [341]

In 1993 Rush was elected to represent Illinois' 1st District in the U.S. Congress. He had left the Black Panther Party in 1974, later telling *People Magazine,* "We started glorifying thuggery and drugs", and "I don't repudiate any of my involvement in the Panther party—it was part of my maturing."[342]

Congressman Rush certainly hasn't repudiated his love of the revolutionary themes that guided the Black Panther Party and today heav-

---

[340] Fred Hampton - "Political Prisoner" [1080p remastered], You Tube video, 1/6/2013

[341] Fred Hampton, Black Panther Party, COINTELPRO, Days of Rage, African American leftism, Elaine Brown, World Heritage Encyclopedia, Project Gutenberg Self-Publishing

[342] "Bobby Rush," By Super User Los Angeles Sentinel, Published January

ily influence the Democratic Party. Calling Rush, "a high -profile activist during the civil rights movement," *Politico* quoted his deep dismay at presidential candidate Joe Biden,

'You would think that after eight years of serving as Vice President under President Obama, Biden would get it, that his frame of reference would be more audacious for the future and less on the obvious incrementalism of the past...' With his statement he has demonstrated that he is wholly out of touch and woefully ignorant of the nuances of the black American experience and that is, in itself, beyond disappointing."[343]

During a radio interview, Rush gave his assessment of President Trump, calling him, "an evil man. I've never seen a man who has done so much harm to this nation." When the interviewer asked Rush to clarify between Trump's policies and his character, Rush reiterated, "Yeah, he's evil. Evil policies, he's an evil man."[344]

More recently, Chicago's Fraternal Order of Police Union mounted a protest outside the office of Cook County State's Attorney Kim Foxx over her handling of the investigation involving Empire actor Jussie Smollett. Congressman Rush jumped to her defense, declaring,

"The FOP is the sworn enemy of black people, the sworn enemy of black people... the FOP has always taken the position that black people can be shot down in the street by members of the Chicago Police Department, and suffer no consequences...let's be clear: Kim Foxx, her battle, is with the FOP and all of their cohorts."[345]

5, 2012

[343] "Bobby Rush rips Biden as 'woefully ignorant' The civil rights activist's statement to POLITICO shows how Biden is still struggling to contain the firestorm over his comments," by Laura Barron-Lopez and Marc Caputo, 06/21/2019

[344] "Chicago Congressman Bobby Rush calls President Trump 'evil'" Interview with Bill Cameron, WLS-AM News, Jan 26, 2018

[345] "Chicago's police union is 'the sworn enemy of black people,' Rep. Bob-

Foxx couldn't resist adding to the conflict, "the injection of white nationalists in this conversation for me, I will tell you personally, I was afraid.... I would certainly hope that the FOP and whatever their disagreements may be, whatever concerns that they may have about my ability or leadership, would at least expect the people of their union to not inject racism or white nationalists into the conversation."[346]

Highly influential black leaders like Bobby Rush continue to inject their communist minded ideology into today's society. They use the same revolutionary battle cries of racism and white nationalism as the Weather Underground. The police are the oppressors. American society is unjust.

Through the Congressional Black Caucus and the Congressional Progressive Caucus, they have effectively formed the alliance envisioned by the Weather Underground with the so-called "anti-racist whites," in the Democratic Party. The Black Lives Matter (BLM) organization came to life and flourished during the Obama Administration. Its goals reflect an acknowledgement of being part of a broader political revolution, just as the Weather Underground, Black Panther Party, DSA, and CPUSA envision.

For the authors of *Prairie Fire*, such an alliance was vital to building a successful revolutionary movement inside the United States-and just as important for the message it gave to other countries struggling to overcome oppressors.

As the Weather Underground fervently believed, "creation of an anti-racist white movement is the necessary foundation for the functional unity of Third World and white enemies of the empire. Anti-racist organizing and action can create this unity."

Regardless of the issues confronting America, the unity envisioned by the Weather Underground abounds within today's radical and revolutionary Democratic Party. With the election of President Barack

---

by Rush says after protest of Jussie Smollett case," by Juan Perez, Jr. 4/6/2019 Chicago Tribune

[346] Ibid

Obama, America returned to the *Days of Rage* and a resumption of the revolutionary attacks on America from the inside. After decades of making progress in race relations and a more peaceful world and watching the former Union of Soviet Socialist Republics collapse, America is now confronted by a new kind of generic, communist ideology.

The 2016 Democratic Party platform asserts, "Democrats believe that cooperation is better than conflict, unity is better than division, empowerment is better than resentment, and bridges are better than walls..." The 2020 platform will likely be even more radical in its approach to immigration reform, racism, white nationalism, and equality. [347]

This is a marked contrast from the attitude of the Democratic Party in January 2001, nine months before the international terrorist attacks on American soil. On January 31, 2001, former Democratic Senator Gary Hart and Republican Senator Warren Rudman released the report of the *"U.S. Commission on National Security/21st Century"*, also known as the *"Hart-Rudman Commission or Hart-Rudman Task Force on Homeland Security."*

Included in the report's conclusions:

"America will become increasingly vulnerable to hostile attack on our homeland, and our military superiority will not help us...All borders will be more porous; some will bend, and some will break...Fragmentation or failure of states will occur, with destabilizing effects on neighboring states...Foreign crises will be replete with atrocities and the deliberate terrorizing of civilian populations...The emerging security environment in the next quarter century will require different military and other national capabilities."[348]

Following the 9/11 attacks, Republicans and Democrats convened the bipartisan 9/11 Commission to explore and make recommendations on how the attacks happened and future attacks could be prevented.

Of note, the ensuing recommendations included broader law en-

---

[347]   Democratic Party 2016 Platform

[348]   "U.S. Commission on National Security/21st Century", 1/31/2001

forcement powers to prevent future attacks before they happen, future threats posed by Iran and the spread of "Islamic jihad," expanding efforts to protect America's borders, and the importance of spreading the word about American values, laws, and institutions to the rest of the world, with the hope they would serve as an example for freedom and liberty.

The Significance of International Solidarity to Black Lives Matter Movement

Today, Black Lives Matter describes itself as follows:

"Four years ago, what is now known as the Black Lives Matter Global Network began to organize. It started out as a chapter-based, member-led organization whose mission was to build local power and to intervene when violence was inflicted on Black communities by the state and vigilantes…In the years since, we've committed to struggling together and to imagining and creating a world free of anti-Blackness, where every Black person has the social, economic, and political power to thrive…"[349]

These are the goals of Black Lives Matter:

- "Our continued commitment to liberation for all Black people means we are continuing the work of our ancestors and fighting for our collective freedom because it is our duty.

- "Every day, we recommit to healing ourselves and each other, and to co-creating alongside comrades, allies, and family a culture where each person feels seen, heard, and supported.

- "We acknowledge, respect, and celebrate differences and commonalities. We work vigorously for freedom and justice for Black people and, by extension, all people.

---

[349]   "Black Lives Matter, What We Believe," https://blacklivesmatter. com/what-we-believe/

- "We intentionally build and nurture a beloved community that is bonded together through a beautiful struggle that is restorative, not depleting.

- "We are unapologetically Black in our positioning. In affirming that Black Lives Matter, we need not qualify our position. To love and desire freedom and justice for ourselves is a prerequisite for wanting the same for others.

- "We see ourselves as part of the global Black family, and we are aware of the different ways we are impacted or privileged as Black people who exist in different parts of the world.

- "We are guided by the fact that all Black lives matter, regardless of actual or perceived sexual identity, gender identity, gender expression, economic status, ability, disability, religious beliefs or disbeliefs, immigration status, or location.

- "We make space for transgender brothers and sisters to participate and lead.

- "We are self-reflexive and do the work required to dismantle cisgender privilege and uplift Black trans folk, especially Black trans women who continue to be disproportionately impacted by trans-antagonistic violence.

- "We build a space that affirms Black women and is free from sexism, misogyny, and environments in which men are centered.

- "We practice empathy. We engage comrades with the intent to learn about and connect with their contexts.

- "We make our spaces family-friendly and enable parents to fully participate with their children.

- "We dismantle the patriarchal practice that requires mothers to work "double shifts" so that they can mother in private even as they participate in public justice work.

- "We disrupt the Western-prescribed nuclear family structure requirement by supporting each other as extended families and "villages" that collectively care for one another, especially our children, to the degree that mothers, parents, and children are comfortable.

- "We foster a queer-affirming network. When we gather, we do so with the intention of freeing ourselves from the tight grip of heteronormative thinking, or rather, the belief that all in the world are heterosexual (unless s/he or they disclose otherwise).

- "We cultivate an intergenerational and communal network free from ageism. We believe that all people, regardless of age, show up with the capacity to lead and learn.

- "We embody and practice justice, liberation, and peace in our engagements with one another."[350]30

Along with the necessary and required updates to account for issues that didn't receive highlighting in the 1960's and 1970's, the Black Lives Matter message is one for the solidarity of the international communist movement.

- "we've committed to **struggling** together and to imagining and creating a world free of anti-Blackness;" "Our continued commitment to **liberation for all Black people**;" "co-creating alongside comrades;" "We see ourselves as part of the global Black family;" "We build a space that affirms Black women and is free from sexism, misogyny, and environments in which men are centered;" "We dis-

---

[350]   Ibid

mantle the patriarchal practice that requires mothers to work "double shifts" so that they can mother in private even as they participate in public justice work:"

- "We **disrupt the Western-prescribed nuclear family structure** requirement by supporting each other as extended families and 'villages.'" **"We cultivate an intergenerational and communal network free from ageism."**[351]

John F. Kennedy would never have dreamed that politicians of his Democratic Party would make decisions rendering America defenseless from insider subversion. President Kennedy's famous call to arms, "ask not what your country can do for you, but what you can do for your country," has been fundamentally transformed.

---

[351]　Ibid

CHAPTER FIFTEEN

The Democratic Party's Attack on America's Bill of Rights

"It would be a short war my friend. The government has nukes. Too many of them..."
Eric Swalwell

For over two hundred years, Americans have individually pursued "life, liberty and the pursuit of happiness," guaranteed by four cornerstones of freedom- the Declaration of Independence; the Constitution of the United States; the Bill of Rights; and the Rule of Law.

America was founded by people who understood that man is easily tempted by power, and that governments will eventually use their power to control others. The Declaration of Independence and U.S. Constitution codify that man is subordinate to his Creator. United States Congressmen and U.S. Senators begin their time in office taking an oath to defend our laws and way of life:

"The Senators and Representatives before mentioned, and the

Members of the several State Legislatures, and all executive and judicial officers, both of the United States and of the several States, shall be bound by Oath or Affirmation, to support this Constitution; but no religious Test shall ever be required as a Qualification to any Office or public Trust under the United States."[352]

Raising his or her right hand and taking the oath of office is the first order of business for a newly elected leader:

"I do solemnly swear (or affirm) that I will support and defend the Constitution of the United States against all enemies, foreign and domestic; that I will bear true faith and allegiance to the same; that I take this obligation freely, without any mental reservation or purpose of evasion; and that I will well and faithfully discharge the duties of the office on which I am about to enter, so help me God."[353]

The signers of the Declaration of Independence made clear, "that all men are created equal, that they are endowed by their Creator with certain unalienable rights."

The "Bill of Rights," of the Communist Party of the United States (CPUSA), declares equality to be the litmus test that determines the relationship between government and citizens. The "communist-minded men and women," of the Weather Underground of the late 1960's plotted to overthrow the government born of the Declaration of Independence. Their strategy was "resistance." Their weapons were "racism," "institutions of racism," "racism of white people," "white supremacy," "male supremacy." Their goal was replacing the constitutional Republic with a socialist government characterized by equality.

The Democratic Socialists of America believe that "we can talk seriously about the transition to democratic socialism through reforms that fundamentally undermine the power of the capitalist system (often referred to as "non-reformist reforms"), such as the nationalization of strategic industries (banking, auto, etc.) and the creation of worker-controlled investment funds (created by taxing corporate profits) that

---

[352] Article VI, U.S. Constitution

[353] Article 6, United States Constitution

will buy out capitalist stakes in firms and set up worker-owned and -operated firms on a large scale."[354]

The 2016 Democratic Party platform ("our most progressive platform in our party's history") has fully adopted major elements of the DSA and Weather Underground (WU) strategies of resistance and their weapon of choice- racism:

"Democrats will fight to end institutional and systemic racism in our society. We will challenge and dismantle the structures that define lasting racial, economic, political, and social inequity. Democrats will promote racial justice through fair, just, and equitable governing of all public-serving institutions and in the formation of public policy. Democrats support removing the Confederate battle flag from public properties, recognizing that it is a symbol of our nation's racist past that has no place in our present or our future. We will push for a societal transformation to make it clear that black lives matter and that there is no place for racism in our country."[355]

The Democratic Party's aggressive push for expanding government programs in areas that touch critical aspects of our lives, along with the Green New Deal, will "fundamentally undermine the power of the capitalist system," just as the Democratic Socialists of America have said they want to do.

The Democratic Party will address "today's extreme levels of income and wealth inequality," by "empowering the United States Postal Service to facilitate the delivery of basic banking services;" taking from one set of Americans and redistributing their wealth to another by, "establishing a multimillionaire surtax to ensure millionaires and billionaires pay their fair share."[356]

The Democratic Party will double up on the Democratic Socialists

---

[354] "Resistance Rising: Socialist Strategy in the Age of Political Revolution, Democratic Socialists of America (DSA) 6/25/2016

[355] Democratic Party 2016 platform

[356] Ibid. Democratic Party 2016 platform

of America wish to nationalize strategic industries, such as banking. They've already started. Referring to the United States Postal Service (USPS) as a "national treasure," their platform includes, "offering basic financial services such as paycheck cashing and removing statutory restraints on services the USPS may offer. It also includes promoting vote-by-mail to increase voter participation and to help address the scourge of voter suppression."[357]

They even have a back-up plan to ensure success, regardless of the outcome of Postal Service banking:

"Democrats will also create an independent, national infrastructure bank that will support critical infrastructure improvements. This bank will provide loans and other financial assistance for investments in energy, water, broadband, transportation, and multi-modal infrastructure projects.

"Democrats will continue to support the interest tax exemption on municipal bonds and will work to establish a permanent version of Build America Bonds as an additional tool to encourage infrastructure investment by state and local governments."[358]

Why does the Democratic Party believe they should exert the influence and power of the United States government into every key aspect of our lives?

"We know that there are barriers standing in the way of that goal, from the enduring scourge of systemic racism to our deeply broken immigration system to discrimination against people on the basis of sexual orientation or gender identity—and we are committed to facing those problems and fixing them. Being stronger together means reaching communities that have been left out and left behind for too long, from coal country to Indian Country to neighborhoods held back by multigenerational poverty..."[359]

---

[357]   Ibid.

[358]   Ibid. Democratic Party 2016 platform.

[359]   Ibid. Democratic Party platform.

The Democratic Party's Great Society has been the blueprint for five decades to address "multigenerational poverty" by redistributing money, using the United States government as a conduit for growing social programs. And yet today, the Democratic Party admits we have "extreme levels of income and wealth inequality."[360]

"In his January 1964 State of the Union address, President Lyndon Johnson proclaimed, 'This administration today, here and now, declares unconditional war on poverty in America.' In the 50 years since that time, U.S. taxpayers have spent over $22 trillion on anti-poverty programs. Adjusted for inflation, this spending (which does not include Social Security or Medicare) is three times the cost of all U.S. military wars since the American Revolution..." the War on Poverty has failed completely. In fact, a significant portion of the population is now less capable of self-sufficiency than it was when the War on Poverty began."[361]

President Lyndon Johnson was a Democrat. His Great Society didn't eliminate poverty, but today's Democrats want voters to restructure America, installing an even bigger, more powerful government to ensure that all men are created with equality- at the expense of "life, liberty, and the pursuit of happiness."

The 2016 Democratic Party platform and most of the Democrats running for president, have made equality, attacking police as racist, free health care and education, the foundation of their campaigns. Capitalism and those they consider wealthy are their targets.

It's important to keep the definition of communism in mind when Democrats continue their discussion of equality in America.

"Though the term "communism" can refer to specific political parties, at its core, communism is an ideology of economic equality through the elimination of private property. The beliefs of communism, most famously expressed by Karl Marx, center on the idea that inequality and

---

[360]   Ibid.

[361]   "The War on Poverty After 50 Years," by Rachel Sheffield and Robert Rector, The Heritage Foundation, September 15, 2014

suffering result from capitalism...

"Historically, such communist revolutions have never yielded their intended utopias of equality. Communist theory predicts that, after the proletariat revolution, special leaders must temporarily take control of the state, leading it toward an eventual "true" communist society. Thus, the governments of the Soviet Union, communist China, Cuba and others were intended to be provisional. In practice, these "temporary" governments have held on to power, often subjecting their citizens to authoritarian control...

"Communist ideology also states that these revolutions should spread across the globe, rather than be limited to individual countries. This helps explain the historical antagonism between capitalist and communist nations — particularly the long Cold War between the United States and the Soviet Union."[362]

Here are a few examples of equality in the minds of Democratic Party presidential Candidates. Their campaign themes, based on equality, have little to do with one of America's most precious tenets-the belief that "all men are created equal," and guaranteed the right to "life, liberty, and the pursuit of happiness."

Beto O'Rourke has focused his sights on another segment of the masses-the LGBTQ community. His webpage is titled, "LGBTQ + Equality." In a section on "Legislative Action to Ensure Full Equality," O'Rourke uses all the right words to cover the issues the Democrats are using to replace our constitutional Republic with a socialist democracy.[363]

He wants Congress to "ensure that every person in our country is safe and respected." He urges passage of an Equality Act to ensure that, "all LGBTQ+ people may fully participate in public life without discrimination in employment, housing, and access to public spaces and

---

[362] "What is Communism?" by Michael Dhar, *LiveScience,* 1/30/2014.

[363] "LGBTQ + Equality," Beto O'Rourke, June 12, 2019

services, such as retail stores and banking services."[364]

O'Rourke's equality plan wouldn't be complete without including criminal justice reform and specifically, "holding police accountable for unlawful actions against the LGBTQ+ community."[365]

O'Rourke's plans for equality also involve a global reach. An entire section of his plan is referred to as, "Protect the LGBTQ+ Community Across the Globe." This initiative would involve improving, "the process for LGBTQ+ refugees and asylum seekers; "working with allies to secure a global treaty through the International Law Commission of the United Nations;" investing in "the Global Equality Fund;" and establishing "a Special Envoy for the Human Rights of LGBTQ+ people within the Department of State."[366]

Several candidates have been critical of the Electoral College. The Electoral College process has become a focus of the Democratic Party's campaign to transform America from a constitutional Republic to a socialist democracy. The party's plan to appeal to carefully developed victim classes (the masses), capture the political heart of America's cities (sanctuary policies), and encourage unlimited immigration over porous borders (granting rights and privileges such as voting to illegal immigrants) is not working fast enough, or proving effective enough, for the Democrats to achieve a political revolution.

They must attack the electoral process to achieve their political revolution. *Fortune* presented the argument for and against: "Why Democrats Want to Abolish the Electoral College—and Republicans Want to Keep It."

"...During a CNN town hall last month, Massachusetts Sen. Elizabeth Warren endorsed eliminating the Electoral College, "my view is that every vote matters. And that means get rid of the Electoral College," she said...

---

[364]   Ibid. O'Rourke

[365]   Ibid. O'Rourke

[366]   Ibid. O'Rourke

"Pete Buttigieg told *The Washington Post,* "It's gotta go. We need a national popular vote."

Beto O'Rourke said "there's a lot of wisdom" in eliminating the Electoral College.

Sen. Kamala D. Harris told Jimmy Kimmel she's "open to the discussion."

"When reached for comment, Miramar, Florida. Mayor Wayne Messam called the Electoral College "an imperfect attempt to provide representation for the states…"

The opposing view is presented by Fortune, "the desire to abolish the Electoral College is driven by the idea Democrats want rural America to go away politically,' Senator Lindsey Graham of South Carolina said on Twitter…"

"Some Republicans say that smaller states and more rural states will have less influence in elections that rely only on the popular vote. But these states already have little power under the current system…

"…Other defenders have argued that doing away with the Electoral College would put white Americans at a disadvantage, a far-right talking point. Former Maine Gov. Paul LePage argued along these lines earlier this year, and suggested big states like California, Florida, and Texas would have more power in deciding the president. 'It's only going to be the minorities that would elect,' he said in an interview."[367]

When looked at in the context of the broader strategy of resistance by the Democratic Party-it becomes obvious that the passion about all things Donald Trump, is in reality a desire to transform America into a socialist democracy. Attacking the nomination of Judge Kavanaugh, the Electoral College, President Donald Trump, those who are opposed to sanctuary cities and illegal immigration, are all positions guided by the Democratic Party push towards a democratic socialist America-to be followed by the communist utopia of which all socialists dream.

President Trump's election obstructed the dream. Part of the plan to get the dream back on track is to terminate the Electoral College. If

---

[367] "Why Democrats Want to Abolish the Electoral College—and Republicans Want to Keep It," by Erin Corbett, *Fortune,* 4/2/2019.

that were to happen, America might never again see a Republican president and the coastal cities will determine who has power and who runs things in the United States. In all but words, the constitutional Republic of United States of America would cease to exist.

The CPUSA and the Democratic Party Unite to "Restructure" the U.S. Government

The Democratic Party has many allies in its quest to transform the United States into a socialist democracy. One of those allies is the Communist Party of the United States (CPUSA)

With high hopes for what some day might happen, the Communist Party has prepared the "Socialist Bill of Rights." The words and ideas presented in the document have an eerie resemblance to the Democratic Party platform of 2016.

"WE MAKE IT ...

"Right now, 99% of Americans share the work of producing all of the products and services of our economy. We work together in person or online. We work in factories and offices. We work in schools and stores. We work in laboratories and in hospitals. And, we work on farms and construction sites.

"THEY TAKE IT!

"But, when it comes to reaping the rewards of this collective labor, things get turned upside down. What the joint labor of millions of Americans has produced ends up being owned by a handful of billionaires. Those same billionaires, without any say-so by the American people, make all the decisions. THEY get to decide to cut pensions, close schools, ship jobs overseas, and pollute the environment.

"A BETTER WORLD IS POSSIBLE!

"In a socialist economy, things get turned right side up. The ownership and control of the means of production would be in the hands of those who do the work. As a result, those of us who produce – the 99% – would make these important decisions together. This would correspond to the way we produce the wealth together.

"WE MUST PUT PEOPLE –AND OUR PLANET – BEFORE PROFITS

"With the people in the driver's seat, corporate profits would no longer be Number One. Instead, the things the American people think are most important would come first. Enough resources would be freed up to do many things. We could fully fund public education and health care for all. We could have mass transit, Social Security, free college tuition, and childcare. At the same time, we could remove lead from our pipes. We, the American people, could set other priorities, too.

"SOCIALISM = 'LIFE, LIBERTY, AND THE PURSUIT OF HAPPINESS'

"In a socialist society, people would get paid for the hard work they do. They would be rewarded for the initiatives they take. The difference? Corporate big shots and hedge fund managers could no longer walk off with trillions of dollars that belong to working families.

"War, racism, sexism, and homophobia would lose their corporate sponsors. We could apply the full power of American ingenuity and technology to reversing climate change and developing green industries. America's rich and diverse heritage could flourish in music and literature. Sports, dance, film, and art would be available to everyone.

"Opportunities would open up for millions of young people to contribute their talents and energy. This would result in well-paying and satisfying careers for our nation's youth. Small businesses would have a role to play in building this vibrant economy. They would be protected from the unfair advantages given to big corporations.

"BILL OF RIGHTS UNDER SOCIALISM

"Socialism in the United States would be built on the strong foundation of our Constitution's Bill of Rights. This includes making the promises of freedom of speech, freedom of religion, and equality for all real. The rights to a job, to health care, and education must also be guaranteed by the Constitution. The criminal justice, police and prison systems must be overhauled from top to bottom to get rid of racial disparity.

"VOTING RIGHTS FOR PEOPLE, NOT FOR CORPORATIONS

"A fairer political system goes hand-in-hand with a socialist economy. To work effectively, socialism needs the active and informed participation of the American people. The American people already agree that corporate money must be barred from corrupting our election system.

"Ten million undocumented workers are a part of our country's working class. They must be welcomed to participate as citizens in a socialist democracy. By the same token, the voting rights of millions of incarcerated Americans – mostly African Americans and Latinos – must be restored.

"In place of voter suppression laws, fair election processes are needed. Universal voter participation is the basis of democracy.

"In both open and hidden ways, racial inequality and sexism are built into the structure of our nation's capitalist economy and society. Rooting it out is a task for the entire American people. That's the only way we can build the unity that we need. It is this unity that will give us the power to build a just and democratic society for every one of us and for future generations. A socialist society also needs checks and balances.

"Organizations at the grassroots level can make sure there are democratic controls. Our country already has great traditions of grassroots organizations: town-hall meetings, tribal councils, and student governments. Our working class has gained valuable experience in operating labor unions, cooperatives, and credit unions. At a local level Americans contribute their talents in PTAs, churches, and charitable organizations.

"WE HAVE A VISION

"Building on this expertise and experience, Americans can have the confidence that together we can build a political and economic system of the people, by the people, and for the people. The unity of America's working people – African American and white, Latino, Asian, Indian and Middle Eastern – is critical to our progress.

"Men and women, LGBTQ and straight, young and old must stand together for each other. This unity cannot be broken if it is based on the working -class principle of "an injury to one is an injury to all."

"This is our vision of a socialist USA."

Democratic Party presidential contenders and other influential Democrats started attacking the Bill of Rights even before the presidential election season was underway.

When Russell Vought was President Trump's nominee to be Deputy Director of the White House Office of Management and Budget, Senator Bernie Sanders attacked his religious beliefs without shame during a public hearing:

"Sanders: Let me get to this issue that has bothered me and bothered many other people. And that is in the piece that I referred to that you wrote for the publication called Resurgent. You wrote, "Muslims do not simply have a deficient theology. They do not know God because they have rejected Jesus Christ, His Son, and they stand condemned." Do you believe that that statement is Islamophobic?

"Vought: Absolutely not, Senator. I'm a Christian, and I believe in a Christian set of principles based on my faith. That post, as I stated in the questionnaire to this committee, was to defend my alma mater, Wheaton College, a Christian school that has a statement of faith that includes the centrality of Jesus Christ for salvation, and . . .

"Sanders: I apologize. Forgive me, we just don't have a lot of time. Do you believe people in the Muslim religion stand condemned...? Is that your view?"

"Vought: Again, Senator, I'm a Christian, and I wrote that piece in accordance with the statement of faith at Wheaton College:

"Sanders: I understand that. I don't know how many Muslims there are in America.

Maybe a couple million. Are you suggesting that all those people stand condemned? What about Jews? Do they stand condemned too?

"Vought: Senator, I'm a Christian . . .

"Sanders (shouting): I understand you are a Christian, but this country is made of people who are not just — I understand that Christianity is the majority religion, but there are other people of different religions in this country and around the world. In your judgment, do you think that people who are not Christians, are going to be condemned?"

"Vought: Thank you for probing on that question. As a Christian, I believe that all individuals are made in the image of God and are worthy of dignity and respect regardless of their religious beliefs. I believe that as a Christian that's how I should treat all individuals . . .

"Sanders: You think your statement that you put into that publication, they do not know God because they rejected Jesus Christ, His Son, and they stand condemned, do you think that's respectful of other religions?

"Vought: Senator, I wrote a post based on being a Christian and attending a Christian school that has a statement of faith that speaks clearly in regard to the centrality of Jesus Christ in salvation.

"Sanders: I would simply say, Mr. Chairman, that this nominee is really not someone who this country is supposed to be about?"[368]

Sanders isn't alone. Hawaiian Senator Mazie Hirono, asked President Trump's nominee for a Federal Court judgeship, Brian Buescher about his membership in a Catholic organization, the Knights of Columbus, and whether it would impact his decisions on abortion, "if confirmed, do you intend to end your membership with this organization to avoid any appearance of bias?"[369]

---

[368] "Watch Bernie Sanders Attack a Christian Nominee and Impose an Unconstitutional Religious Test for Public Office," by David French, National Review, 6/7/2017

[369] "Democrats Accused of 'Anti-Catholic Bigotry' by Knights of Columbus

In a series of written follow up questions from the same hearing, Presidential candidate Kamala Harris questioned Buescher about his religious beliefs:

"Since 1993, you have been a member of the Knights of Columbus, an all-male society comprised primarily of Catholic men. In 2016, Carl Anderson, leader of the Knights of Columbus, described abortion as 'a legal regime that has resulted in more than 40 million deaths.' Mr. Anderson went on to say that 'abortion is the killing of the innocent on a massive scale.' Were you aware that the Knights of Columbus opposed a woman's right to choose when you joined the organization?

"Harris wasn't finished. Follow-ups included 'Were you aware that the Knights of Columbus opposed marriage equality when you joined the organization?' and 'Have you ever, in any way, assisted with or contributed to advocacy against women's reproductive rights?'[370]

Senator Dianne Feinstein, who many think of as a Democratic Party moderate, engaged in the same religious attacks on President Trump's nominee, Amy Coney Barrett. for another judicial position. Barrett, who is Catholic, listened as a United States Senator, who has taken an oath of office to preserve, defend and protect the Constitution of the United States, publicly assailed her religious beliefs.

'The dogma lives loudly within you,' Feinstein asserted. She went on: 'Dogma and law are two different things. I think whatever a religion is, it has its own dogma. The law is totally different...' "Why is it that so many of us on this side have this very uncomfortable feeling?' she asked."[371]

United States Congressman Eric Swalwell actively supports a ban on the possession of military-style semiautomatic assault weapons.

Over Trump Judicial Nominee Questioning," by Nicole Goodkind, *Newsweek*, 12/24/2018

[370] Ibid. *Newsweek*

[371] "The Dogma Lives Loudly Within You and that's a Concern," C-Span Video of Congressional Hearing, *The Washington Post,* 9/7/2017

Swalwell believes that the government should buy back these weapons and/or actively encourage people to turn them in. For those who decide against turning their weapons into the government, Swalwell supports searches, seizures, arrests, and criminal prosecution of those refusing to abide by any law which would ban them.

Getting into an online Twitter battle with an opponent of Swalwell's position, who told the congressman such a move would start a war, Swalwell fired back, "… And it would be a short war my friend. The government has nukes. Too many of them. But they're legit." Swalwell later claimed he was joking, but his joke is irrelevant.[372]

The clear implication Swalwell conveyed to an American citizen was that the government is far stronger than all of us. The government, if run by the Democratic Party, will use that power on anyone who contests the coming *"fundamental transformation."* The transformation will involve a frontal assault on America's Bill of Rights.

The Democratic Party is also involved in a series of wide -ranging attacks on the Rule of Law in America, creating "sanctuary cities," releasing thousands of prisoners convicted of violent crimes, changing guidelines for criminal conduct, modifying definitions for the elements of a crime that constitute a felony, and specifically targeting the systemic racism of the American police.

The Presidential Administration of Barack Obama and his Vice-President, Joe Biden can take direct responsibility for unleashing this assault, based directly on the dogma of the Weather Underground and the Black Panther Party.

Presidential candidate Joe Biden is eager and ready to continue these unfounded attacks. He has explained his approach to the criminal justice system and America's police on his campaign website.

"Expand and use the power of the U.S. Justice Department to address systemic misconduct in police departments and prosecutors' offices. Using authority in legislation spearheaded by Biden as senator, the

---

[372] "That time Eric Swalwell threatened to go nuclear on gun owners. Literally," by Becket Adams, *Washington Examiner*, 7/8/2019.

Obama-Biden Justice Department used pattern-or-practice investigations and consent decrees to address circumstances of "systemic police misconduct" and to "restore trust between police and communities in cities such as Ferguson."[373]

Wide-ranging attacks on the beliefs that underscore the Declaration of Independence, the Constitution of the United States, Bill of Rights, and Rule of Law in America, are consistent with the Democratic Party's intent to replace our constitutional Republic with socialist democracy. The incremental installation of a communist utopia guided by a Socialist Bill of Rights will follow. An all- powerful U.S. Government will make certain "equality" works- by controlling all aspects of our lives.

ELECTORAL COLLEGE NO LONGER WORKS

---

[373] "Joe Biden's Criminal Justice Policy," joebiden.com

CHAPTER SIXTEEN

Incremental Communism-the Strategy of Today's Democratic Party

---

"The ongoing attack on our constitutional republic is a direct result of the imposition of incremental communism reflected in the ideas and policies of today's Democratic Party."
Brian Shepherd, retired FBI agent

The language in the Weather Underground's *Prairie Fire* leaves little doubt about the goals of 1970's *"communist-minded"* men and women, who claimed credit for at least twenty bombings directed at U.S. Government and other targets during four years between 1970 and 1974.

"...We need strategy. We need to battle for a correct ideology and win people over. In this way we create the conditions for the development of a successful revolutionary movement and party. We need a revolutionary communist party in order to lead the struggle, give coherence and direction to the fight, seize power and build the new society. Getting from here to there is a process of coming together in a disciplined way around ideology and strategy... mobilizing a base among the US people, building principled relationships to Third World struggle, and accumulating practice in struggle against US imperialism."[374]

The Black Panther Party's *Ten Point Plan*, by co-founders Huey Newton and Bobby Seale, stressed how far the Black Power revolutionaries were willing to go with their demands on the United States. Recall that Huey Newton described the Panthers as Maoist/Leninist communists who desired to collapse the United States Government.

"...We believe that this racist government has robbed us, and now we are demanding the overdue debt of forty acres and two mules... We will accept the payment in currency which will be distributed to our many communities...we feel that this is a modest demand that we make."[375].

The alliance formed by black extremists and "anti-racist" white revolutionaries was forged to bring down the United States Government forty-five years ago. The heirs of that revolution have found a "strategy," "a correct ideology," are "mobilizing a base among the US people," "building principled relationships to the Third World struggle," and "demanding the overdue debt."

Describing themselves as activists, progressives, and democratic socialists, the true believers in the ideology of communism do their work inside government as elected Congressmen and women in the

---

[374] "Prairie Fire: The Politics of Revolutionary Anti-Imperialism: Political Statement of the Weather Underground, July 1974," for the Weather Underground by Bernardine Dohrn, Billy Ayers, Jeff Jones, Celia Sojourn, published and copyrighted by Communication Company.

[375] Marxist History: USA: Black Panther Party, The Ten Point Program, Huey P. Newton, October 15, 1966 (from the *War Against the Panthers*).

House of Representatives and United States Senate. Many are endorsed, and assisted in their elections, by the Communist Party of the United States. Retired FBI Agent Brian Shephard, who worked Soviet counter-intelligence and the Communist Party of the United States in the FBI's New York City office throughout the 1970's and 1980's, calls the ongoing attack on our constitutional Republic incremental communism.

The following is illustrative of the daily activities that have consumed elected Democratic Party officials endorsed by the Communist Party of the United States of America (CPUSA), and Democratic Socialists of America.

Raul Grijalva

Raul Grijalva is a Democratic Party Congressman from Arizona's 3rd District.

"Arizona Rep. Raul Grijalva, the ranking Democrat on the House Natural Resources Committee recently caused a stir by sending letters to seven university presidents seeking background information on scientists and professors who had given congressional testimony that failed to endorse what is the conventional wisdom in some quarters regarding climate change...

"Though the congressman lacked legal authority to demand information, his aggressive plan which came to light in late February, should not be a surprise at a time when power holders from the White House on down are employing similar means against perceived enemies...[376].

"Mr. Grijalva left a clue about how he operates in 2013 when the magazine In These Times asked about his legislative strategy. 'I'm a Saul Alinsky guy,' he said, referring to the community organizer and activist who died in 1972, 'that's where I learned this stuff.'"[377].

---

[376] "Grijalva: Climate Letters Went Too Far in Seeking Correspondence," by Ben Geman and National Journal, *The Atlantic*, 3/15/2015

[377] "The Alinsky Way of Governing: What happens when those in power adopt 'rules for radicals' to attack their less powerful opponents," by Pete Pe-

Grijalva graduated from the University of Arizona with a degree in sociology and began his career as a community organizer. He became a leader and activist in groups like the Chicano Liberation Committee:

"They had long hair, wore military fatigues and brown berets and were angry and confrontational,' 'Fists in the air, Chicano student activists in the late 1960s marched on high school and college campuses throughout the American Southwest with voices so loud it was impossible for history to forget them..."[378]

Sheila Jackson Lee

Congresswoman Sheila Jackson-Lee represents the 18th Congressional District in Texas. In 2010, she:

"...entered into Acres Home Multiservice Community Center, walked to where the voting booths were...

"... Jackson-Lee loudly stated to the crowd in the voting area, "I've heard a lot of complaints about voter intimidation by poll watchers. I am not going to allow voter intimidation." Lee then reportedly went to the poll watcher and asked, "What's your name? Who do you represent?" The presiding judge then asked Congresswoman Lee to leave."[379].

In 2005, Jackson-Lee was one of the speakers at the *Million More Movement* rally on the National Mall, where the red, green and black flag of Black Power and Black Liberation was prominently displayed.

The featured speaker at the rally was Nation of Islam Minister Louis Farrakhan. The president of the Cuban National Assembly spoke to the crowd through videotape, criticizing the United States and ex-

---

tersen, *Wall Street Journal*, 4/9/2015

[378] "Anniversary sparks MEChA reunion," by Bryon Wells, *Arizona Daily Wildcat*, November 10, 1997

[379] "Forget Black Panthers - Congresswoman Warns DOJ of Tea Party Voter Intimidation," by Meredith Jessup, *the Blaze*, 10/28/2010

pressing Cuba's solidarity with America's poor. Other speakers focused on the prison system and the plight of political prisoners such as Mumia Abu-Jamal, Jamil Abdullah Al-Amin (formerly H. Rap Brown) and Leonard Peltier.

Common themes were police brutality, reparations, voter disenfranchisement, LGBT oppression, immigrant rights, economic and political empowerment, education and health, the role of art and culture in the struggle for social justice.

In 2014 Jackson-Lee participated with other Democrats on the House Floor in gesturing with the "Hands Up-Don't Shoot sign support for Michael Brown who was killed in a police shooting that triggered the Ferguson, Missouri violence. Other participants were Reps. Hakeem Jeffries, Yvette Clarke, and Al Green. Jeffries addressed the House saying the gestures were "a rallying cry of people all across America who are fed up with police violence."[380]

Grace Meng

Congresswoman Meng traveled to China in 2013 with several other members of Congress, including one Republican.

In 2015 she spoke at a conference organized by the Committee of 100, titled, *"Trade Secrets and Economic Espionage: Legal Risks in Advancing Technology between the U.S. and China."*

Her remarks concerned racial profiling in economic espionage cases.

"...the Committee of 100 has been committed to pursuing the full political, social, and economic inclusion of Chinese Americans in the United States. In 1999, the Committee led a coalition to raise national awareness of the denial of due process in the Wen Ho Lee case of alleged espionage and has since been involved in cases such as that of

---

[380] "Lawmakers make 'hands up' gesture on House floor," By Lucy McCalmont, *Politico,* 12/02/2014

Sherry Chen."[381]

The Committee, along with six other Asian Pacific American organizations, asked for Attorney General Loretta Lynch to look into racial discrimination in the criminal investigations of Asian Americans. In November 2015 she joined other colleagues and asked the Attorney General to investigate cases where Chinese Americans were accused of espionage, but the charges were later dismissed.

Raul Ruiz

Democrat Raul Ruiz, who represents California's 36th Congressional District, has been arrested twice during protests on behalf of Native Americans. A self-described activist, Ruiz was arrested in 1997 at a Thanksgiving Day protest at Plymouth Rock.

During a similar protest in 1999, Ruiz offered his support for Mumia Abul-Jamal, the convicted murderer of a police officer. He also read a letter from an unidentified Marxist on behalf of Leonard Peltier, the convicted murderer of two FBI agents on the Pine Ridge Indian Reservation in the 1970's.

"...Leonard Peltier's most serious crime is that he seeks to reside in the past, and in his culture, in his roots, the history of his people, the Lakota. And for the powerful, this is a crime, because knowing oneself with history impedes from being tossed around by this absurd machine that is in the system."[382]

---

[381] "Committee of 100 Releases White Paper Analyzing Economic Espionage Act Cases," https://www.committee100.org/press_release/committee-of-100-releases-white-paper-analyzing-economic-espionage-act-cases/, 4/5/2018

[382] "Congressional Candidate Supported Convicted Killer of FBI Agents in 1999 Audio Tape," by Michael Patrick Leahy, *Breitbart,* 10/18/2012

Carolyn Maloney

New York Democratic Congresswomen from the 12th District, Carolyn Maloney, led the fight to get American citizen Lori Berenson released from a Peruvian prison. Berenson was convicted of committing terrorist acts to overthrow the government of Peru:

"I am delighted that Lori has been released... she will now be able to begin to live her life in freedom.

"Lori's parents live in my district and sought my help starting in 1995 when she was first arrested, and I have tried to be helpful in the effort to free her... In 1997, I traveled to Peru and met Lori in prison.... She has not had an easy time."[383]

Berenson was involved with the Tupac Amaru Revolutionary Movement (MRTA), in a series of terrorist attacks in Peru. Authorities discovered a safe house rented under Berenson's name. They found at least a dozen other terrorists affiliated with MRTA, along with explosives, weapons and other lethal means to initiate terror attacks.

Berenson denied any involvement with MRTA, then said the group was a revolutionary movement, not a terrorist organization, and finally admitted, "It might not have been intentional, but the bottom line: I did collaborate with them." [384]

In 1986, Maloney greeted peace marchers who had hiked 3500 miles to New York City with a message of nuclear disarmament. A week later, *People's Daily World*, the newspaper of the Communist Party of the United States, held a reception for the same marchers.

Maloney endorsed David Dinkins for New York City Mayor in 1990. Dinkins was a member of the Democratic Socialists of America and backed by members and supporters of the Communist Party of the United States.

---

[383] "Rep. Maloney Statement on Release of Lori Berenson," Press Release, Rep. Carolyn B. Maloney, May 26, 2010

[384] "It might not have been intentional, but the bottom line: I did collaborate with them," by Jennifer Egan, *The New York Times Magazine*, 3/2/2012

James Clyburn

James Clyburn represents South Carolina's 6th District.

As part of a delegation from the Congressional Black Caucus, Clyburn visited Fidel Castro and Cuba in June 2000. Castro offered full scholarships to 500 American students and the opportunity to study in medical school in Cuba. They could then return to the United States to work among the poor areas of the country, where there was a shortage of doctors. Clyburn believed that Castro had a "great sense of history and a great sense of self."

Castro wrote of his visit with Clyburn and other members of the Congressional Black Caucus:

"In May 2000, another Caucus delegation visited us. It was presided over by the then Caucus President James Clyburn, from North Carolina, and was made up of Bennie Thompson from Mississippi and Gregory Meeks from New York. These congressmen were the first to learn from me of Cuba's disposition to grant a number of scholarships to low-income youths, to be selected by the Congressional Black Caucus, so that they could come to Cuba and study medicine…

"When the anti-Cuban pressures and activities of the Bush administration were intensified with respect to travel and the presence in Cuba of persons under U.S. jurisdiction, Black Caucus legislators addressed Secretary of State Colin Powell and managed to secure a license that legally allowed American youths to continue their medical studies – which they had already begun – in Cuba…"[385]

In March/April 2010, Clyburn dispatched an aide to Cuba in a "fact-finding mission to understand the importance and culture of U.S. policy toward Cuba." The trip was paid for with a grant from the Institute for Policy Studies.

The Institute for Policy Studies is:

"…an avowedly radical organization formed in 1963 by Richard J.

---

[385] "The Seven Members of Congress Who Are Visiting Us," by Fidel Castro Ruz, *Monthly Review: An Independent Socialist Magazine*, 4/6/2009

Barnet and Marcus G. Raskin… noticeably active in radical movements, , including the anti-Vietnam war-movement; Barnet traveled to Communist North Vietnam during the war, and both Barnet and Raskin were reported to have had contact with representatives of the Communist government of Hanoi in Paris during-the same period…"[386]

Eddie Johnson

Congresswoman Johnson is a member of the Congressional Black Caucus and Congressional Progressive Caucus. In 2001, while the chairperson of the Congressional Black Caucus, Johnson wrote an article for the *People's Daily*, the newspaper of the Communist Party of the United States.

Johnson represents the 30th Congressional District in Texas. In 2005, Johnson and a staff member, Murat Gokcigdem, spent three days in Havana, Cuba "to explore first-hand the issues facing the people of Cuba…An opportunity to foster a more pragmatic approach towards dealing with the Cuban government and finding constructive solutions to US/Cuba policy concerns". Johnson's travel cost of $1,555.29 was financed by the Christopher Reynolds Foundation. [387]

She founded, *A World of Women for World Peace*. The organization holds an annual conference. "I began my initiative, A World of Women for World Peace, to bring a greater visibility to the role of women who are victims of war and aggression…It is my hope that we continue this dialogue to promote peace around the world."[388]

---

[386] Institute for Policy Studies, archived document, *The Heritage Foundation*, 4/19/1977

[387] American Radio Works website: Trips sponsored by the Christopher Reynolds Foundation (retrieved from KeyWiki, 9/28/2019)

[388] "Congresswoman Eddie Bernice Johnson Hosts Her 13th Annual A World of Women for World Peace Conference," ebjohnson.house.gov, 05/06/13

Debbie Stabenow

In July 2007, Michigan Congresswoman Debbie Stabenow, sent a staffer to Cuba to attend a "fact-finding mission to learn more about Cuba's leadership transition and ongoing program of reforms in Cuban government." The staffer's travel costs were paid by the Institute of Policy Studies. [389]

Stabenow co-sponsored legislation in 2009 that would open up more U.S. agricultural exports to Cuba.

Debbie Stabenow traveled to Cuba in 2013 with Senator Patrick Leahy, Democratic senators Sherrod Brown, Sheldon Whitehouse, Republican Senator Jeff Flake and Democratic congressmen James McGovern and Chris Van Hollen.

She has had extensive support in her political career from the Democratic Socialists of America and the Institute for Policy Studies.

Stabenow traveled to the Soviet Union in 1989 with the co-founder of the Democratic Socialists of America, Millie Jeffries, to attend the *Women for a Meaningful Summit Conference* as a delegate. She and Jeffries went to China in 1995 as part of the *Fourth World Conference on Women*.

When Millie Jeffries died in 2004, Stabenow wrote:

"...today I have lost a very dear friend, as have the people of Michigan and hundreds of thousands of people across the country. Millie Jeffery is an icon in the State of Michigan and in our country for civil rights, women's rights, and workers' rights. Her life has epitomized the principles by which we all strive to live our lives-justice, equality, and compassion... Millie is the "political godmother" for many of us, and we are extremely grateful for her love and support."[390]

---

[389] Legistorm: *Center for Democracy in the Americas - Sponsor of Congressional Travel* (retrieved from *KeyWiki* on 9/28/2019)

[390] "Mildred McWilliams "Millie" Jeffrey, by Debbie Stabenow, I SPY, 40,000 Politicians, Millions of Facts, 3/24/2004

Edward Markey

Edward Markey, U.S. Senator from Massachusetts, endorsed the platform of the nuclear freeze organization called SANE (Smarter Approach to Nuclear Weapons) early in his political career.

In 2007 Markey entered a tribute into the Congressional Record on the death of nuclear freeze activist Randall Forsberg:

"Randy Forsberg was the mother of the Nuclear Freeze movement. When she was a doctoral candidate at the Massachusetts Institute of Technology in 1980, she put forward a simple and inspired proposal: to end the 'testing, production, and deployment' of all nuclear weapons everywhere. With her 'Call to Halt the Nuclear Arms Race,' and her tireless advocacy for a nuclear weapons freeze, Randy galvanized a national grassroots campaign to end the threat of nuclear weapons."[391]

In 2012, and again in 2014, Markey sponsored legislation (the SANE Act) to cut "$100 billion in spending on outdated, wasteful nuclear weapons and related programs over the next ten years. Let's cut new nuclear weapons and not programs for the poor, the elderly, the sick and the children of our country." [392]

In 2013 Markey was endorsed by the Democratic Socialists of America, "...Markey is the clear progressive choice, especially on foreign policy, abortion choice and the environment. He is a member of the Congressional Progressive..."[393]

Markey was endorsed in his Senate run by the group, Peace Action, "...Rep. Ed Markey is a key leader in Congress on abolishing nuclear weapons. He is the U.S. co-president of Parliamentarians for Nuclear Non-proliferation and Disarmament, and his "SANE Act," named

---

[391]   "ON THE DEATH OF RANDALL FORSBERG," by Hon. Edward J. Markey, *Congressional Record*, 10/23/2007

[392]   Congressional Record: Proceedings and Debates of the ... Congress, by United States Congress, Vol. 158, Part I, 2/9/2012

[393]   DSA Connections: DSA Endorsement: Ed Markey, *Key Wiki*, Ed Markey

for Peace Action's predecessor organization, calls for cuts in spending on nuclear bomb production facilities, nuclear-armed bombers and submarines, the end of U.S. bombers' nuclear mission, and reduction in number of deployed weapons."[394]

William Lacy Clay

In June 2019 Missouri Congressman William Lacy Clay was involved in a Congressional hearing on the *Federal Response to White Supremacy*. He referenced a study titled the *Plain View Project*, implying that it concluded, "white supremacists infiltrated law enforcement agencies."

In 2017, William Lacy Clay chose a painting by artist David Pulphus depicting police officers as pigs as part of the United States Congressional Art Competition." The painting intended to capture the unrest in Ferguson, Missouri, and how it became the springboard for the Black Lives Matter movement. In the painting, two of the officers "carry guns while protesters march towards them carrying signs that read 'history,' 'stop killing' and 'racism kills.' Clay hung the painting on a wall inside a walkway under the Capitol building. It was eventually removed through the authority of House Speaker, Paul Ryan.

In April 2005 Congressman Clay joined the Communist Party of the United States in supporting a student hunger strike at Washington University in St. Louis, Missouri. The strike ended when the university committed a million dollars over two years toward higher salaries and better benefits for low-paid contract employees. Congressman Clay spoke at a victory rally, saying, "you students risked a lot. But it was a worthwhile victory."[395]

Missouri state representative Maria Chappelle-Nadal told the

---

[394] Massachusetts Peace Action Party for Ed Markey for Senate, "email blast," 4/28/2013

[395] "Victory for Wash U students in living wage," *People's World, Continuing the Daily Worker*, April 29, 2005

Communist Party USA's *People's Daily World*, "these courageous students fought their butts off. Never, for one moment, did they think about giving up." During the last weekend of the sit-in, Chappelle-Nadal joined the students on the hunger strike and slept in the admissions office with the students.[396]

"Nineteen days is a long time," said Joan Suarez, a member of *Democratic Socialists of America, the Worker's Rights Board* and *Jobs with Justice.* "Everyone talks about the courage of these students."[397]

"*Socialist Worker's Alliance* learned from like-minded groups across the country," said Danielle Christmas… "we saw other students take power into their own hands. We knew that if things were going to change here, we had to take power into our hands."[398]

In 2000, Congressman Clay brought Lew Moye, a union activist and Communist Party of the United States affiliate, onto his staff as a campaign adviser.

From May 22-25, 2008, the Communist Party USA founded Coalition of Black Trade Unionists held their 37th International Convention in St. Louis, Missouri. Clay, Jr. was a speaker at the May 22 opening session.

Gregory Meeks

When Hugo Chavez of Venezuela died in 2013, President Obama sent Congressmen Gregory Meeks and William Dela Hunt of Massachusetts to represent the United States at his funeral. Raul Castro of Cuba and Mahmoud Ahmadinejad of Iran were part of the group of 30 world leaders who also attended the services for Chavez. Meeks had these comments about Venezuela under Chavez and its future without him:

---

[396]   "Victory for Wash. U students in living wage," by Tony Pecinovskiy, *People's World*, 4/29/2005

[397]   Ibid.

[398]   Ibid.

"There were world leaders from many of our allies–Colombia, all of the Caribbean, and everyone who was there–so it was an opportunity to talk to them also about where we go from here and how we can improve relationships. ... Before Chávez was president, poor people had no hope. Chavez gave them hope and that someone was on their side...

"...Chávez was democratically elected three times... I would never disparage a people's choice for their president just like I don't want anyone to disparage the American people's choice for president."[399]

Meeks said he would never disparage a "people's choice for president", referring to the election of Chavez three times in Venezuela. He later commented on the Electoral College victory of President Trump. "My deep concern is that President Trump's obvious racism and obliviousness will continue to be embedded in his policies... One must question... his evident prejudice."[400]

Jan Schakowsky

Jan Schakowsky represents the 9th Congressional District in Illinois. On October 13, 2011 Congresswoman Schakowski joined a protest organized by the Occupy Movement and Young Communist League. Amid chants, "this is what democracy looks like," the crowd shouted, "Chairman Mao."

Among signs that read "Fuck the Lobbyists," and "FUCK THIS SHIT," a fellow wearing a shirt emblazoned with "YCL," for Young Communist League, explained that "real democracies are where corporations don't run everything...that's what socialism is...democracy without big interests that control everything...had a revolution in 1776...need a second one to take it back again..."

Bea Lumpkin of the Chicago chapter of the Communist Party of

[399] "Congressman Gregory Meeks Reports Back After Attending Hugo Chávez's Funeral," by Colin Campbell, *Observer*, 3/11/2013

[400] "CPUSA Marches With Jan Schakowsky At #Occupy Chicago," Youtube, 10/13/2011

the USA was asked during the protest about socialism. Her response, "that's not the issue today...the issue is getting a little more democracy." When the interviewer asked whether President Obama should be more open about embracing democratic socialism, Bea Lumpkin told him "you're ridiculous, you're stupid ...you're a big fake."

As the interviewer caught up with Schakowski, who was at the protest, to ask her about the movement, Schakowski replied, "these are ordinary Americans who are protesting peacefully because they think the economy is not fair."[401]

Schakowsky has maintained close ties with the Democratic Socialists of America, dating back to the 1970's. Early in her political career, she became friends with a United Farm Workers union leader named Eliseo Medina. Rising through the ranks, Medina is currently the vice-president of Service Employees International Union (SEIU) and an honorary chair of the Democratic Socialists of America.

In 1998 and 2000 she was endorsed by the Democratic Socialists of America (DSA), which called her, "an old friend of DSA and a real fighter." She was given the DSA Eugene Debs, Norman Thomas, Michael Harrington award in 2000 for honoring their "legacy of struggle for social justice." [402]

Sponsored by the Democratic Socialists of America, the *Institute for Policy Studies*, and George Soros, Schakowsky has been a speaker at DSA annual conferences since 2004.

In 2011 Schakowsky endorsed a manual published by the Democratic Socialists of America, titled, *Organizing for Social Change: Midwest Academy Manual for Activists.*

Jan Schakowsky and Danny Davis, paid tribute to Frank Lumpkin, long -time leader of the Chicago chapter of the Communist Party of the United States, at his funeral in April 2011.

---

[401]   "A Brief History of the Debs- Thomas- Harrington Dinner," https://archive.vn/na77f, 5/5/2000

[402]   "Video Reportedly Shows Dem. Rep. Receiving Award From Communist Media Arm," by Jonathon M. Seidl, *the Blaze*, 3/12/2012

In 2013 Schakowsky joined other Democratic Congressional members endorsing a proposal asking President Obama to award the Presidential Medal of Freedom to a deceased community organizer Fred Ross, Jr. He was an adherent of the Saul Alinsky *Rules for Radicals*, and helped elect Ed Roybal, a member of the Communist Party of the United States of America, to the Los Angeles City Council.

In 2015 Schakowsky spoke at a dinner in Washington, D.C. honoring Congressman John Conyers' fifty years of service. Other attendees at the dinner included Democratic Congressmen Charles Rangel, Steve Cohen, and Alan Grayson. Irvin Jim, a self-proclaimed Marxist-Leninist, represented the National Union of Metalworkers of South Africa.

Schakowsky joined fifteen Congresspeople who met with members of the Freedom Road organization and Committee to Stop FBI Repression. The groups were complaining about the FBI investigating, serving grand jury subpoenas and searching homes of people involved in international solidarity work and anti-war organizing. Keith Ellison, John Conyers, Maxine Waters, Danny Davis, Luis Gutierrez, and Raul Grijalva were especially sensitive to the groups, with Ellison sending a letter to Attorney General Eric Holder.

Danny Davis

Danny K. Davis was first elected to the United States Congress from the 7th District of Illinois in 1996. Davis was endorsed by the Teamsters, AFL-CIO, ACORN, Sierra Club and Democratic Socialists of America, of which he is a member, Davis ran as both a Democrat and as a member of the New Party. At the time, New Party was just beginning in some areas of the U.S. and the process of a candidate receiving nominations from more than one party and allowed to have his/her name on the ballot in more than one place, was called "electoral fusing."

The New Party was a progressive party, drawing its support from the community organizers of ACORN and some of Chicago's labor unions. In the 1996 Illinois Senate election, Barack Obama was endorsed by the New Party.[403]

On March 4, 2012, Congressman Davis visited the Chicago Headquarters of the Communist Party of the United States (CPUSA) and received the Chris Hani/Rudy Lozano Social Justice Award. The award was named after two prominent Chicago "progressives." Lozano was a Chicago community organizer who was killed in his own home after failing to pay a $7000 drug debt. Hani was assassinated in South Africa after taking over the leadership of the South African Communist Party in 1991.

Davis' award honored his lifetime achievements of inspiring adherence to the care of social justice. The award ceremony was written up in the "People's World" CPUSA news website. Davis was also filmed leaving the CPUSA Chicago Headquarters with CPUSA members. He was interviewed by a Rebel Pundit reporter:

Unidentified Female: "Excuse me who are you with?"

Rebel Pundit (RB):" I'm just a citizen, does it matter?"

Unidentified Female: "Yeah kind of, alright."

RB: "Are you aware that this is the home of the Communist Party USA in Chicago Congressman." "How do you feel that the African American community feels about you accepting an…"

Unidentified male: "You're disgusting."

RB: "Do not touch me…" "Why am I a disgusting human? Get out of my space."

RB: "You know what the Community Center is?"

Congressman Davis: "It's the home for…the Communist Par-

---

[403] "How to Push Obama," John Nichols, The Progressive, January 2009.

ty USA…People's World…"

RB: "What was the award for today?"

Congressman Davis: "Lifetime of inspired leadership." "I thought you're just a citizen? Why are you worried about the Communist Party?"

RB: "I shouldn't be worried about the Communist Party?"

Cong. Davis: "No."

RB: "Are you proud to be accepting an award from People's World."

Congressman Davis: "Well I'll tell you what, I don't think I'll be answering any more questions about it. Thank you very much."

In 2004, Danny Davis stumped for Barack Obama and introduced him to the Teamsters as Obama ran for the U.S. Senate. Obama said this about Davis, "You just heard from one of the best Congressmen in the country and the reason he's one of the best Congressman in the country is he shares our values"

President Obama Normalizes Relations with Cuba

In March 2016, President Obama visited Cuba in a major step to normalize relations with the communist nation. He was accompanied by Nancy Pelosi and a delegation from the House of Representatives. The delegation included Karen Bass, Cheri Bustos, Sam Farr, Rosa De-Lauro, Barbara Lee, Charles Rangel, Kathy Castor, David Cicilline, Steve Cohen, Jan Schakowsky, Peter Welch, Alan Lowenthal, Jim Mc-Govern and Lucille Roybal-Allard, and Eliot Engel. Democratic Party Senators traveling with Obama were Amy Klobuchar of Minnesota,

Dick Durbin of Illinois, Heidi Heitkamp of North Dakota, Patrick Leahy of Vermont, Tom Udall of New Mexico and Jeff Flake, the sole Republican on the trip. (Leahy and Flake co-sponsored the Freedom to Travel to Cuba Act of 2015).

In 2018, Senators Patrick Leahy, Vermont; Ron Wyden, Oregon and Gary Peters, Michigan, accompanied by representatives Kathy Castor, Florida; Jim McGovern, Massachusetts and Susan Davis of California, traveled to Cuba and met with Raul Castro. According to a statement issued by the Cuban government, the delegation discussed matters of interest to both countries.

President John F. Kennedy was inaugurated on January 20, 1961. The young President understood the threat facing America. He was proud of America's history. He was excited and optimistic about its future.

"Let the word go forth from this time and place, to friend and foe alike, that the torch has been passed to a new generation of Americans—born in this century, tempered by war, disciplined by a hard and bitter peace, proud of our ancient heritage—and unwilling to witness or permit the slow undoing of those human rights to which this nation has always been committed, and to which we are committed today at home and around the world."

Today's Democrats are not the Democrats John F. Kennedy knew. Today's Democratic Party is critically ill with the ideology of communism.

That is the real existential threat facing America today.

SOCIALISTS CRY
"POWER TO THE PEOPLE"
AND RAISE THE
CLENCHED FIST
AS THEY SAY IT.
WE ALL KNOW
WHAT THEY REALLY MEAN—
POWER OVER PEOPLE,
POWER TO THE STATE.
- MARGARET THATCHER

CHAPTER SEVENTEEN

"I support a Green New Deal that will
aggressively tackle climate change, economic
inequality, and racial injustice"
Elizabeth Warren

In early 2019, Democratic Senator Ed Markey introduced Senate Resolution 59 and Congresswoman Alexandria Ocasio-Cortez, House Resolution 109, which are commonly referred to as the Green New Deal. Global warming proponents have come roaring back from America's rejection a decade ago of former Vice- President Al Gore's, An Inconvenient Truth.

The Green New Deal

The Green New Deal is Gore's Inconvenient Truth on asteroids. While Gore argued that future hurricanes hitting America would have far greater destructive power than Hurricane Katrina in 2012, sinking many of the nation's southern coastal areas under floods of biblical proportion, Ocasio-Cortez has updated Gore's climate forecast with this urgent warning, "we're, like, the world is going to end in 12 years if we don't address climate change."[404]

Democratic Party presidential candidates have fallen quickly into line. Senator Bernie Sanders has exclaimed, "every candidate running for president has got to answer the following very simple question: At a time when we need to address the planetary crisis of climate change, and transform our energy system away from fossil fuels and into energy efficiency and sustainability, should we continue to give $135 billion in tax breaks and subsidies over the next decade to fossil fuel companies?[405]

Senator Cory Booker endorsed the Green New Deal, "climate change is a clear and urgent threat to our communities and our future… its effects are disproportionately borne by our most vulnerable populations, namely communities of color, and low income. We must take bold action on climate change and create a green economy that benefits all Americans."[406]

Senator Elizabeth Warren, speaking for the Green New Deal, delivered a speech on the floor of the United States Senate; "I support a Green New Deal that will aggressively tackle climate change, economic inequality, and racial injustice…I don't accept the Republicans' argument that boldly addressing climate change and having the world's strongest economy are incompatible. I believe that the exact opposite of that is true. Tackling our climate challenges will provide us with the opportunity to grow our economy, protect public health, and propel the United States to become the world leader in innovation in the twenty-first century."[407]

---

[404]   "Ocasio-Cortez: 'The World Is Going to End In 12 Years If We Don't Address Climate Change,'" by Tim Harris, *Newsweek*, 1/22/2019

[405]   Betterworld.net

[406]   "Cory Booker Backs 'Green New Deal' On Climate Change in Latest Appeal to Party's Left Wing," by Herb Jackson, *North Jersey Record*, 12/14/2018

[407]   "Warren Delivers Floor Speech on Climate Change Leadership," 3/26/2019.

Former Congressman Beto O'Rourke sounded a dire warning in response to a question on the campaign trail, "let us all be well aware that life will be a lot tougher for the generations that follow us, no matter what we do. It is only a matter of degrees. Along this current trajectory, there will be people who can no longer live in the cities they call home today. There is food grown in this country that will no longer prosper in these soils. There is going to be massive migration of tens or hundreds of millions of people from places that are going to be uninhabitable or under the sea...This is the final chance. The scientists are unanimous on this. We have no more than 12 years to take incredibly bold action on this crisis."[408]

Under the guise of climate change, Senator Kamala Harris wants to ban fracking and tell Americans how much meat they can eat, "... there has to be also what we do in terms of creating incentives of what we will eat in a healthy way, that we will encourage moderation, and that we will be educated about the effect of our eating habits on our environment. And we have to do a much better job of that. And the government has to do a much better job of that."[409]

United Nations and Climate Change

Interestingly, Harris' comments seem to echo a United Nations report on how we treat our planet. "scientists say a shift away from eating meat toward plant-based diets could yield big dividends in the fight against climate change. Reduced meat consumption means lower emissions from livestock and the fertilizer needed to sustain them but also provides an opportunity to reforest land that farmers would have otherwise used for grazing. Rethinking the human diet across the globe could

---

[408] "AP Debunks Beto O'Rourke Claim That World Has Just 12 Years to Combat Climate Change," by Valerie Richardson, *The Washington Times,* March 19, 2019

[409] "Harris Would Change Dietary Guidelines, Food Labels to Discourage Red Meat Consumption," by Susan Jones, *CNS News,* 9/5/2019

drive emissions reductions of up to 8 gigatons annually, according to the report, greater than an entire year of emissions in the U.S."[410]

Mayor Pete Buttigieg's Climate Plan

Indiana Mayor Pete Buttigieg has detailed a major climate plan he would implement if elected president. His plan will affect every aspect of American life and radically alter our country's national security priorities.

"When I first became mayor of South Bend, I toured our city's emergency operations. I hoped I'd rarely have to return. But during my time as mayor, we've had to activate it twice just for floods that are supposed to occur once in a millennium.

"…From hurricanes devastating Puerto Rico to fires ravaging the Amazon, climate change is affecting everyone, everywhere. It is the security challenge of our time, and a wall on our southern border won't stop it.

"For too long, Washington has chosen denial and obstruction. But the timeline that compels us to act isn't set by Congress -- it's being dictated by science. With climate catastrophe on the horizon, we've reached a now-or-never moment in our history. To meet this crisis, we must channel all of our energies into a national project -- one that draws on the resources of every American, from big cities to rural communities, and seizes the tremendous opportunity of a new era of climate action…

"…First, we'll set an ambitious goal to transform America into a net-zero emissions society no later than 2050 -- and spur the innovation to get us there. We'll nearly quadruple R&D investments in advanced wind and solar, battery storage, and carbon capture to $25 billion a year -- more than the Manhattan Project. Many of these investments will be financed by Climate Action Bonds, modeled on World War II war bonds, which will allow every American to own a piece of our clean

---

[410] The Intergovernmental Panel on Climate Change," United Nations, 2019.

energy future.

"Industrial America...was built on oil and gas. But just as my community has moved forward, so must our country. So, we'll launch a 21st-century Industrial Revolution, investing in mass transit, transitioning to electric vehicles, and making buildings and homes more energy efficient. And with scientists indicating our soil can absorb as much carbon as the global transportation system emits, we'll put American farmers at the center of our climate revolution...Through investments in soil management and other technologies, we can make a farm in Iowa as much a symbol of confronting climate disruption as an electric vehicle in California.

"To discourage the pollution that accelerates climate change at home and abroad, we'll set a price on carbon-and offset the cost to consumers by giving that money back as a dividend to working Americans. Instead of subsidizing harmful fossil fuels, we'll support communities and workers from Appalachia to Nevada as they transition from coal, oil, and gas. By establishing new industries and revitalizing entire regions, we'll create 3 million new jobs, many of them good union jobs.

"Second, my administration will prioritize resilience to climate shocks. That means building green infrastructure that can withstand extreme weather and sea level rise. We'll also establish next-generation regional resilience hubs, supplemented with $5 billion annual grants focused on rural communities... And we'll bring young people together in a Climate Corps to help make communities more sustainable through their service work.

"As growing food and water insecurity increases migration and political unrest from Syria to sub-Saharan Africa, we must integrate climate management into every aspect of our national security planning. To achieve that, we'll place a senior climate security adviser on the Secretary of Defense's staff and create a Climate Watch Floor to monitor climate-related risks. By retrofitting existing facilities and noncombat vehicles, and making new ones zero emissions, the Department of Defense will lead the way in clean energy.

"Finally, we'll rebuild international relationships and ensure that

America – not China -- leads the world on climate. I was proud to join more than 400 mayors in committing to upholding the Paris Climate Agreement goals, despite the current administration's withdrawal. When I'm president, the United States won't just rejoin the Paris accord, we'll redouble our commitment. We'll encourage other countries to adopt their own price on carbon. And because so much of our global leadership flows from our local communities, in my first 100 days in office we'll convene a Pittsburgh Summit of regional, state, and local leaders to support locally-created solutions…."[411]

What's in the Green New Deal

The Democratic Party has compared the Green New Deal with President Franklin Roosevelt's New Deal. The provisions of the Green New Deal would involve the U.S. Government in just about every aspect of daily living

- "Guaranteeing a job with a family-sustaining wage, adequate family and medical leave, paid vacations, and retirement security to all people of the United States."

- "Providing all people of the United States with – (i) high-quality health care; (ii)

- affordable, safe, and adequate housing; (iii) economic security; and (iv) access to clean water, clean air, healthy and affordable food, and nature."

- "Providing resources, training, and high-quality education, including higher education, to all people of the United States."

- "Meeting 100 percent of the power demand in the United States through clean, renewable, and zero-emission energy sources."

---

[411]　https://peteforamerica.com/policies/climate/ "Rising to the Climate Challenge"

- "Repairing and upgrading the infrastructure in the United States, including . . . by eliminating pollution and greenhouse gas emissions as much as technologically feasible."

- "Building or upgrading to energy-efficient, distributed, and smart power grids, and working to ensure affordable access to electricity."

- "Upgrading all existing buildings in the United States and building new buildings to achieve maximal energy efficiency, water efficiency, safety, affordability, comfort, and durability, including through electrification."

- "Overhauling transportation systems in the United States to eliminate pollution and greenhouse gas emissions from the transportation sector as much as is technologically feasible, including through investment in – (i) zero-emission vehicle infrastructure and manufacturing; (ii) clean, affordable, and accessible public transportation; and (iii) high-speed rail."

- "Spurring massive growth in clean manufacturing in the United States and removing pollution and greenhouse gas emissions from manufacturing and industry as much as is technologically feasible."

"Working collaboratively with farmers and ranchers in the United States to eliminate pollution and greenhouse gas emissions from the agricultural sector as much as is technologically feasible."[412]

Communist Party Support of the Green New Deal

The Ocasio-Cortez Green New Deal is supported by the Communist Party of the United States. In an article titled, "American Communists Unite Behind Green New Deal, the Washington Times goes inside

---

[412] Democratic Party 2016 Platform

a General Session:

"One of the Communist revolutionary's eternal problems — making a living while also pursuing the socialist dream — was thrown into relief at the party's national convention during a spirited discussion over the Green New Deal. That the world stands on the precipice of catastrophe was a given among the roughly 300 delegates, and the Communist Party of the USA remains solidly behind the expensive plan to overhaul the global economy and its current reliance on fossil fuels and gas.

"'It is important we not underestimate the fact we are facing a situation of mass extinction on this planet,' said Michael, a Communist from Houston who addressed the general session on 'The US Working Class, Climate Change and the Green New Deal.

"He went on to discuss the 'acidification of the ocean.' and even blamed the calamity of Hurricane Harvey that smashed into Houston and southeastern Texas in 2017 on global warming.

"In the end, he said mankind faces a stark choice between 'socialism or extinction.'

"...As the session came to a close, an energetic Communist... grabbed a microphone...leading the CPUSA members in a growing chant.

"'Same struggle, same fight, 'Climate justice, worker's rights.'"[413]

DSA Supports Green New Deal

The youth movement inside the Democratic Socialists of America is ready and willing to force Americans to accept the Ocasio-Cortez Green New Deal, whether they like it or not:

"In the likely case we don't completely end capitalism in the next decade, we need a plan for effectively dealing with climate change anyway. Winning a transformative GND will require massive leverage over

---

[413]   "American Communists Unite Behind Green New Deal," by James Varney, *Washington Times*, 6/22/2019

the political and economic system. We need the ability to force these changes over the objection of broad sections of the capitalist class, who are fiercely unwilling to lose their profits. The confrontational tactics and electoral challenges of the growing GND movement are essential parts of the leverage we need, but we think history shows they won't be enough. We will also need direct leverage against the capitalist class, right in the places where they make their money…

"Who has that leverage? In short, working people, united and organized. The working class not only has the numbers as the majority of society, but it also stands in direct antagonism to the capitalists causing the climate crisis."[414]

Democrats Promote Climate Change to End Capitalism and Install a Socialist Government

The 2016 Democratic Party platform outlined its support for climate change. Referring to the failure to tackle climate change in the context of the alleged additional burden it places on the poor and disadvantaged of our society, the platform declared anyone failing to support the Democratic Party's ideology was guilty of **"environmental racism,"** and that it was vital to pursue **"climate justice."**

Increasingly, the Democratic Party raises the possibility of prosecuting for fraud, any individual or corporation that presents an opposing view to their "facts" and "science" in support of climate change.

There are those who have argued that the climate change passion that can be seen in the Communist Party of the United States, Democratic Socialists of America, and Democratic Party isn't about climate change. But about using climate change as the rationale to transform America into a socialist nation. Ocasio-Cortez former Chief of Staff and climate guru, Saikait Chakrabarti, has said as much.

---

[414] "A Class Struggle Strategy for a Green New Deal," by Keith Brower Brown, Jeremy Gong, Matt Huber and Jamie Munro, *Socialist Forum,* a Publication of the Democratic Socialists of America, Winter, 2019

Chakrabarti, who was forced to step down as a result of an ongoing investigation into campaign financing irregularities, had a meeting with Washington Governor Jay Inslee's climate change adviser, Sam Ricketts, resulting in this account from the Washington Post:

"Chakrabarti had an unexpected disclosure. 'The interesting thing about the Green New Deal.' he said, 'is it wasn't originally a climate thing at all.' Ricketts greeted this startling notion with an attentive poker face. 'Do you guys think of it as a climate thing?' Chakrabarti continued. 'Because we really think of it as a how-do you- change-the-entire-economy thing.'

"'Yeah,' said Ricketts. Then he said: 'No.' Then he said: 'I think it's, it's, it's, it's dual. It is both rising to the challenge that is existential around climate and it is building an economy that contains more prosperity. More sustainability in that prosperity — and more broadly shared prosperity, equitability and justice throughout.'

"Chakrabarti liked the answer. 'The thing I think you guys are doing that's so incredible is ... you guys are actually figuring out how to do it and make it work, the comprehensive plan where it all fits together,' he said. "I'd love to get into a situation where everyone's trying to just outdo each other.' But Chakrabarti couldn't help adding: "' I'll be honest, my view is I still think you guys aren't going big enough.'

"Ricketts seemed unfazed by the critique. 'Well, you know, we're not done. When it comes to a nationwide economic mobilization, there's more to come on this front, for one. And other key components we're going to be rolling forward speak to some of the key justice elements of this...ensuring every community has got a part of this'

"Nationwide economic mobilization. Justice. Community. Ricketts kept laying down chords in Chakrabarti's key. It was an acknowledgment of just how far inside establishment Washington the progressive movement has reached. Everything is intersectional now — including decarbonization.

"Ocasio-Cortez' priorities and approach offer the purest expression of the progressive movement in Congress…"[415]

The Democratic Party Green New Deal is an intrusive plan that would limit the freedom of Americans to travel where they please, to eat what they wish, and to reject the ideas they don't accept. This is the only Democratic Party vision for America's future. It is a vision supported by hundreds of progressive front organizations, and international bodies like the United Nations.

The Washington Post account of Chakrabarti's meeting illustrates a specific intent to curtail freedom of thought and begin the process of transforming production and distribution systems in the United States. It confirms a willingness on behalf of the Democratic Party to cause turmoil to the nation's economy on their road to installing a progressive socialist democracy under the guise of climate change.

Weather Underground on the Destruction of Capitalism and Transformation to Socialism

The Weather Underground warned of the turmoil that would exist, during the time between the destruction of capitalism and the transformation to socialism.

"After a long struggle, power will be in the hands of the people. Society will have to be reorganized, toward the integration of each with the whole, where people can realize themselves in peace and freedom. There will be rebuilding to do, but the tremendous power of creative human energy —revealed now in flashes of liberated space and in struggle— will be freed to fulfill its potential. Freed from the constrictions, prejudices and fearful anxieties of imperialist society, people can be better…

"Our values are collective and communal. Birth and death will be celebrated with dignity, old people will have respect, children will have rights. We will eliminate waste from our society, all the people can eat

---

[415]   "AOC's Chief of Change," by David Montgomery, *Washington Post Magazine*, 7/10/2019

healthy food. The cities can be real human gardens. We will have to rebuild them, reclaim idyllic rivers and forests, and the dying species. Wielded in the interest of everyone, technology can serve us; no labor need be unproductive. Our art, music, poetry, theater will interpret and awaken the relationship of ourselves to Third World forces, acting on each other. Our culture will be insurgent, celebrate people's victories and record the history of the struggle. We will support those who are still fighting and continue fighting ourselves. We will awaken our sense of being part of a world community."[416]

As part of their climate change plans, the Democratic Party, wants to see the cars Americans drive convert to all renewable fuels in the near future. The entire country could potentially become hostage to government bureaucracies and authoritarian politicians trading food and energy for freedom.

This is how Saddam Hussein's Iraq was run. Food and energy were hostages to secure allegiance to the government. This is the manner in which all totalitarian societies have been run in the past. And will be in the future. America is not immune. Many are already blaming current power outages in California on political decisions made by the Democratic Party that runs the state.

National Security Consequences of Electromagnetic Pulse (EMP) Technology

There is another dangerous national security consequence in the push to eliminate fossil fuels and convert to renewable energy sources, like electricity. The People's Republic of China has made major advances in an area of research called "electromagnetic pulse technology." Ten years ago, the U.S. Government became aware of Chinese intelligence officers pursuing collection efforts regarding electromagnetic pulse technology as a potential weapon of interest towards gaining military superiority over the United States.

---

[416] *Prairie Fire*

During the past decade, the Chinese have invested extensive funding in EMP research. They have expanded their understanding of how EMP can be used to kill civilians in a time of war. This is important in any discussion of climate change that entails phasing out gasoline powered cars, and gas heat for homes and businesses, in favor of electricity as a primary power source.

An EMP attack would limit options for civilians to take care of themselves, pending restoration of order following such an attack. All the systems that contribute to quality of life and depend upon electric power, such as transportation, production, and distribution would be critically impacted.

"China is building specialized nuclear warheads so potent that a single one may be enough to devastate America with its enhanced electromagnetic pulse (EMP), according to a report the Department of Defense (DoD) recently declassified.

"The report, *Nuclear EMP Attack Scenarios and Combined-Arms Cyber Warfare,* was written by Dr. Peter Vincent Pry for a congressionally mandated commission investigating the threat from EMPs to the United States.

"The report warns that future wars may look entirely different than past wars due to people's increasing reliance on technology. China, alongside Russia, Iran, and North Korea, have recognized America's extreme reliance on electricity, electronics, and technology, and subsequently adapted their military plans to target this dependence.

"Detonation of a single generic nuclear bomb between 30-400 kilometers above earth will create an EMP that propagates outward towards earth with a radius of between 600 and 2,200 kilometers. The effects of an EMP would be catastrophic and could plunge a nation into indefinite darkness. There would be widespread destruction of computers, nuclear power plants, satellites, phones, refrigerators, transformers, and more.

"The EMP commission estimates a full 90 percent of the American population could die within a year of an EMP attack."[417]

Democratic Party assertions that climate change truly constitutes an "existential threat" to America are unsupported by the facts. Democrats view "climate change deniers" as the real problem facing the country. They advocate prosecution of corporations who "talk back" with a different view of climate change. At the same time, the evidence is clear and overwhelming that the People's Republic of China is *the* "existential threat" to the United States of America- militarily, economically, and politically.

Democrats have responded to the climate change threat with a plan to immediately transform and restructure America through the installation of a democratic socialist government. They have responded to the growing threat posed by China with Congressional hearings.

Lacking more credible justification for the harsh transformation the Green New Deal would place on every aspect of American life, it can only be seen as a subterfuge in furtherance of their plan to expand government control over our society and beliefs. In short, it is all about power.

---

[417] "China's EMP Weapons Pose Grave Threat to America, Newly Declassified Report Shows," by Daniel Ashman, *The Epoch Times,* 1/30/2019.

CONCLUSION

The Democratic Party Platform of 2016 is a mirror image of the Weather Underground's *Prairie Fire* manifesto of 1974. The leadership of the Democratic Party, and the majority of its candidates for President in 2020, have adopted the strategy of the revolutionary radicals of the 1970's-the Weather Underground and Black Panther Party for Self-Defense. They wanted to destroy America's constitutional Republic and replace it with a communist utopia. Today's Democratic Party is pursuing the political phase of that same revolution.

THE OLD REVOLUTION

The Weather Underground understood that, "...revolution is a fight by the people for power. It is a changing of power in which existing social and economic relations are turned upside down."

The Communist Party of the United States of America envisions a "revolutionary transformation of society and the economy toward socialism and then communism. "

Influential leaders in today's Democratic Party have directly related to the 1970's revolutionaries and their impact on America.

When he was Attorney General, Eric Holder told the Race Card Project, "time for a Third Revolution... this is a revolutionary country... they saw inequality, they saw unjust system and they resorted to revolution..."

Talking with *New Yorker Magazine* about his travels to Cuba and El Salvador in the 1980's when those countries were at the center of communist revolutionary movements, Mayor Bill DeBlasio said, "I was involved in a movement that I thought made a lot of sense, and it began, and the reason I got involved, was because of United States foreign policy."

THE NEW RESISTANCE

The Weather Underground identified the, "many faces to militant resistance... attacks on the police... International Women's Day marches... demands for control and power through seizures of institutions..."

Hillary Clinton pledged, "I'm going to do everything I can to support the resistance." Nancy Pelosi impressed upon her followers, "... this resistance summer is so important."

USING RACISM AS A WEAPON

The Weather Underground looked at America and concluded, "institutionalized racism is mainlined and perpetuated over the generations by the schools... immigration laws, birth control, the army, the prisons."

The 2016 Democratic Party platform pledge was "... Democrats will fight to end institutional and systemic racism in our society. We will challenge and dismantle the structures that define lasting racial, economic, political, and social inequity."

Elizabeth Warren declared "... our criminal justice system: It's racist...front to back."

Beto O'Rourke believes "this country... was founded on racism... and is racist today..."

After five Dallas police officers were killed and seven wounded by a man who said he "wanted to kill white people," President Obama, speaking at the memorial for the officers, said:

"... when African Americans from all walks of life, from different communities across the country, voice a growing despair over what they perceive to be unequal treatment; when study after study shows that whites and people of color experience the criminal justice system differently, so that if you're black you're more likely to be pulled over or searched or arrested, more likely to get longer sentences, more likely to get the death penalty for the same crime...it hurts."

USING EXTORTIONATE DEMANDS AS WEAPONS

The Black Panther Party demanded reparations as part of their Ten Point Program, "...We believe that this racist government has robbed us, and now we are demanding the overdue debt of forty acres and two mules."

When asked about reparations for Black Americans, New York City's Mayor Bill DeBlasio answered, "... reparations have to be taken seriously..."

DEPLOYING THE "MASSES"

The Weather Underground painted a portrait of the victim class that constitutes the masses in its *Prairie Fire* manifesto. The masses would join in international solidarity to topple the Republic. The masses would reverse a history of oppression and subjugation against-"Black, Puerto, Chicano, and Indian people... women."

New York City Mayor DeBlasio spoke against inequality as it related to Black people and the... "oppression of... Latinos, Native Americans, Asian and women..."

THE STRUGGLES

The Communist Party of the United States recognized, "the United States has a proud history of revolutionary struggles...the struggles for the immediate demands and reforms needed by working people..."

The Weather Underground wrote, "those who carry the traditions and lessons of the struggles of the last decade, those who join in the struggles of today..."

Bernie Sanders has told his followers they are in a "struggle for justice," and that, "the struggle continues."

Shortly after he became President of the United States, Obama told the assembled Turkish Parliament, "The United States is still working through some of our own darker periods in our history…Our country still struggles with the legacies of slavery and segregation, the past treatment of Native Americans…"

SOLIDARITY WITH CHINA, CUBA, RUSSIA, AND 1970's REVOLUTIONARIES

Congresswoman Judy Chu traveled to the People's Republic of China in 2011 to visit her ancestral home/province. While traveling in China, she proclaimed, "I am a daughter of China, now I am coming home… I am truly coming home…"

Congresswoman Barbara Lee has traveled to Cuba at least two dozen times in the past several decades. Fidel Castro referred to her as "Dear Comrade."

Sitting in a sauna, sipping vodka with Soviet officials in the former Union of Soviet Socialist Republics in 1988, Bernie Sanders is, "heard extolling the virtues of Soviet life and culture, " on a video of his travels.

New York Congressman Jerry Nadler, chairman of the House Judiciary Committee, worked for years on behalf of former Weather Underground fugitives Susan Rosenburg, Linda Evans, and Judith Clark, to secure their release from prison. Nadler succeeded, despite the fact that they were involved in crimes that resulted in the killing of police officers during the *Days of Rage*.

When asked about Susan Rosenburg's complicity in the 1981 Brinks armored car robbery in Nyack, New York, Nadler responded, "a couple of cops were killed…she proclaimed that she was innocent of that…she was sentenced to 58 years in jail, which is a hell of a sentence, you know, 59 months for this stick of dynamite…"

THE TRANSFORMATION OF AMERICA

In *Prairie Fire,* the Weather Underground described itself as "communist women and men." Co-founder of the Black Panther Party Huey Newton, called it a "Maoist/Leninist" organization. Both groups realized they would need to guide America through an unstable period of socialism, on their way to the perfect state of communism they envisioned for America.

Huey Newton described this as a "total transformation" of America. The Communist Party of the United States calls it a "revolutionary transformation of society and the economy toward socialism and then communism." The Democratic Socialists of America calls it, "socialist transformation." The Democratic Party Platform of 2016 referred to the "societal transformation."

Barack Obama, proclaimed before he moved into the White House, that his presidency would bring about the "fundamental transformation of America."

In the waning days of his Presidency, Obama told an audience of students in South America, "So often in the past there has been a division between left and right, between capitalists and communists or socialists... You don't have to worry about whether it really fits into socialist theory or capitalist theory. You should just decide what works..."

IDEOLOGY OF COMMUNISM- THE UNDERLAYMENT OF REVOLUTION

Leading Democratic Presidential candidate Bernie Sanders espouses, "peace... economic, social, racial, and environmental justice...." Sanders has the endorsement of Congresswoman Alexandria Ocasio-Cortez, who has declared that, "capitalism is irredeemable." Ocasio-Cortez, a member of the Democratic Socialists of America, introduced the New Green Deal. It has the endorsement of Bernie Sanders.

Sanders and Ocasio-Cortez are marching in line with the Communist Party, USA, when it chants, *"peace, justice, and equality. We need socialism."*

The Weather Underground terrorists of the 1970's, the Black Panther Party of Self-Defense, the Communist Party of the United States, the Democratic Socialists of America and today's Democratic Party are bound by the ideology of communism.

The Students for a Democratic Society (SDS) was born in 1960, as an organization opposed to the war in Vietnam. SDS engaged in protests and civil disobedience against the war in Vietnam. SDS evolved from a group called SLID or Student League for Industrial Democracy. SLID was the student organization of the League for Industrial Democracy, founded by Michael Harrington.

When SLID transitioned into the SDS in 1960, Harrington left the League for Industrial Democracy. He founded the Democratic Socialists of America. By 1969, the Weather Underground grew out of the SDS. The founders of the Weather Underground believed only revolutionary violence and not political compromise, would change the capitalist system.

Bill Ayers, one of the authors of the Weather Underground's *Prairie Fire* manifesto still refuses to rule out violence in pursuit of revolution.

Angela Davis, who purchased a firearm used in the murder of a judge in a brazen jailbreak inside a Marin County courtroom; Mark Rudd, a former member of the Weather Underground; and other heirs of the 1970's revolutionaries found work as professors in America's universities and colleges.

Barbara Lee, Bobby Rush, John Lewis, and Keith Ellison are just a few prominent Democratic officials who have made their way to the halls of Congress, from the radical revolutionary battle fields of the 1960's and 1970's.

If the 2016 Democratic Party platform looks like the Weather Underground's *Prairie Fire* and the Black Panther Party's Ten Point Plan, it's because current and former members of the Congressional Black Caucus, the Congressional Progressive Caucus, and their advisers, consultants and front organizations drafted the 2016 party platform.

Representative Barbara Lee worked in the office of the Black Panther Party in Oakland in the late 1960's. She admired Huey Newton and Bobby Seale, co-founders of the party.

The website for the Center for American Progress begins with this caption, "Transforming the Culture of Power, Women," and aims to "dismantle the culture of power that fuels gender- based violence…"

Luis Gutierrez, former Congressman from Chicago endorsed the League of Revolutionary Struggle and belonged to the Puerto Rican Socialist Party-a Marxist/Leninist organization, in the 1980's.

Cornel West, well known activist and professor, is quoted as believing, "in a time in which Communist regimes have been rightfully discredited and yet alternatives to neoliberal capitalist societies are unwisely dismissed, I defend the fundamental claim of Marxist theory: there must be countervailing forces that defend people's needs against the brutality of profit driven capitalism."

Democrats want President Trump out of the White House because he has interfered with their plan to impose so-called "democratic socialism" on the United States. Their true intent is the incremental implementation of communism. The underlayment that connects the Weather Underground, Black Panther Party, Communist Party of the USA, Democratic Socialists of America, and today's Democratic Party is the ideology of communism.

The evidence is clear. It's *In Their Own Words.*

Epilogue

It's not the purpose of this book to rehash vast amounts of information from the Hillary Clinton email, Trump/Russia and Trump/Ukraine investigations. The report of Special Counsel Robert Mueller, and two reports of Department of Justice Inspector General Michael Horowitz constitute the only factual record of what happened inside the FBI and Department of Justice (DOJ) during the waning days of the Obama Administration and early days of the Trump Administration.

Report on the Investigation into Russian Interference in the 2016 Presidential Election (The Mueller Report)

Former FBI Director Robert Mueller, III was appointed as Special Counsel of the investigation into allegations of Russian interference in the 2016 election by Deputy Attorney General Rod J. Rosenstein on May 17, 2017. The FBI had initiated an investigation into the suspicious activities and involvement of several of President Trump's advisors with Russia in July 2016. The FBI investigation was code-named Crossfire Hurricane.

Special Counsel Mueller released to the public the results of his efforts on April 18, 2019, in the *Report on the Investigation into Russian Interference in the 2016 Presidential Election.* He answered questions about his report before the House Intelligence Committee on July 24, 2019.

The Mueller investigation took two years to complete, cost $32 million, involved nineteen attorneys, forty FBI agents and staff, and ended with over one hundred criminal charges against three Russian companies and thirty-four individuals, including six advisors to President Trump. Despite these numbers, reflecting a significant commitment by the United States Government to ascertain the truth surrounding Russian interference in the 2016 election, Volume I of the Mueller Report concluded:

"Although the investigation established that the Russian government perceived it would benefit from a Trump presidency and worked to secure that outcome, and that the Campaign expected it would benefit electorally from information stolen and released through Russian efforts, the investigation did not establish that members of the Trump Campaign conspired or coordinated with the Russian government in its election interference activities."

Volume II of the Mueller Report examined issues related to President Trump's firing of FBI Director James Comey on May 9, 2017 and whether it constituted obstruction of justice by the President. Mueller's team concluded:

"The evidence we obtained about the President's actions and intent presents difficult issues that would need to be resolved if we were making a traditional prosecutorial judgment. At the same time, if we had confidence after a thorough investigation of the facts that the President clearly did not commit obstruction of justice, we would so state. Based on the facts and the applicable legal standards, we are unable to reach that judgment. Accordingly, while this report does not conclude that the President committed a crime, it also does not exonerate him."

"A Review of Various Actions by the Federal Bureau of Investigation and Department of Justice in Advance of the 2016 Election" (The DOJ OIG Report on Midyear Exam, June 2018)

Long before the completion of the Special Counsel's investigation into Russian interference in the 2016 election, significant questions had arisen concerning the FBI investigation into Hillary Clinton's use of a private email server. Codenamed Midyear Exam (commonly referred to as Midyear) and initiated in July 2015, the Midyear investigation has become synonymous with how not to conduct an FBI investigation.

The DOJ Office of Inspector General released its first investigative report on the conduct of Midyear in June 2018. "A Review of Various Actions by the Federal Bureau of Investigation and Department of Justice in Advance of the 2016 Election" found:

- Text and instant messages among five FBI agents expressing hostility towards Donald Trump and support for Hillary Clinton. The OIG concluded, "the conduct by these employees cast a cloud over the FBI Midyear investigation and sowed doubt the FBI's work on, and its handling of, the Midyear investigation. Moreover, the damage caused by their actions extends far beyond the scope of the Midyear investigation and goes to the heart of the FBI's reputation for neutral fact finding and political independence."

- Text messages between FBI Deputy Assistant Director Peter Strzok and Lisa Page, Special Counsel to the Deputy Director, "created the appearance that investigative decisions were impacted by bias."

- "…Numerous FBI employees, at all levels of the organization and with no official reason to be in contact with the media, who were nevertheless in frequent contact with reporters… We have profound concerns about the volume and extent of unauthorized media contacts by FBI personnel that we have uncovered during our review. In addition, we identified instances where FBI employees improperly received benefits from reporters, including tickets to sporting events, golfing outings, drinks and meals, and admittance to nonpublic social events."

- Attorney General (AG) Loretta Lynch instructed Comey to refer to the Midyear investigation as a "matter," when talking to Congress and the media.

- AG Lynch had an unplanned meeting on her plane on the tarmac at Phoenix Airport when former President Bill Clinton walked aboard unexpectedly. Lynch became concerned about appearances when it "was just too long a meeting to have had."

- FBI Director Comey decided the DOJ was under a cloud over the Clinton email investigation and that in order to protect the FBI's credibility, he would write and read a public statement about the investigation and announce that no charges would be recommended. He would not tell the DOJ ahead of time.

- On July 5, 2016 Director Comey spoke with AG Lynch and Deputy AG Sally Yates and told them of his media appearance the same afternoon but did not share the substance of what he planned to say. AG Lynch never questioned him or asked to see his statement.

- On July 6, AG Lynch and the DOJ declined any prosecution of Hillary Clinton or any of her staff over the email server issues, based upon the FBI's recommendations.

- FBI agents in New York City serving a search warrant on former Congressman Anthony Weiner (husband of Clinton confidante Huma Abedin) found 347,000 emails from the State Department on Weiner's laptop on 9/27/2016. They immediately contacted the Midyear Case Agents, appropriate FBI Assistant Directors and Deputy Director McCabe at FBIHQ on the same date. Despite further contacts and reminders to invite the Midyear agents to New York to view the emails, no actions occurred until New York finally used the U.S. Attorney's Office to channel the information they possessed. It was not until October 27, 2016 that McCabe seemed to see the urgency of the situation and sent an email requesting a meeting with Comey, "if you have any space on your calendar."

- Director Comey told the OIG, "he did not know what this email was about when he received it and did not initially recall that he had been previously notified about the Weiner laptop." He also didn't connect Weiner as the husband of Abedin. When the Midyear team briefed Comey about the email discovery later on 10/27, McCabe was asked not to participate. He recused himself from the investigation on November 1. Comey approved a search warrant as a result of the briefing and expressed concern that the month delay in responding to the development had major consequences.

- When interviewed by the OIG as to the delay in their decisions to review the emails found by New York agents on Weiner's laptop, FBIHQ agents and officials involved provided four reasons why there was a month delay in taking action. These included: waiting for additional information, the need for consent or a new search warrant, Crossfire Hurricane was a priority over Midyear, and the belief that the newly discovered emails were insignificant. The OIG concluded all the given reasons were "unpersuasive."

- Comey decided to make Congress aware that the Midyear investigation was being reopened to examine the emails. He asked his Chief of Staff, James Rybicki, to notify AG Loretta Lynch and Deputy AG Sally Yates. Comey never called the AG personally, and when Rybicki relayed a message from the AG that the DOJ didn't think it was a good idea to tell Congress, but did not order Comey to stand down, he believed he had the authority to proceed to do what he thought best. According to the OIG Report, it was Comey's "view that candidate Clinton was going to win the presidency and that she would be perceived to be an illegitimate president if the public first learned of the information after the election."

- When Andrew McCabe was the FBI's Assistant Director of its Washington Field Office, his wife received $675,288 from "then Governor McAuliffe's Political Action Committee (PAC) and from the Virginia Democratic Party. In addition, on June 26, 2015, Hillary Clinton was the featured speaker at a fundraiser in Virginia hosted by the Virginia Democratic Party and attended by Governor McAuliffe."

- When McCabe was promoted to Deputy Director of the FBI, he played an active role in the Midyear and Clinton Foundation investigations. The OIG Report concluded, "FBI ethics officials and attorneys did not fully appreciate the potential significant implications to McCabe and the FBI from campaign donations to Dr. McCabe's campaign."

The OIG Report made nine recommendations to address the issues it discovered during its investigation. There were so many questions about the FBI's conduct and potential connections between the Midyear and Crossfire Hurricane investigations prompted by the OIG Report, that a second OIG investigation was undertaken to answer them.

Review of Four FISA Applications and Other Aspects of the FBI's Crossfire Hurricane Investigation **(The DOJ OIG Report on Crossfire Hurricane, December 2019)**

In December 2019, the OIG for the DOJ released a "Review of Four FISA Applications and Other Aspects of the FBI's Crossfire Hurricane Investigation," to the public. The OIG review examined:

- Whether the opening of Crossfire Hurricane and individual investigations on Trump advisors Carter Page, Michael Flynn, Paul Manafort, and George Papadopoulos, complied with DOJ and FBI policies.

- The FBI's relationship with Christopher Steele.

- The FBI's filing of four Foreign Intelligence Surveillance Act (FISA) warrants with the FISA Court to surveillance Carter Page.

- The role played by DOJ attorney Bruce Ohr in dealing with

Christopher Steele, the State Department, Glenn Simpson of Fusion GPS, Ohr's dealings with other DOJ attorneys on a criminal case against Manafort, and the employment of Oh's wife by Fusion GPS.

- The FBI's use of Undercover Employees and Confidential Human Sources in Crossfire Hurricane and how those sources were used in connection with the Trump campaign.

The OIG Report concluded that, "based upon the information known to the FBI in October 2016, the first application (for a FISA on Carter Page) contained... seven significant inaccuracies and omissions." These included:

- Failure to include that Carter Page was an operational source for another U.S. Government agency from 2008-2013, having contact with one of the Russians of interest in the FISA.

- Overstating the degree of corroboration of Christopher Steele's past reporting, without approval from Steele's handling agent.

- Omitting information on the questionable reliability of a sub-source of Christopher Steele.

- Stating in the FISA that Steele did not provide election related information to Yahoo News for a 9/23/2016 article, and only provided his information to the FBI and his client, Fusion GPS. This was contradicted by information possessed by the FBI that Steele also provided his information to the State Department.

- Omitted George Papadopoulos' consensually monitored statements denying anyone in the Trump campaign was collaborating with Russia or any other outside groups, such as Wikileaks.

- Omitted Carter Page consensually monitored statements that "he literally never met" Paul Manafort and that Manafort never responded to his emails, which contradicted claims that Page was engaged in a conspiracy with Manafort on behalf of the Trump campaign.

- Included statements in the FISA that Page had made to a Confidential Human Source that were consensually monitored and fit the FBI theory of the Crossfire Hurricane investigation while omitting statements that he made which were inconsistent with it.

The OIG found ten additional "significant errors in the three renewal applications" of the FISA, in January, April and June 2017.

- Steele's sub-source made statements in January 2017 raising questions about the allegations made in the FISA application.

- The FISA application of June 2017 failed to include that another U.S. Government agency told the FBI that Carter Page had a prior relationship with them. An Office of Legal Counsel attorney altered an email from the other agency, so that it would indicate that Page was not a source, when in fact he was. The FBI affiant signed the FISA, thinking that the other agency confirmed Page had never had a relationship with them.

- The FISA omitted negative information from other sources directly related to Christopher Steele's reputation, trustworthiness, and credibility.

- The FISA omitted information obtained from Bruce Ohr, DOJ, that Steele was sending his reporting to Hillary Clinton's campaign, that Glenn Simpson of Fusion GPS was paying Steele to discuss information with the media, and that Steele was passionate and desperate about keeping Donald Trump from being elected president.

- The FBI never updated information in the FISA renewals to

indicate Steele was connected to Glenn Simpson, Fusion GPS, the Democratic Party and/or DNC.

- The FBI never corrected the FISA record prior to its third renewal that Steele was actually the source of information for the 9/23/2017 Yahoo News article even after some officials learned in 2017 that Steele admitted to having a interactions with the news media in the summer of 2016.

- The FISA omitted advising the FISA Court that Steele's reporting in the FBI criminal programs had been "minimally corroborated." Instead, the FISA Court was told that Steele's information had been used in criminal proceedings.

- The FISA omitted statements by George Papadopoulos in 2016 denying that the Trump campaign had any involvement in the DNC email hacking.

- The FISA "omitted information indicating that Page played no role in the Republican platform change on Russia's annexation of Ukraine."

- The FISA "omitted Joseph Mifsud's denials to the FBI that he supplied Papadopoulos with the information Papadopoulos shared with the Friendly Foreign Government (suggesting that the campaign received an offer or suggestion of assistance from Russia."

Regarding the four Carter Page FISA applications in their entirety, the OIG concluded:

"We identified at least 17 significant errors or omissions in the Carter Page FISA applications...These errors and omissions resulted from case agents providing wrong or incomplete information to OI and failing to flag important issues for discussion. While we did not find documentary or testimonial evidence of intentional misconduct on the part of the case agents who assisted OI in preparing the applications...

we also did not receive satisfactory explanations for the errors or problems we identified. In most instances, the agents and supervisors told us that they either did not know or recall why the information was not shared with OI, that the failure to do so may have been an oversight, that they did not recognize at the time the relevance of the information to the FISA application, or that they did not believe the missing information to be significant."

Finally, the OIG determined that after Christopher Steele was closed by the FBI as a Confidential Human Source, Bruce Ohr met with the Crossfire Hurricane team thirteen times between November 21, 2016 and May 15, 2017 to provide the results of his meetings with Steele and/or Glenn Simpson. Ohr requested the meetings, however, the FBI agents who debriefed him maintained notes of their discussions and continuously advised him to keep them updated.

Despite identifying 31 examples of poor judgments, significant omissions in the four Carter Page FISA applications, and highly questionable conduct involving some of the highest level FBI and DOJ officials in the Midyear and Crossfire Hurricane investigations (as well as the continued de facto operation of Christopher Steele after he was closed as a source of the FBI), the OIG concluded there wasn't any bias in the Midyear investigation and that the predication of the Crossfire Hurricane investigation was in accordance with DOJ guidelines and policies.

The Consequences of a Compromised FBI to America's National Security

Perhaps those conclusions are accurate. Regardless, they raise serious questions about the ability of today's FBI to protect America from national security threats, emanating from inside and outside the country.

During a recent campaign appearance with Senator Bernie Sanders, Alexandria Ocasio-Cortez said, "This is about a movement that has been decades in the making."

In Their Own Words has described in detail what Ocasio-Cortez really means but will not say. Sanders and Ocasio-Cortez talk of socialism in America, but their words and actions reflect the ideology of communism touted by the "communist minded men and women" of the Weather Underground many decades ago. That is the movement of which she speaks.

The FBI stood in the way of the revolutionary violence of the Weather Underground and Black Panther Party movement then. Today's FBI may not be up to the challenge of defending America against the attack from today's generation of "communist-minded men and women," who work from inside the Democratic Party.

It will be up the voters this time to protect our constitutional Republic from the grand deception called "democratic socialism"- which is nothing more than an iteration of the socialist virus of decades past. This mutation of the ideology of communism will destroy America, just as it has destroyed every country it has touched throughout history. If the Democrats succeed in their quest for ultimate government power, America's future is on the line. Nothing less than our individual freedom and liberty is at stake.

Federal Bureau of Investigation

July 16, 2013

Dear Honorable Comey,

Thank you for your comments about us at your confirmation hearing. Employees of the FBI truly are "united by a fierce desire to do something good for [our] country." By all accounts, that fierce desire will report to you soon. It is both an amazing power and an awesome responsibility. Congratulations and welcome to the Bureau. You will find that FBI employees have an incredible capacity for perseverance and loyalty. We will pursue all leads to their logical end, not just clearing the tangled shrubs in the way, but paving new roads when necessary. Given a worthy Mission, we will march steadfastly and tirelessly, and we will keep marching at great personal sacrifice until the Mission is accomplished.

This letter is part of our march. Several of us have gathered to compile a brief welcome and a sincere plea which we hope to deliver, unfiltered, to your hands. Each of us comes from a unique perspective. We are Agents and Support staff, Headquarters and Field Division employees. We are management and rank & file, some near departure, some just beginning our journey with the FBI. But we all have something in common: we share a hope that we will contribute great things to the FBI and one day retire, fondly leaving both the Bureau and the Nation a *better* place for our having been there. Our contribution lies not only in promoting the good within the FBI, but in recognizing and uprooting the bad; and in holding ourselves and our organization accountable to the citizens we are honored to serve. We have taken this unconventional step of reaching out to you because we are convinced that we stand at a crossroad as an organization and as a Nation, and we cannot afford any further delay.

Our concerns have a common thread: The FBI's true Mission of law enforcement/ national security is so obscured by competing agendas that our effectiveness has been diminished. Decisions now pass through a lens of political correctness, expanding approval layers, and an inappropriate expense/improper distribution of resources. There is also significant discrimination, despite (and ironically, as a result of) the prominence and ever-expanding activities of the FBI's office of Equal Employment Opportunity Affairs (OEEOA) and the Diversity and Inclusion Section. In the interest of time and space, we limit our examples:

- **Political correctness.** The FBI "Active Shooter Awareness" mandatory online training failed to mention that Nidal Hasan shouted "Allahu akbar" prior to his rampage, despite the testimony of eyewitnesses which was available and well-established at the time the training was produced. The subject matter expert (SME) and all those in the approval line allowed this inaccurate text and audio: "…the shooting at Fort Hood remains a mystery and investigators still do not have the exact motivation for the attack…" This statement was finally removed eight months after the problem was first brought to the attention of the responsible HQ unit by a Field Agent, but only after repeated contacts. Scant seconds can mean the difference between life and death in shootings. If another similar tragedy occurred, this time in Bureau space, would employees have been properly prepared?

- **Expanding management.** A Special Agent in the field (pay grade GS-I0 through GS-I3) is three layers from the Director through a Supervisory Special Agent, Assistant Special Agent in Charge, and finally, a Special Agent in Charge. A Special Agent at FBIHQ (none with less than a GS-I4 pay grade) is *nine* (9) layers from the Director, through a wearying maze of

Unit Chiefs, Section Chiefs and their Assistants; as well as all the permutations of the Executive, Assistant and Deputy Directors and their respective Assistants. Many Field Agents who accept 18 month Temporary Duty Assignments (TDY) and report to FBIHQ have claimed they are shocked by the culture of cowardice and self-preservation that keeps HQ locked in a loop of inefficiency. The most significant complaints: a) the additional layers work; b)some of HQ management are inexperienced and unsuited for their tasks, having either only been in the field briefly or having been at HQ for so long that they have forgotten how the field operates; c) those with no prior law enforcement or military experience(hired specifically to introduce a corporate mentality into the Bureau) often have no understanding about how to advance the Bureau Mission and are ineffective at best, obstructionist at worst.

- **Inappropriate budgetary expenses/improper distribution of resources.** Bureaucracies and wasteful spending historically go hand-in-hand, but we refuse to accept that this is inevitable in the FBI. We recognize our real bosses are the American taxpayers, and we would like to see their money treated with greater respect. Not only would the dollars stretch farther, but decision-makers would be more careful about who and what was being paid out of the FBI budget. We would also encourage a closer inspection of the distribution of Special Agents (traditional criminal and cyber work vs. terrorism and intelligence work), inasmuch as it appears quotas are set for the assignment of resources, whether or not the work load justifies the staffing level. Some additional budgetary issues follow:

  o Special Agents earning GS-10 through GS-14 salaries are now spending nearly one-half of their time on administrative duties that used to be handled by GS-7,8 or 9 support staff(i.e., scanning, indexing, uploading, and routing official Bureau documents; entering case evidence; recording time & attendance; documenting mileage; updating personal information; etc). In addition, some of the computer systems are so cumbersome that an entire day may be spent trying to accomplish what ought to have been completed in an hour. When one considers that there are well over 12,000 Special Agents, not only is the wasted money staggering; but the loss of time toward the investigative and intelligence-gathering effort is arguably comparable to an FBI with 6,000 fewer Agents on board.

o   In the midst of "sequestration," with furloughs looming, there is money enough to fund projects that do not involve law enforcement or national security- many which are considered divisive and inflammatory. Some employees will argue that the FBI is overfunded and that the sequestration was a welcome relief. Just last month (dubbed "Lesbian, Gay, Bisexual and Transgender (LGBT) Pride Month" in the FBI), the employees of one Division were encouraged to use their afternoon Bureau time to view a gay propaganda movie, followed by free food and a trivia game with prizes. When an agent dared to question the expenditure of scarce taxpayer resources on this, he was silenced by upper management and the event proceeded. This was by no means an isolated event.

o   In just one Division, taxpayer monies have already paid the salaries of FBI employees who, on Bureau time, a) tutor students, b) make sandwiches at a local community food pantry, and c) engage in sporting events with inner-city youth. In August of *2013*, the same Division's employees will spend an entire day building a house, cleaning up residential areas and boarding up vacant buildings in a blighted neighborhood. These events, and others, are orchestrated as part of the FBI's "Community Outreach" program. This Outreach (a Bureau-wide initiative) has expanded from delivering anti-drug school lectures and hosting the "Citizens Academy," to supplementing the budgets of charities with FBI resources. It should be noted that individual FBI employees must report any volunteer work they choose to do on their personal time to the Security Unit so that it can be reviewed for a potential conflict of interest. It is unclear how the FBI selects the charities (especially considering these amounts to an endorsement) and whether these entries or their leaders are vetted to try to minimize the chance of future scandal to the FBI. While we agree that charity work is vital to a compassionate society, we simply propose that it ought not to be done with the hard-earned taxpayer money that the government has collected for federal law enforcement and national security purposes. This is particularly relevant now, at a time when some Agents complain about a lack of necessary training and supplies, and others bemoan the near abandonment of support to both remote Resident Agencies and the local Police and Sheriffs with whom we once enjoyed a close cooperative relationship. Our community outreach is most profoundly accomplished when we complete our mission with justice and fairness; when we excise the criminal element from a community, leaving the citizens to raise their families in peace; and when we convey to our colleagues in local law enforcement that we'll be there when they need us.

o   Every year, narrow categories of race (excluding white), national origin (excluding European), gender (excluding male) and sexual orientation (excluding heterosexual) each receive an *entire month celebration* replete with e-mails and color posters from FBIHQ panel discussions[broadcast Bureau-wide], quizzes, movies, luncheons and award ceremonies. The entire budget, including staffing supplies, comes from the hard-earned tax dollars that are entrusted to the FBI for law enforcement and national security matters. Even the bonus money awarded to an SAC is based, in part, on how much he or she supports these off-Mission activities. The continuation of activities, advisory committees and promotions convey the impression that the budgets for the OEEOA and the "Diversity and Inclusion Section" have been unaffected by sequestration. We believe that both these HQ sections are counterproductive and should be eliminated or reduced to the minimum required by any applicable law. As one Agent so aptly stated: "HQ wants us to be liked by everyone, both inside and outside the Bureau. I'd rather be respected. Our diverse make-up does not make us stronger, it just makes us different. Our accomplishments make us stronger." Incidentally, Agents who have died in the line of duty are only commemorated for one day out of the year.

- **Discrimination.** The free exercise of religion is specifically protected in the constitution and identified in the civil Rights Act of 1964, yet the entire protected class of Religion is ignored or marginalized within the Bureau; whereas sexual orientation, which does not command the same legal protections as Religion, is celebrated with great fanfare. Those who adhere to Christianity are systematically offended, mistreated and discriminated against, often by the very people who took an oath to uphold the constitution. One employee was instructed by a supervisor to remove Bible quotes placed on the employee's own office wall because they had "offended" a supporter of the LGBT agenda. Another employee was told she could not post her prayer meeting notice on the electronic billboard, although other groups were free to list their meetings and events. And every June, thousands of Christian FBI employees are forced to endure the FBI's active promotion of homosexuality, bisexuality and transexuality in the workplace, despite the fact that these lifestyles are contrary to their protected religious beliefs. Not only does this create a hostile work environment, but for those who find these celebrations inappropriate, nearly every announcement about an LGBT event technically meets the FBI's own definition for "sexual harassment." Offense Code 5.20 states:"…unwelcome conduct of a sexual nature by a… coworker…can constitute sexual harassment." The OEEOA and the Diversity and Inclusion Section's social-engineering agenda further aggravates by focusing all the attention of the categories' members on what they *are* and not what they *have done* to contribute to the law enforcement mission of the FBI. The result is disastrous, but HQ seems to be the only group that does not realize it. Common sense tells us that there can be no favouritism toward one class without necessarily offending another. Beyond illogical, this position is harmful to the Bureau by sowing the "victim" mindset in some and causing resentment in others who see the special treatment as arbitrary, unearned and undeserved.

It needs to be said: In any workplace, in any discussion; the dignity of a person is reduced when they are told to rely on the color of their skin or the gender of their sex partner to gain respect and admiration. In a properly ordered organization, it is the character of a person and the quality of their contribution that ought to draw the attention of their colleagues. Moreover, the FBI is a law enforcement /national security agency- not a social service agency. We cannot be everything to everyone and when we dedicate resources to issues that are unrelated to our true mission, we dilute our efforts and necessarily reduce our effectiveness.

Fidelity, Bravery and Integrity. It is the motto of the FBI and something that should be at the very core of the Bureau's Mission, always and everywhere. The Bureau is still an amazing law enforcement and national security agency, full of dedicated employees who march valiantly to protect the citizens of this beloved Nation. We know that our work is ultimately good vs. evil and that anything that takes us away from this Mission is a diversion, a calculated distraction that makes us less than we ought to be. We pray that you recognize the dangerous territory into which the FBI has been purposefully led. It can only be corrected with Godly wisdom, strength and fortitude; and you have our prayers and our support as you embark on this historic journey.

The FBI once enjoyed the reputation as the finest law enforcement agency, serving the citizens of the greatest Nation on earth. We believe that place of honor is still within our reach.

Godspeed Honorable Comey.

In your service, we remain,
The committed employees of the FBI.

[signature page to follow]